More Praise for James Ishmael Ford and *Zen Master Who?*

"Apart from Rick Fields' classic *How the Swans Came to the Lake,* reportage on the history of Zen in the West has tended to center on one or at most two traditions, e.g., Japanese Soto and Rinzai schools. James Ishmael Ford has instead taken a broad perspective, covering not only the Japanese and Chinese pioneers and influences but also extending his coverage to Korean, Vietnamese, and the syncretic Harada/Yasutani lineages. I found his clear account of the Korean Kwan Um school's Dharma transmission model to be especially interesting. Informal in tone and extensive in coverage, *Zen Master WHO?* should prove both informative and absorbing reading for a new generation of Zen students and teachers alike."
—John Daishin Buksbazen, author of *Zen Meditation in Plain English*

"James Ford brings to all his work a keen mind grounded in a thorough understanding of Zen practice and the nuances which pervade its development in the Western world. His insights are clear and unbiased and aim at presenting an honest picture of the development of Zen."
—Diane Eshin Rizzetto, author of *Waking Up to What You Do*

"*Zen Master WHO?* gives us colorful portrayals of Zen's major figures from a respected Zen Master."
Ruben Habito, author of *Living Zen, Loving God* and *Healing Breath*

ZEN
MASTER
Who?

ZEN
MASTER
Who?

A GUIDE TO THE
PEOPLE AND STORIES OF ZEN

JAMES ISHMAEL FORD

FOREWORD BY BARRY MAGID

WISDOM PUBLICATIONS • BOSTON

Wisdom Publications, Inc.
199 Elm Street
Somerville MA 02144 USA
www.wisdompubs.org

Library of Congress Cataloging-in-Publication Data

Ford, James Ishmael.
  Zen master who? : a guide to the people and stories of Zen / James Ishmael Ford.
    p. cm.
  Includes bibliographical references and index.
  ISBN 0-86171-509-8 (pbk. : alk. paper)
    1. Zen Buddhism—North America—History.   I. Title.
BQ9262.9.N7F67 2006
294.3'9270973—dc22

                  2006020147

ISBN 0-86171-509-8
First Printing
10 09 08 07 06
5 4 3 2 1

Cover design by TLrggms. Interior by Dede Cummings
Set in Grajon 11.5/16pt.

DEDICATED TO THE MEMORY OF RICK FIELDS— whose large-hearted study of the Dharma in North America, *How the Swans Came to the Lake,* first written some twenty-five years ago, inspired this book in so many different ways.

CONTENTS

SECTION 3:
THE FUTURE OF ZEN IN THE WEST

FOREWORD

Zen Master WHO? is a veritable Who's Who and What's What of contemporary American Zen. Anyone seeking to understand the evolution of the many faces of Zen in America—Japanese, Chinese, Korean, Vietnamese, and American—will find this an invaluable resource.

James Ishmael Ford not only offers beginners a clear account of the basics of Buddhist practice common to all forms of Zen, and sound advice on what to look for in a Zen teacher, he delineates the often subtle difference in teachings, training, ordination, and transmission in the various schools and lineages. Even seasoned practitioners will find much to ponder in his exploration of the way different teachers and training centers define what it takes to become a Zen teacher, what it means to be a monk or a priest, and the role of lay teachers in religious practice.

This is the most thorough account yet of the great diversity of ways in which Zen is adapting itself to modern America, of what is being preserved of Zen's monastic origins and what is changing due to its increasing secularization and liberalization, and of Zen's increasing interface with modern science, psychology, and social activism.

Zen Master Who? is a comprehensive survey of the Asian masters who first brought Zen to America and of their American students who have been empowered to carry on the legacy. It tells the story of American Zen clearly—and honestly, because the tale includes many renowned teachers of great insight who nonetheless engaged in destructive, inappropriate behavior with their students. As Ford rightly notes, "these two truths sit closely side by side—and contain all the difficulties and possibilities of our humanity and the Zen way." This seeming contradiction creates a koan about the nature of enlightenment that remains at the center of American Zen practice. By telling the story of real people, with real problems and real accomplishments, Ford makes us ponder just what it is we expect from practice, from teachers, and from ourselves.

Barry Magid

Barry Magid is a Dharma Heir of Charlotte Joko Beck, and the author of *Ordinary Mind: Exploring the Common Ground of Zen and Psychoanalysis*

PREFACE

*T*HERE ARE MANY BOOKS on Zen practice, including wonderful anthologies of Dharma talks by masters both Eastern and Western. Some, like Philip Kapleau's *The Three Pillars of Zen,* Shunryu Suzuki's *Zen Mind, Beginner's Mind,* and Charlotte Joko Beck's *Everyday Zen* deserve to be called true Western spiritual classics. And there are detailed studies of the subtle arts of *shikantaza* and koan study. Thank goodness!

However, except for parts of the late Rick Field's pioneering study *How the Swans Came to the Lake: A Narrative History of Buddhism in America* and Thomas Tweed's *The American Encounter with Buddhism,* there has been no book-length look at the many people, ancient and modern, who have helped shape the institution that has become Western Zen.

I hope that this book will help to fill this niche.

At the same time I need to make a clear disclaimer: this book is not a scholarly work, and does not purport to offer a "history" in any academically rigorous sense.

Zen Buddhism exists within a web of stories. Some tell of our being both one and many—and of the need to drop even *that* insight, if we hope for true liberation for ourselves and the world. Some tell the real and fabled tales of our founding teachers, deep and wise and subject—like ourselves—to every failing of the human condition.

Each story, like a facet of a jewel, reflects the whole of our world and our potential. I hope my presentation of these stories, in addition to familiarizing you with some (though by no means all!) of the *whos* and *whats* of Zen, also points to deep truths about our human condition. I tell these stories—of institutional formation and expansion, of personal questing and teaching, of collective creating and revisioning—out of a deep love for the tradition of Zen, and a desire to welcome and orient an interested person to it.

I believe these ancient and modern stories of the Zen path—stories of those who have walked it before us and of those who walk it with us even now—have a mysterious healing quality. I deeply believe they point to who and what we are as well as what we might become.

Additionally, while telling these stories, throughout the book I will from time to time add my own comments as both an observer of the historic phenomenon of Western Zen and as a Zen teacher. I've given nearly forty years of my life to Zen practice and study, and more than the last decade to teaching Zen in various capacities. My aim is to present the teachers and founders of our Western Zen as living human beings, including their faults as well as their many gifts.

Our authentic humanity is, after all, the way of the buddhas. I hope the reader will find this commentarial, occasionally instructional voice adds life to my presentation of Zen's emergence as a distinctive spiritual path, and helps convey a more vivid picture of what the Zen tradition offers us in our culture, today. I also hope my observations will further the ongoing conversations—among students, teachers, clerics, scholars, and laypeople—about the shape of Zen as it settles into its Western home.

Finally, I hope this book will aid those seeking a Zen center or a Zen teacher who may find themselves unable to make sense out of the wonderful mess of different lineages, practices, and teachers among which they have the historically unprecedented opportunity to choose.

This book comprises three parts of unequal length and differing styles. Part One of this book explores the ancient and sometimes legendary stories of the Zen way, their resonances within Buddhism as well as how they begin to diverge from what might be thought of as the erstwhile mainstream of Buddhist practice. When I first began my own practice, I was informed simply by these *myths* of Zen, using that term in all its richness. I believed in the exclusively ahistorical and romanticizing presentations of many early Western exponents of the Zen way. This book will delve more deeply into these myths and the truths they contain and, occasionally, obscure.

There should be no doubt that Zen has now become a "Western" phenomenon. Its vital lineages have sunk roots throughout Europe, South America, and Australia (which is culturally, if not geographically, Western). Nevertheless, the densest locus of Western Zen seems to be North America. And North America is where I give my greatest attention in this book. While this exploration is by no means a complete account of Western Zen (or even, for the matter, of North American Zen), I hope such details as I provide offer a useful snapshot of Zen in the West, with North America in deepest focus.

Part Two is a consideration of the true stories of those very real people critical to the transmission—across centuries, cultures, and vast distances—of this Zen way to us in America and the West. This section will introduce many of the missionaries from China and Japan and Korea and Vietnam who have left indelible marks upon the Western Zen heart. In this part of the book we will also look at the early generations of Western teachers and the institutions they and their students established.

Finally, Part Three contains my own reflection on the larger story of modern Zen, my own best insights into what Zen is and how I feel it might most successfully manifest within Western culture. I hope you may find it illuminating as you set out on your own path—a path which, even in its uniqueness, is precisely the same as the path walked by buddhas and ancestors since time immemorial.

Some scholars suggest it takes Buddhism at least two centuries to settle into a new culture—and that we in the West are nowhere near a point where we can with any certainty describe the direction or final form Western Zen will take. I know this is true. Yet many shoots have been planted here in our rich loam, roots have begun to sink into that soil, and any number of flowers, however fragile, have begun to blossom. This book is an exploration of the garden that is the Zen way today—or, more properly, the *ways* of Zen as we can see them now.

I hope you will find this book useful in understanding the development of Zen and its particular expressions in the West. I hope this reflection will intrigue and entice. The Zen way is vast and graceful and holds within its teachings and practices nothing less than hope for a suffering world. It is worth careful attention and the devotion of a lifetime.

However accurately this volume describes where Zen has come from and where it is going, it is due to my many friends and guides, and the many scholars on whose careful research I myself rely. Any errors that remain here, sadly, are my own. May this book help to further the establishment of the Dharma in the West, healing the great hurt and saving the many beings. Any merit this volume creates is joyfully dedicated to that hope.

James Ishmael Ford
Zeno Myoun Osho
Boundless Way Zen
West Newton, Massachusetts

A Note about Personal Names

Japanese Soto teachers are usually called by their family name followed by title. Japanese Rinzai masters, on the other hand, are usually called by their Dharma name followed by title—although, at least in the West, they too often use their family name followed by title. I, for the most part, try to retain this convention in this book.

SECTION 1

THE EMERGENCE OF ZEN BUDDHISM IN THE EAST

ONE

The Founding Stories

A special transmission outside scriptures;
Not depending on words or letters:
Directly pointing to the mind;
Seeing into one's nature and attaining the Way.

THIS VERSE IS ATTRIBUTED to Bodhidharma, the semi-mythical founder of *Chan,* as Zen is called in China. In this verse, we have the traditional expression of Zen's vision. In it, too, we have an assertion of our true nature, our ability to comprehend reality with this very mind-body—independent of any outside power, person, or teaching.

Attaining the Zen way ultimately has nothing to do with the sacred texts of Buddhism, and nothing to do with secret initiations, ordination certificates, or seals of approval. While these various things do have significance (if in a secondary way), and I certainly will discuss these matters in some detail in this book, they are nonetheless not the heart of Zen. Rather, Zen is the discovery of the True Self, what is sometimes called "your face from before when your parents were born." This discovery is as intimate as intimate can be. Zen is about our individual awakening to things as they are, and how that awakening manifests in the world we share.

Zen is a direct pointing to who and what we are. It is an invitation and it is a method. But, as with a cookbook filled with photographs of delicious food, at some point we should put the book down and turn on the oven. In the last analysis, Zen teachings simply show the path that each of us must make our own. The proof of Zen, always, is in our living it.

The Zen we encounter today in centers, temples, and monasteries around the world took shape over many generations, and Zen has given its own unique style of teaching and use of language. But even with their many common threads, the many Zen communities are astonishingly different.

Some historical perspective can be part of our own direct knowing of Zen's heritage, and one of the useful ways to explore the history, teachings, and emerging reality of Zen in the West is through stories. It appears we human beings actually do tend to think in stories, in metaphor and simile.

Indeed, much of Zen's unique contribution to meditation disciplines is the use of stories, poems-fragments, and folktales as opportunities for reflection that often lead to surprising realizations. If we can *engage* these stories without clinging to them, we can investigate what each of them may point to about ourselves, and move toward a profoundly personal moment of discovery.

The Life and Teachings of the Buddha

The foundational Buddhist story is that of a man born in the foothills of the Himalayas near the border of what is now India and Nepal, sometime between the sixth and fifth centuries before the Common Era. While he was undoubtedly a historical person, nearly all details of the Buddha's life are debated among scholars. Moreover, the various tellings of his story have been and continue to be shaped by the needs of the different schools that claim him as their founder. This certainly is no less true of the Zen schools.

The man was called Siddhartha Gautama. (Gautama was his family name, Siddhartha his personal name.) He was born into the *Kshatriya* caste, the caste of warriors and rulers. He was a prince, the son of a king. Still, Siddhartha's story can be seen, in many ways, to be our story. Like each of us Siddhartha was born with all the potential of the world before him. Yet, though his father was a king, no amount of money or power could shield the young Siddhartha from sickness, old age, and death—just as no circumstance, however fortunate, can shield us from such things.

Upon seeing the truths of sickness, old age, and death—and upon seeing a yogic renunciant manifesting a life about something more deeply real than comfort—Siddhartha gave up his throne and abandoned his family to become a wandering mendicant and pursue for himself the deepest truths of being, and to find out if there were any way he could free himself from the seemingly inescapable worldly suffering.

Siddhartha's abandonment of his wife and newborn son is a source of recurring conversation (and occasionally outrage) among Western practitioners. On one level, it seems a selfish act. It appears to suggest that family life and a life of spiritual liberation are incompatable. Let it suffice for us to simply raise these questions here, but let me also suggest while this was Siddhartha's path, this choice need not be part of our own. One of the profound gifts of the Zen tradition is its teaching that we can find freedom even amid the complexities of a worldly life.

After studying with many of the great teachers of his day and practicing their paths of asceticism and self-torture, he saw that a life of extreme privation, just like his life of endless indulgence, did not bring him any closer to freedom. Siddhartha determined to find something else, a middle way.

Recalling a moment in his childhood when he had had a glimpse of tranquillity and inner peace, he sat down under the canopy of a Bodhi tree and began to look carefully at his mind. He focused silent but persistent attention to what was arising and passing away in each moment.

Days passed and fell away, but he knew, intuitively, that freedom lay within this relentless watching; indeed, he intuited that his very life, and vastly more was at stake. While he was not certain of the outcome—how could he have been?—he felt the Great Matter was intimately at hand.

Then, miraculously—or perhaps as naturally as a ripe apple falls from a tree—Venus, the morning star, crossed the horizon in the crisp air, and Siddhartha gazed at the wonder, horror, and astonishing beauty of it all—and in less than the time it takes to draw a breath, Siddhartha understood it, whole and complete. He *awoke*. He awoke from the beginningless slumber that had filled his entire life; he awoke to liberation, equanimity, and conditionless joy.

In the Zen tradition, it is said that his first words upon this momentous event, which even now reverberates through space and time, were "I see in this moment all the beings of the world and I awake together." And Siddhartha—once and no longer a prince, a renunciant, a seeker—became the Buddha, "the awakened one."

Shortly after his great enlightenment, the Buddha expounded the "First Turning of the Great Dharma Wheel," the essence of the Buddha way. The word *dharma* has many facets. One way to translate it is "law," in the sense of the laws of the universe. The word is also used to refer to Buddhist teaching and even reality itself. In beginning to turn the Dharma Wheel, the Buddha was beginning to teach us how to see the truth.

In this first sermon, he proclaimed the way human beings can heal themselves and the world. These teachings are summarized as the Four Noble Truths, whose story and presentation mark what many of us in the West consider to be "Buddhism."

The Four Noble Truths and the Eightfold Path

Some contemporary Western Buddhists suggest we might more appropriately call these insights the four *simple* truths. "Simple" is a commendable choice, but there is also something to be said for the more traditional "noble." It has been pointed out many times over the years since the time of the Buddha that *noble* means "worthy of respect," and *noble* also means "courageous." And *truth?* In Buddhism, *truth* is simply "that which is real."

The first of Buddha's noble truths is the assertion that human life is characterized by dukkha. *Dukkha* is a Pali term usually translated as "suffering." This translation is arguably accurate but perhaps not quite sufficient. Two modern Western teachers, Robert Aitken and Stephen Batchelor, each suggest the word *anguish* may better illuminate certain aspects of dukkha. I suspect as Buddhism finds a home in the West, *dukkha* (like *dharma* and a handful of other terms) may be a word that simply needs to be carried untranslated into English—or other Western languages in which the Dharma takes root.

Dukkha refers to all types of suffering, anguish, and angst. It is that general sense of dissatisfaction that seems to characterize the human condition. It is not having what we want, and not wanting what we have. It is the sense of *dis-ease* that shadows our lives, the dreadful spoiler of all accomplishments that follows even our sweetest successes. But dukkha cannot be reduced to just its psychic features. This profound dis-ease is not merely about the pain of cancer or the horrors of children starving to death in war-torn countries. It means even more.

It has to do with inevitability: the inevitability, for instance, of our own deaths and the deaths of everyone we know and love, the inevitability of our enounter with the mysteries of change itself. Sickness and death, hunger, and the very tearing apart of our planet itself are all within dukkha. This last important point is frequently missed in our psychologized era, when things are too often reduced to concerns of ego, or self. But dukkha is bigger than that.

The Buddha's second truth explains the cause of dukkha. And here is where the personal and impersonal meet. The Buddha taught that our psychological and physical experiences influence each other—to some degree, they *co-create* each other. Each of us and each part of us arises together with everything else, in all its and our aspects. Our emotions, thoughts, every blessed part of us *just as it is,* arise and fall together with the rising and falling of everything else in the cosmos. Co-arising—of the universe and I, the universe and you—is not about ego; it's about intimacy, being deeply intimate with the deepest truths of our being and every bit of the universe.

The second noble truth speaks of clinging, and the Buddha urges the rejection of clinging in favor of a profound and possibly terrifying openness. The Buddha is not advising us to withdraw from life or hide from the world. How, after all, would we really do that? Rather he is showing us that clinging to anything—holding tightly onto *anything* in the hope that it never change, never leave us—is like grasping at water rushing wildly downstream in an effort to halt its riparian flow. It's not that it shouldn't be done; it *cannot* be done.

The human-suffering aspect of dukkha follows any attempt to cling to that which passes. Of course, the desire to cling to this or that appears to be a consequence of ordinary human consciousness. We have an innate and astonishing ability to divide things. This amazing ability of our mind allows us to distinguish, to compare and contrast, and to analyze everything. It allows us to build a dike or cultivate corn, and to kill each other very efficiently.

Like the knowledge of good and evil that came to Adam and Eve upon eating the forbidden fruit, our ability to divide the cosmos does make us like gods. We can change our environment, transmit knowledge across space and time, communicate faster than sound itself—and, of course, with a single weapon take millions of lives.

For good and ill, the mind's power to divide up the world distinguishes us from the creatures on the planet.

Before we human beings discovered our ability to divide the cosmos, we simply lived and died, never making any distinctions. This is the *pre*human condition, and when trying to put it into words, we find language fails us. Before language, life and death are not two. Yet language is not itself bad, not itself a problem. Indeed it is with language that we become human. With the separating of life and death, we have the terrible knowing, even as we're born, that we'll die. In our divided universe, mortality haunts everything.

Becoming aware of death, our natural reaction is to recoil from it, deny it, hide from it. Instead of embracing our full reality, we tend to attribute permanence, substance, and unchangingness to constructs that cannot live up to these qualities. We cling to loved ones and to our own lives, desperately wanting them to be everlasting. But, if we are instead lucky enough to find within ourselves a seed of what motivated Prince Siddhartha two and a half millennia ago, we might begin to investigate what the alternative to clinging is.

It is important to know that *not* clinging does not mean turning away or giving up. In fact, Zen teachings suggest that the true spiritual action of letting go never involves turning away. The way to wisdom is to hold all things, including ourselves, in open hands. In this difficult but necessary way, we discover how we can return to our authentic heritage, our true home. We can learn to use the fire of our minds to good purpose. This is all contained within the Buddha's second truth.

The third truth has to do with the fact that even though we are amid, surrounded by, and pervaded with dukkha, we don't have to suffer. Each of us can join all our parts and find our true selves—and we can do it *before* dividing up the cosmos. Pain may be inevitable, but, as the old saw goes, suffering turns out to be optional.

The promise of the Buddha is that we human beings can attain peace and more, we can find who we really are, our true nature, and our true possibility. The spiritual disciplines in Zen are about husbanding and creating the container within which to hold the fire of our lives, and in so doing learning to live peacefully with that fire. Our lives are combusted, but we are not burned.

How can this be so? I believe it has to do with a *turning* of the heart and mind. This is what we might do as we notice the shape of our thoughts and determine to do something about it. This is the great secret of our human condition. The past is gone, the future is not yet come, but in this moment, right now, we can *choose* what happens. We can react from our conditioned habits, binding ourselves ever more tightly to the cycle of suffering, or we can look deeper.

Choosing this second thing means noticing, really attending to what is going on within us, within our thought processes as well as within our deepest feelings, really examining the nature of our inner experience. When we do this, another choice, an option other than blind reaction, opens up for us: we find we can act from wholeness, from compassion, from freedom, in a way that doesn't perpetuate our beginningless suffering. It is that simple—and it can be very difficult, as well.

The fourth noble truth is "the path." The Buddha's path is a middle way that shows us how to hold all things—our loved ones, ourselves, the cosmos itself—without crushing the life out of them. In that first great sermon of the Buddha, the middle way is described as an eightfold path. This consists of right (or "correct" or even "profitable") view, resolve, speech, conduct, livelihood, effort, mindfulness, and concentration.

Helpfully, this eightfold path can be divided into three larger parts: meditation, morality, and wisdom.

Meditation has to do with how we direct our consciousness. Wisdom has to do with the truths that arise out of our deep knowing of intimate connectedness. And wise conduct, or morality, has to do with living in harmony with the world we encounter, a life in which we cause ourselves and others ever less and less harm.

Wise conduct, right morality, is a core element of the middle way, and this may surprise people who have read or thought of Zen as being free of all constraints. The cosmos and everything in it is a web of interwoven relationships—in which case, of course, everything we do matters.

Buddhist moral constraints have nothing to do with pleasing some higher power and have *everything* to do with discovering a sense of harmony with all things and respect for the "passingness," beauty, and uniqueness of all things. Buddha's basic (nonmonastic) code of behavior consists of five precepts that call for us not to kill, not to steal, not to lie, not to misuse sex, and not to become intoxicated.

Later in this book, we will see how these precepts are expanded as the sixteen "bodhisattva" precepts, the precepts by which an "enlightenment being" lives her or his life, and as the *Vinaya,* the hundreds of precepts associated with traditional monastic ordination.

The Story of Bodhidharma

The second great story of Zen is of another Indian man, a monk by the name of Bodhidharma, who crossed the perilous seas to bring to China the seeds of what would become the Zen way. Although Buddhism in one form or another had been in China for some time, Bodhidharma is the figure to whom the Zen way of awakening is always traced. With the story of Bodhidharma, Zen begins to take its distinctive shape.

In this story, Bodhidharma encounters a great emperor who asks what "merit" he has generated with his royal acts of beneficence, such as the funding of numerous monasteries and hospitals. The cultivation of merit is a continuing theme in Mahayana Buddhism, the larger school of Buddhism of which Zen is a part, and so this was a sensible question for the king to ask.

This traditional understanding could be called a "spiritual

economy" in which laypeople "earned" spiritual merit by materially supporting the spiritual practice of monastics. Indeed, laypeople traditionally practiced Buddhism primarily by making donations to the ordained sangha that led to the creation of merit. And the emperor, of course, knew all of this—as did Bodhidharma. So imagine the emperor's shock when Bodhidharma replies, in what I always imagine to be a measured baritone, "No merit. No merit at all."

Part of the Zen teaching here is that each of us must find meaning and completeness in our own lives and actions, our own practice. Good deeds are, of course, good to do. But there is no cosmic ledger keeping track of those good deeds or our many harm-causing ones. Nonetheless the account is kept in our heart, in our very life itself. And it is in our life itself that we must find the fruits, the rewards, of Buddhist practice.

When the outraged emperor demands to know who this impertinent monk is, Bodhidharma replies simply, "Don't know." And with that, this enigmatic monk from India just turned and walked away from the emperor. That "don't know," that not-knowing mind, resonates right down to the present. It has become the uniquely Zen way of expressing Siddhartha's awakening together with all other beings, indeed with the whole world.

According to the Zen tradition, when Bodhidharma left the emperor, he then settled into a cave where he sat facing a wall in silent meditation for nine years. Here we get the first intimation of Zen's particular discipline in sustained silent and dedicated presence. And, calling back to this story, in Zen we may speak of "wall-gazing," when refering to this primary Zen practice. One modern Zen master invites us to take this even more deeply, asking us to "face a wall without facing a wall."

Bodhidharma is also revered as the founder of China's great Shaolin temple, and is claimed, perhaps confusingly for devotees of the essentially pacifistic Zen traditions, to also be the founder of certain schools of martial arts. Among the legends that have gathered around his name, it is also recounted that Bodhidharma, as testament to his determination to never again fall into deluded slumber, ripped the very lids from his eyes—and where they fell the tea plant grew.

Amid such obvious fables, it is unclear what is factual in any story of Bodhidharma. Historical records seem to show there was a real figure, if shadowy, called Bodhidharma; but those historical documents don't begin to portray the character we encounter in this and other, frankly, later stories of a man by that name. We can only assume much of those stories of Bodhidharma are myth and legend. However, in some important sense, all this doesn't matter. The story of Bodhidharma, be he legendary or real, points us to a path beyond words and letters; it points directly to the human heart, and the healing of humanity's great hurt.

Bodhidharma and the Teachings of Emptiness

The story of Bodhidharma's encounter with the Chinese emperor points to an important theme in the Zen school's teaching: *shunyata*. *Shunyata* is a Sanskrit word which is usually translated as "emptiness." When Bodhidharma tells the emperor, "No merit," he is pointing to shunyata. When he answers "Don't know" he is speaking from shunyata. When he sits for years facing a wall, he is dwelling in, facing, and manifesting shunyata.

We first find shunyata in the sutras of the Pali Canon, the sacred texts attributed as words of the Buddha himself. Here it is primarily associated with the fundamental impermanence of things, helping further to explain specific terms as *anitya,* "impermanence, or transitoriness," and *anatman,* "the impermanence of persons, of selves." By the beginning of the first century BCE, the Prajnaparamita cycle of sutras begins to emerge, and foremost among these Mahayana sutras is the Heart Sutra, beloved of Buddhist practitioners throughout the world. In the Heart Sutra, the emptiness that is shunyata is extended to the categories of mind and, beyond that, to all *dharmas,* all the structures of creation. Moreover the Heart Sutra offers the following revolutionary, categorical statement: *Form is exactly emptiness and emptiness is exactly form.*

The exact identity of form and emptiness, of the phenomenal world and shunyata, is a critical understanding within Zen. Actually it is the *central* understanding. Setting out on the Zen path, one need not know what it means that "form is emptiness," and "emptiness is form." But if we can follow Bodhidharma's advice to the emperor, and simply allow ourselves to *not* know, we are well on our way to this insight. It is sufficient to simply know the fact that Zen teaches this, and to allow our not-knowing of this to be a goad, a beacon calling us ever farther on the path.

Our lives are dynamic: first this, now that. Understanding this allows us to perceive all things as they are. No thing has a separate reality. Wisdom *is,* in fact, action. We are all one, yet every aspect of that one is open, unbounded, and empty. Realizing this, we can begin to walk the true path of the Zen way. This path has nothing to do with retreating from the world, nothing to do with denying our genes, history, or place in the great flow of all that is. Living Zen is about our most intimate connection with the world, wherever we find ourselves: meditating in a monastery, washing dishes at home, or doing business in the financial district.

Huineng and the Way of Sudden Awakening

The third great story of Zen is the story of Huineng, set in China at the beginning of the seventh century. This story is somewhat more complex in nature and implication, and so I will give it in brief outline, pausing at intervals to explore some of what this story has to teach us.

With the story of Huineng we begin to see most clearly into Zen's perspective on awakening, the discovery of the healing quality of our attending to the ordinary, to this very moment. We have a single source for this story, the *Platform Sutra of the Sixth Ancestor,* a text that is itself not necessarily an objective account. Nonetheless, in some very real ways it is the seminal text of Zen.

Dajian Huineng's father died when he was three, and due to his family's extreme poverty, he was forced from a very early age to help support his mother by cutting and selling firewood. One day as he was carrying a load of kindling into town, he overheard someone reciting a line from a sacred text: "You should activate your mind without it dwelling anywhere." Just hearing these words was enough for this young woodcutter to have a dramatic experience. The boy, who was ripe for this moment, awakened fully.

There are several points for us to see here. One is that awakening is not something "out there" or "down the line." It happens in a mysterious, curious, wondrous moment; completely beyond any planning or hope. This is an important teaching: it tells us the possibility for awakening, for freedom, is always available to us right here, right now. Moreover, we don't *earn* it. This awakening arose within the mind of an ordinary woodcutter, not a Buddha or a saint, or even a master meditator. This is wondrous good news— and I really want to underscore this point—for it shows that awakening is something such ordinary folk as you and I can achieve, just as we are.

But it's also important for me to point out that, with all this talk of "awakening," the conventions of language are beginning to fail us. Awakening is not a thing, nor is it a thought, nor is it even an *experience*—rather it is noticing what is: the first time perhaps dramatically, but then over, and over, and over, and deeper and deeper and deeper, in each undramatic moment of our lives.

When the boy asked the wanderer the source of these "turning words," he was told they came from a traditional Buddhist text, the Diamond Sutra. It had been taught to the speaker by the Zen master Daman Hongren. Recalling the story of the Prince Siddhartha, you may remember that when the great urge to awakening pulled him to the path, he abandoned his family. Huineng's story takes place amid China's culture of filial duty—and so the faithful youth quickly made arrangements for his mother's care before heading north toward Hongren so that he could explore and deepen his understanding.

While on this journey, he met a family that included an elderly nun. As he began explaining the meaning of obscure texts to her, it was immediately obvious to the nun that while untutored (indeed, according to the story, illiterate) young Huineng had great natural wisdom. She encouraged reflections on the sacred texts she read to him. She also told others about this young prodigy. Friends and neighbors began to gather to hear his teachings, and soon people were traveling for miles to hear the young sage speak of the way of a mind that is active but rests nowhere.

Before long, however, Huineng thought: "I seek great wisdom. Why should I stop halfway?" And so he continued on to the monastery of Master Hongren. At this point in the tale, we catch another critical aspect of the Zen way: While one must necessarily achieve insight for and by oneself, our initial insight, authentic as it is, is also likely to be somewhat shallow, and perhaps incompletely integrated into the whole of our lives. A taste of water and the ocean itself are of course both water, but one offers greater depths to plumb. So our awakening needs checking, confirmation, and constant deepening. In short, even though we must take every step for ourselves, we will almost always need a teacher along the way.

The human mind is a powerful thing, and our ability to deceive ourselves is almost limitless. So on the Zen way, a teacher is essential—someone who has walked the path and can vouch personally for its efficacy, someone who has learned about the traps, pitfalls, and dead ends, someone who can urge us deeper and prod us from complacency. Though we are all naturally self-realized, to go to the depths of self-realization, we need companions and guides.

Eventually Huineng arrived at Hongren's monastery. In a private interview with the master, Huineng was asked where he came from and why he wished to enter the community. Huineng replied that he came from the Guangzhou in the south, and wished to become a buddha.

The master laughed and said no one in the south has buddha nature. This would be like someone in Boston saying no one from Kansas has buddha nature; it was a joke that surely reflected certain prejudices of that time and place—but it was also an invitation to a deeper encounter, a Zen master's deliberate prod.

The young Huineng rose to the challenge. He corrected the teacher: "Within common understanding, it can be said there are northerners and southerners. But can that be true within buddha nature?" When the alert mind does not settle into one thing or another, how can there be discrimination?

This is also good news for those of us who practice Zen today. Whether we think ourselves smart or dim, healthy or sick, young or old, privileged or challenged, burdened by our upbringing or strengthened by it—none of this matters in the Zen way. Awakening is available to all of us, equally, without discrimination.

It was obvious to Hongren that the boy's insight was not shallow, and at the same time, Hongren seems also to have recognized that the boy's understanding needed some time to ripen. Huineng was accepted into the community and set to work husking rice.

Huineng settled into the rhythms of monastic life. During this time he probably had no further encounters with the teacher other than perhaps occasionally hearing him lecture. As a lay practitioner, the young Huineng may not have even been allowed to sit in the meditation hall, a space reserved for monks. Nonetheless all this time that active mind settled nowhere, continuing to deepen.

We should pause here and notice that the "official" story of one of Zen's founding teachers doesn't have him spending a great amount of time with his teacher or formally sitting in the meditation hall, nor even being ordained. The Zen school of course makes great use of meditation practices, as they are among the authentic gifts of the Zen way. But the true essence of Zen resides in a place deeper and broader than the bare term *meditation* can imply.

Returning to our story: About eight months after the young man was set to husking rice old Hongren decided it was time to name his successor, the person who would formally carry on his teaching responsibilities in his monastic community. As the story goes, Hongren decided to frame a contest to find that successor. He declared: "The great way is difficult to understand. I don't want you simply regurgitating what I've said to you all these years. Instead, I want each of you, my students, to compose a brief verse that demonstrates your own intimate understanding."

It is said that only one person, the head monk, Yuquan Shenxiu, wrote such a verse. After all, Shenxiu was the head monk for a reason. Why should any of the junior monks expect their understanding to surpass their seniors? This the traditional monastic hierarchy. Nonetheless, hesitant to bring his poem directly to his old teacher, Shenxiu wrote it anonymously on the wall of the great hallway:

The body is the tree of wisdom.
The mind but a bright mirror.
At all times diligently polish it,
To remain untainted by dust.

The master saw the verse and declared, "Very good, very good!" But in private he was concerned that the writer, whom he was certain was Shenxiu, had not yet penetrated to the real depths of the matter.

Shenxiu's verse admirably described the work-in-progress of awakening, but it was not itself the statement of an awakening master. Fortunately, before Hongren was left with no choice but to confer transmission on an unworthy successor, Huineng came into the hallway and saw the verse. Because he was illiterate, he had to ask a monk what it said. Hearing it read to him, he said, innocently and simply, "No, that's not it." Then he had the monk transcribe another verse:

The tree of wisdom fundamentally does not exist.
Nor is there a stand for the mirror.
Originally, there is not a single thing,
So where would dust alight?

When the master saw this poem, he knew it had been written by the successor he was seeking, penetrating deeply into emptiness and ultimate reality. He also somehow knew it was written by the young lay practitioner he'd set to work husking rice eight months before. Nonetheless he announced, "This is written by someone who has yet to understand the matter fully," and Master Hongren had it erased.

That night, at midnight as the story goes, in the secrecy of his private chamber, Hongren formally transmitted the Dharma to Huineng, and with this Huineng became a "master"; his understanding verified as the equal of his teacher's.

This secret meeting, which seems like it might be the culmination of Huineng's tale, is in fact its midpoint. With this exchange the teacher gives him the traditional signs of transmission, formal acknowledgment of Huineng's realization. These signs were the old master's own robe and eating bowl, which had been passed down to him (so says the story) through successive teachers from Bodhidharma himself.

Hongren and Huineng agree, however, that the rest of Hongren's community is not yet ready to accept this newcomer, this unlettered, untrained youth, as the leader of the monastery, the holder of the Dharma—and it's important to note too that Huineng is still not even ordained. And so Huineng departs, under cloak of darkness, with robe and bowl in hand, and the seal of his teacher's Dharma on his heart.

At the beginning of Huineng's flight from the monastery, he has a fateful encounter with another monk, a former general, who catches up with him and demands that Hongren's robe and bowl be returned, saying Huineng has no right to carry them.

The most important point in this story, however, is how Huineng responds: Knowing these signs of transmission are merely symbols, not realization itself, Huineng simply sets them down. "Please," he says, surely without aggression, "take them." And then, the story takes a sharply allegorical turn: the old general finds that, try as he might, he cannot lift the robe and the bowl.

The monk who had been a general can read allegory as well as anyone, it seems, and instantly repents his grasping after mere trappings, offers to stay with the young sage, and entreats the young man to teach him the true meaning of realization, of awakening.

Huineng does teach him, and eventually, receives ordination and founds a monastery, teaching countless more seekers after authentic wisdom. His lineage, known at the time as the "Southern School of Zen" is now known only as Zen. All of us who walk the Zen way—whatever our nationality, whatever our culture, whatever our Zen sect—are Huineng's heirs.

The story of Huineng lays open in an almost archetypal fashion many crucial themes, themes that are an essential part of Zen even to our own time: the role of the teacher and of confirmation, the meaning and necessity of "transmitting" the Dharma, the nature of lineage, and, most important, the nature of realization itself.

TWO

Ancient Teachers and Nascent Institutions

Lineage, Ordination, and Transmission

The Zen stories tell of a line of teachers leading directly back through Huineng, who has since come to be known as the Sixth Chinese Ancestor, to Bodhidharma (the First Ancestor in China), and back to India through a line of twenty-six teachers leading eventually to the Buddha himself.

However, there is limited objective basis for believing in the veridical historicity of this lineage. The Indian lineage list is a hodgepodge collection of prominent Indian Buddhists put together in a rough chronology, and even the Chinese list of five ancestors, leading up to Huineng, can be traced only to the documents of Huineng's own school.

Moreover, while some of what the Buddha taught is open to debate—and is debated with great passion—scholarly opinion suggests that the early sutra collections, the traditional anthologies of the Buddha's teachings, are largely authentic, quite likely a fairly accurate record of what the Buddha actually said and taught. And in those sutras the Buddha was unambiguously clear there would be no personal succession following his death. He named no one heir. Rather he wanted to be succeeded by the rule of the Order, the ordained Sangha itself, and his teachings.

So the ideas of lineage and tradition in Zen are more or less a Chinese creation. Indeed, much of the particular flavor and many of the foci of Zen all arise in China. While Zen is clearly a Buddhist school, its origin is very much Chinese, and as such owes much to the insights of the Watercourse Way, or Taoist path, and to a lesser degree to Confucian perspectives.

Thus any exploration of Zen's modern manifestations must give consideration to its history in China. Indeed, every question we are exploring and debating in the establishment of Western Zen has its origins here in China. Zen's meditative disciplines, its focus on transmission and lineage all take shape here. To have some sense of these perspectives will allow our conversations to take deep root, and perhaps to flower.

As early as the fourth century, there are records of Chinese Buddhists practicing forms of meditation. By the sixth century the remarkable Zhiyi, one of the founders of the Tiantai school, was writing Chinese-influenced meditation manuals. Throughout the sixth century various Chinese meditation masters began teaching, some gathering large followings of monks and nuns, and some influencing government officials.

By the seventh century, with some but not all the mythic structures in place, Zen institutions are still nascent. Nevertheless, at the time when Hongren is guiding the brilliant young Huineng, a school of meditation—with characteristics distinct from both its Indian ancestors and other schools of Chinese Buddhism—is clearly emerging.

It isn't until the eighth century, however, that we find the first clear idea of a *lineage* in Zen. This occurs when one of Huineng's successors, the monk Heze Shenhui, delivers a polemical attack on the most prominent of Hongren's other successors, Shenxiu (who plays the part of the unfortunate head monk in the Platform Sutra).

At the time of these attacks, Shenxiu's is the primary Zen lineage. His school emphasized practice, study, and the gradual cultivation of wisdom.

Countering this approach, Shenhui asserts that the authentic core of Zen is an immediate and unmediated experience of who we truly are. In many ways this is at least a big piece of modern Zen's teaching. But Shenhui also asserts that his own is the only authentic succession from Hongren, master of both Shenxiu and Huineng. And with these polemics, of Shenhui against Shenxiu, we have the first sectarian notion of "lineage" in Zen.

But lineage is more real than polemic. As we will see later in this book, lineage also helps a seeker know what kinds of Zen practices, which approaches, she or he will encounter with a given teacher. And there is also something even more profound here, for the lineage of Shenhui has to do with realization itself, and involves, for the first time in history, a seal of approval given by master to student, thus joining that student with the teacher and with her or his teacher, going back at least to a real founding teacher, Huineng, if not literally to the Buddha himself.

If at the time of Huineng the act of transmission was shrouded in mystery, story, and myth, within one more generation transmission would be a formal reality. This transmission—perhaps more correctly with a capital *T*—was clearly about spiritual authority. It was the acknowledgment of realization and of the right to teach in the name of the lineage. This Transmission was now clearly distinguishable from simple ordination into the monastic sangha.

But what is this Dharma transmission, sometimes called by the even more mysterious name "mind-to-mind transmission of the Dharma"? One great master, Eihei Dogen (about whom we will learn much more below), speaks of "correctly transmitting the Dharma to oneself" (yet it should be noted that this transmission "to oneself" is what happens even when one "receives" Transmission "from" one's teacher—curiouser and curiouser!).

But what Transmission is and what "receiving" it precisely means is a subject scholars and monastics can and do debate at great length. But on a practical level, it has certain implications for a modern explorer on the path of Zen. The fact of Dharma transmission indicates the reality that within the Zen tradition, people become teachers only with the "permission" or "authorization" of their own teachers, after having their own insights examined and verified.

The spiritual path is a subtle one, and a good guide is important. Knowing whether your teacher has "received Dharma transmission" is a valuable piece of information for assessing that teacher's relationship to the Zen tradition as it has been practiced and handed down for centuries. And yet, the fact that a person has not received formal Dharma transmission does not *in itself* mean that person cannot be teaching real truths of genuine spiritual utility. But it may mean that what she or he is teaching is not, precisely, the Zen path. Whether this fact is important is something a potential student should investigate for her- or himself.

Significantly, even in ancient China, laypeople received Dharma transmission—making even more clear the undeniable divergence of ordination and Transmission that began with Huineng.

Within just a few generations, the broad shape of what we understand as Zen took form. We've already encountered the famous verse attributed to Bodhidharma—although undoubtedly it is a later construction—that proclaimed the rhetoric of the Zen way:

A special transmission outside the scriptures,
Not based upon words or letters;
Directly pointing to the mind
Seeing into one's true nature, attaining the Buddha way.

The focus of Zen is direct realization not bound by texts or even oral traditions. We can point to this realization, but each of us must find the Great Way for ourselves. Several ironies followed the grand assertion of this verse, not least of which is that this tradition "outside words and letters" has produced an amazingly prodigious body of literature! And, too, this way of "direct pointing" and personal realization has a long history of formal institutions. Over generations various schools, lineages, and styles of teaching have flourished and passed away, while others continue to this day.

In the eighth century, Mazu, known also as Great Master Ma, gained fame for his direct and sometimes even violent presentation of the way. His lineage, passing through Master Linji and then later, in Japan, through Master Hakuin, has come to be known in the West as the Rinzai school.

The other significant personality of this formative period was the profoundly intellectual Shitou, who presented a more refined and gentle Zen. His lineage, passing through Master Dongshan and later, in Japan, through Master Dogen, would become known in the West as the Soto school.

The heirs of one teacher would tend to emphasize the immediate and direct experience of awakening; the heirs of the other emphasized the identity of practice and enlightenment. And as with so much we encounter in Zen, these two things are both profoundly different and ultimately the same.

We'll now turn our attention to the stories of some of these seminal people of Zen, and later on we will spend more time exploring the practices they taught.

The Zen of Words and the Practice of Silent Illumination

Linji Yixuan lived in first part of the ninth century. He entered the monastic life as a boy, spending a number of years studying both the Vinaya, the monastic codes, and the sutras. Eventually dissatisfied with his lack of deeper insight into the meaning of the traditions, he entered Master Huangbo's monastery. After several years of intense study Linji had his great awakening and received the approval of his teacher.

He settled at a temple in northern China from where his reputation as a teacher gradually extended. It is said he had twenty-two Dharma successors by the time of his death in 866.

Linji's style, following in the line from Mazu to Baizhang to Huangbo, was dynamic and vital. The school that emerged from this line of teachers was named for master Linji; it is called Rinzai in Japan. It is characterized by the practice of *kanhua chan,* the Zen of words, or *koans,* the teaching stories of Zen. It is one of two principal lines of Zen flourishing today.

The other great Zen exemplar was Dongshan, an eleventh-generation master of the Chinese Zen path. Dongshan became a monk at the age of twenty-one having already practiced for several years. He visited many of the great Zen masters of the time before becoming a disciple of Yunyan, under whom he experienced awakening and from whom he received Dharma transmission. Eventually he settled at Mount Dongshan, by which name he became known. Together with his student Caoshan Benji, Dongshan founded the Caodong school, better known by its Japanese pronunciation, *Soto.* This is the school noted for *mochao chan,* the Zen of silent illumination.

For many commentators on the Zen way, these two schools are used as examples of the two principal styles of Zen. Certainly Dongshan's line of Zen, along with Linji's, has flourished for generations. One is characterized as championing the way of simple presence as the living way; the other, championing the way of intimate examination of phrases and words, stories, bits of poetry, and fragments of folklore—all vital opportunities for shaking off layers of assumption.

The reality is more complicated. Silent illumination is consistently taught within the koan lineages, and koan introspection as well as other forms of koan study are frequently practiced within the silent-illumination lineages. At the same time the schools who claim Linji and Dongshan as their founders have tended to separately emphasize the two primary practices of Zen, Linji/Rinzai focusing on koan introspection and Caodong/Soto on silent illumination.

Let's turn our attention to koans and "just sitting"—the practices of the mature Zen school.

THREE

The Practices of Zen

ROM ITS FIRST EMERGENCE as an independent school, Zen has focused on the arts of meditation. Yet meditation has always been central to Buddhist practice. Traditionally, there are three main styles of meditation practice: *shamatha, metta,* and *vipassana.* Shamatha is a practice of concentration and calmness. Metta is the discipline of reorienting consciousness into a realm of persisting loving-kindness. And vipassana is the Buddha's way of insight.

All Zen practices are based in what might be seen as shamatha-vipassana, the blending of shamatha with vipassana, a practice of concentration and an opening to the insights that arise amid it. But in their transmission through China, these disciplines take on the specific flavors of Zen's formative personalities. Echoing the two dominant perspectives of Zen, one practice emphasizes *shikantaza,* "just sitting" or the way of silent illumination, while the other follows the sudden insight that deep introspection with koans can reveal.

There is constant tension between these two great streams and their dominant practices, and there are examples, in the literature of various eras, of advocates of one denigrating the other. But each of these disciplines can take us successfully on our journey to depth and wisdom. Personally, I follow a tradition that sees how these two approaches complement each other. Though in no way new, this view seems to be becoming increasingly common, especially among Western Zen teachers and practitioners.

It's impossible to understand Zen without some perspective, ideally firsthand, on its great spiritual disciplines. So let us look briefly at the two core meditation practices of shikantaza and koan introspection. We will then explore, in brief, the other common element of the Zen way: the precepts of right action, particularly its expression in ordination and monastic life.

Shikantaza and the Matter of Awakening

Shikantaza means quite simply "just sitting." Some trace the root of this word to the Japanese pronunciation of the Sanskrit *vipassana,* though this is far from certain. Vipassana practice attends to various details such as labeling thoughts or noting shifts in sensation. However, even this brief description is complicated by the fact many meditation teachers, including Zen meditation teachers, offer what I've already called shamatha-vipassana. Shamatha is a practice of "stopping" or "settling," through the cultivation of concentration, which is joined with and supports the practice of insight.

The term shikantaza describes a practice that happens not only as we sit, but also as we stand, walk, and engage in all of our waking activities. It sometimes even infuses our sleep, becoming the content of our dreams. This practice is sometimes called "silent illumination," or "serene contemplation." While "just sitting" is really just a simple way of saying "being present," people often have trouble grasping what that really means. Shikantaza reveals the ancient nature of our human minds.

The rhetoric of shikantaza can sometimes be challenging, however. Consider the following words of the great master Yaoshan Weiyan, who lived from the first half of the eighth century through the first quarter of the ninth century. When asked what he thought while sitting in meditation, he replied, "I think of not-thinking." When asked how he did that, he replied, "beyond-thinking." Sometimes simple doesn't seem simple!

I recall many years back, I was guiding a small sitting group in Berkeley, California. Someone who had been sitting for several years with another Zen group had begun sitting with us. After a month or two she said she was going back to her old center. I asked if there was anything I should know. She said there was: while our group sat for twenty-five-minute periods before moving into *kin-hin,* a simple form of walking meditation, the other group sat for forty-minute periods. And she explained she could only experience "theta waves" after a half an hour of continuous sitting.

This kind of misunderstanding of the practices of Zen is not that uncommon. Western Zen teachers often refer to such people as "samadhi junkies," and there have been quite a few meditators who have left my own sitting groups for organizations that offer longer meditation periods or more of them, seeking opportunities for deeper states of samadhi.

Samadhi is a Sanskrit term, literally meaning "to make firm" (one's concentration) and refers to deep experiences of unity that arise in meditation, particularly in longer sitting periods or meditation retreats. No doubt, experiences of samadhi can be powerful and compelling. But samadhi is not itself the end of the Zen path. Without a good guide, people can and often do get "stuck" (in a psychological sense, of course, not a literal one) in their samadhi experiences.

The Platform Sutra itself teaches the identity of samadhi and *prajna,* or deepest wisdom. But one-sided attention to samadhi quickly becomes problematic. People who've experienced these states of deep oneness without understanding those states' connection to wisdom can easily miss the real purpose of Zen—finding an authentic way of being present to everything that is—and instead trade that "what is" for a deep but passing sensation of peace.

"Just sitting" shouldn't be understood as mere quietism; nor is it a way to dwell in states of bliss, suppress our thoughts, or cultivate any kind of blankness. Shikantaza invites us to intimately be within the spaciousness that includes thought, as well as the space outside the thoughts and the very thoughts themselves. We are invited to simply experience the natural expansiveness of our mind and whatever it may reveal—even if what it reveals is an experience of contraction!

Because shikantaza is such a simple practice, there often isn't a lot of instruction in Zen meditation. While rooted in the practices of vipassana, shikantaza lets go of the minute and detailed focus of the traditional vipassana discipline. Often in traditional settings—both ancient and modern—the sum total of *zazen* instruction really amounts to little more than to "sit down and hold still."

Many contemporary Japanese teachers report that this "sit down and hold still" was all they were told as young novices. But for most of us in our culture, such limited instruction is not very helpful.

(I would point someone looking for more detailed explanation to *The Art of Just Sitting: Essential Writings on the Zen Practice of Shikantaza,* a broad and deep anthology of ancient and modern teachings, edited by John Daido Loori.)

In formal meditation posture, we may soon discover that the "spaciousness" of our mind is elusive. Instead of just being present, we're fretting about the past, scheming the future, worrying, resenting, fearing, hating, grasping, desiring—anything but experiencing spaciousness.

So today in the West most Zen teachers offer some form of meditation technique to help us get to spaciousness. Most commonly this involves using a form of breath-counting or breath-awareness as an anchor for the wandering mind.

Hongzhi, Dogen, and Shikantaza

Hongzhi Zhengjue, who lived from the end of the eleventh century through the middle of the twelfth, was the first great theorist of the way of "silent illumination," and this is the term most often associated with his teaching. At the beginning of his classic treatise translated in Taigen Dan Leighton's *Cultivating the Empty Field*, Hongzhi declares: "The practice of true reality is simply to sit in silent introspection." Hongzhi describes a dynamic experience, one that avoids the seductions of inner bliss states as well as the wandering roads of ideas—thus pushing us to engage actively in finding our essential spaciousness, our nondual reality.

The principal exponent of the practice of shikantaza *per se* was the great thirteenth-century master Eihei Dogen (whom we will learn much more about when we explore Zen in Japan). The term *shikantaza* appears to have been coined by his teacher Tiantong Rujing, but it was Dogen who carried it forward, explaining and expanding what it can mean for us as a living practice. In his *Fukan-zazengi,* or "Universal Recommendations for Zazen" (which can be found in the collection translated as *Dogen's Extensive Record*), Dogen explains the practice.

He suggests finding a clean, dry place, if possible cool in summer and warm in winter. He goes on to describe the use of a *zafu,* or small round pillow one sits upon, and the *zabuton,* or larger square, flat cushion under the zafu, which supports the ankles and knees. He then describes the basic posture—sitting erect, with hands in the lap, eyes cast downward—as "the method used by all Buddha ancestors for zazen."

"Therefore," Dogen continues, "put aside the intellectual practice of investigating words and chasing phrases, and learn to take the backward step that turns the light and shines it inward. Body and mind of themselves will drop away, and your original face will manifest." He concludes by echoing that famous dialogue with

Yaoshan: "Think of not-thinking. How do you think of not-thinking? Beyond-thinking."

Just sitting is the universal solvent. It is the way to confirm all the teachings presented in all of Zen literature, the way to confirm our original awakening, our true nature, and the way to heal this world.

Dahui, Hakuin, and Koan Introspection

No one knows the precise origin of koan introspection, though some trace it to the Taoist tradition of "pure conversation." Rinzai Zen priest and scholar Victor Sogen Hori, the premier writer on koan introspection in the English language, advances a compelling argument that the distant ancestor of koan study can be found in the Chinese tradition of literary games. Whatever its origins, two teachers in particular gave koan study the shape that most Western Zen practitioners will encounter: the Chinese monk Dahui Zonggao and the Japanese monk Hakuin Ekaku.

Dahui, a twelfth-century Linji-lineage master, is often identified as one of the first teachers to exclusively emphasize koan study. Having read the *Record of Yunmen* as a young man, he was inspired to undertake the Zen way. His first teacher, Zhan Tangshun, pointed out that the young monk's inability to achieve awakening was due to his pride and intellectual acumen. Dahui's understanding of the outside prevented him from entering the inside.

On his deathbed, Dahui's teacher directed him to go to master Yuanwu Keqin—the master who would be remembered as the compiler of *The Blue Cliff Record,* one of the most important collections of koans. Eventually, Yuanwu gave his Dharma transmission to Dahui who in 1137 would become abbot of Nengren Temple. While there he began to collect a multivolume anthology of koans and became a strong advocate of using the koan known as "Zhaozhou's Dog." (We will explore this in more detail below.) In Dahui's teachings it is possible to see the beginnings of the approach that would flower with the eighteenth-century Japanese master Hakuin.

In the ensuing years, war and famine plagued the country, and more than half the hundred monks in Dahui's monastery died. In 1158 he became abbot at Mount Jing near Hangzhou, and it was during these years that Dahui began to publicly criticize the overemphasis on silent illumination and to hold up the possibilities inherent in koan introspection. While he was personally quite close to Hongzhi—who would, in fact, request Dahui be his executor following his death—the great division between koan introspection and shikantaza began at the temples of these two great teachers.

Personally, I find it wonderfully compelling that the masters of these monasteries were in fact friends, each respecting the other while at the same time criticizing a too-one-sided clinging to this practice or that. I find this a powerful model for us as we engage our various Zen practices today. Sadly, however, in the ensuing centuries, this division would continue to exist, with sectarian narrow-mindedness raging strong.

Over time, koan introspection would gradually ossify, losing its dynamism and becoming more an exercise in formalism, mere study, though surely there were some who continued to find insight through studying koans. The next major development in koan introspection came in the eighteenth century, with Japanese master Hakuin Ekaku (about whom we will learn more when we explore Zen in Japan).

For our purposes here, suffice it to say that Hakuin is of particular importance for his systematization of the practice of koan introspection, helping forge it into a reliable tool of training that, when wielded by a master, could serve to awaken students and bring powerful nondual insights. Dahui and Hakuin gave koan introspection its unique shape and placed it as a clearly distinct practice within the Zen schools.

What Koan Introspection Is, and What It's Not

What, in fact, is koan introspection? What does it mean to engage in it? These are important questions worth exploring, as koans and koan study are some of the most perennially misunderstood elements of Zen. Indeed, the practice at the heart of koan introspection, however, is unique to the Zen school and has no significant corollary anywhere else.

Unfortunately, most of what has been published in the English language clouds the matter. This is partially the fault of the Zen tradition itself, which tends to guard the koan way as an esoteric treasure. And it is partially the fault of some European and American commentators, who frequently misunderstand both Zen and koan study.

The various scholars who have taken up the subject of koan introspection often seem like the blind men described by the Buddha: exploring the elephant and interpreting the leg, tail, or trunk as the whole. As Sogen Hori writes, these scholars explore Zen's "nondual epistemology, its ritual and performance, its language, [or] its politics," and indeed, some such perspectives can help clarify how the koan can be engaged at different levels; some point to the shortcomings of Zen institutions; some examine how koan study can be and in fact *is* abused or misused: all speak to one truth or another. But none of these considerations captures the essence of koan introspection.

It should be said that koans are also engaged by some Soto Zen teachers, though this is usually in a discursive way, as objects of conversation among practitioners. These conversations are guided by mature practitioners who often have great insight but little or no formal training in koan introspection, in wielding the tools of Master Hakuin's refined system. Without a doubt, contemporary Soto practitioners can profit from this engagement, as can we all. We and they may find moments of startling clarity or gentle prodding toward greater depth in our practice. In fact this dialogistic approach is one (among several) of the "orthodox" uses of koans.

The Linji/Hakuin legacy of koan practice, however, is more dramatic and intimate than the critical engagement of a spiritual literary tradition, even when it is grounded in shikantaza. To distinguish these disciplines, let us consider the emerging use of the term "koan introspection" for the Linji/Hakuin style. Traditional Linji koan introspection is about our possible awakening, our turning in a heartbeat from delusion to awakening. To achieve this, Zen practice requires three things: great doubt, great faith, and great determination. These become particularly obvious through koan introspection.

The idea of great doubt might seem startling in this context. Matters of religion often seem to be about faith and sometimes, sadly, even about the crushing of doubters. In Zen, however, great doubt must be turned onto ourselves. And as such, this "great doubt" must not be confused with a merely dismissive variety of skeptical doubt. We can see one of the true meanings of great doubt in a reply from Robert Aitken, one of the elders of Western Zen, when asked what he thought about contemporary deconstructionist philosophy: it could be valuable so long as it includes the necessary step of deconstructing itself. Turning doubt on ourselves, we strive to manifest the truth behind that delightful bumper sticker: DON'T BELIEVE EVERYTHING YOU THINK.

Koans cultivate and make use of this great doubt. Contrary to what some might say on the subject, koans are not meaningless phrases meant to break through to a transrational consciousness (whatever we may imagine that means). Rather they are a direct pointing to reality, an invitation for us to "taste water" and to know for ourselves whether it is cool or warm.

While there is an aspect beyond discursive thought, koan introspection very much includes our experiences of judging and assessing. One of my koan teachers suggested that shikantaza is a mature practice for mature people, but that for more difficult cases such as the likes of *me,* koans could shake us up and put us on the right path. I had spent the first ten or so years of my practice engaged in shikantaza, and today it is again my baseline practice. But it wasn't until I found the koan way that I found myself opened up, my heart broken and restored, and my place in the world revealing itself.

In koan introspection, doubt and faith travel together. It is our relentless presence to doubt and faith that takes us to the gate of nondual insight. Indeed both the path to the gate and the gate itself are discovered within that relentlessness.

From an instrumentalist view of koan introspection, words like *Mu* or phrases like "What is the sound of the single hand clapping?" or "What is your original face from before your parents were born?" are often mistakenly assumed to be meaningless. It is assumed that the "point" of such koans is to simply startle the discursive mind into some kind of transrational state. But this understanding of koans simply posits a new dualism: a lower discursive consciousness and a higher nondiscursive state. That is not what koan introspection is about.

Rather, as we push through any koan—experiencing great doubt, great faith, and great determination—we find the exact identity between our ordinary consciousness and fundamental openness. Nondual reality includes subject and object, each itself and freely transposing with the other; first this, now that, sometimes one drops away, sometimes the other, sometimes both drop away, sometimes one emerges from the other, sometimes both emerge together—but we *rest* nowhere. Resting nowhere and moving fluidly among these perspectives is the true practice of koan introspection.

Let us return for a moment to the question of what koans actually are and explore the ways they are used in training. The word *koan* is believed to be derived from the Chinese *kung* and *an. Kung* means "public" and *an* means "case"—like a legal document. A koan can be a single word, short phrase, a bit of traditional poetry, or a story. Most commonly it is an anecdote about an encounter between a student and teacher.

In China and Korea the primary form of koan engagement is through a *huatou* (in Chinese; *wato* in Japanese), which literally means "word head." In this practice, we are given one single koan for a lifetime. This koan becomes a touchstone of our practice: it is a place to put our doubt, to cultivate great doubt, to allow the revelation of great faith, and to focus our great energy.

But in Japan and the Japanese-derived koan lineages in the West, koan study has taken on a new dimension. By the eighteenth century, various Japanese Rinzai teachers began introducing koan "curricula." These were programs of koan study through which a student might "pass" after many years. While there is some dispute over who actually developed this system, it is usually believed to have culminated in the work of the great master Hakuin Ekaku and his principal students or, at least, in that of teachers who followed them. This program is used by orthodox Japanese Rinzai to this day. And it is the source for the single modern reform used in some Soto schools: the so-called Harada-Yasutani curriculum.

This form of koan study begins with a step reminiscent of the Chinese original: the new student is given a "breakthrough" koan, a case specifically meant to elicit an initial experience of nonduality. The Japanese term for this koan is *shokan,* or "first barrier." A student might spend years struggling with it; only rarely does someone pass through the breakthrough koan quickly.

A breakthrough koan might be "What is your face before your parents were born?" or Hakuin's own question "What is the sound of the single hand clapping?" But most commonly it is Zhaozhou's *Mu.* This simple koan is the gateway to all koan practice, without which additional explorations cannot begin.

Zhaozhou Congshen was a ninth-century Chan master and Dharma heir of Nanquan. While he had thirteen Dharma successors of his own, his particular line eventually died out. But he continues to live as a Zen teacher through his record and the numerous citations of his encounters with students in the various koan collections.

Zhaozhou is best known for the following koan, offered here in its entirety: A monk asked Zhaozhou, "Does a dog have buddha nature?" Zhaozhou said, "No." (This koan is also known in shorthand by Japanese translation of Zhaozhuo's answer, Mu.) Let me take just a little time to explore this.

Now, assuming that the questioner knew that the "theologically correct" response is that all things have buddha nature—or, more properly, are buddha nature—we can also assume that the student's question is hinting at a deeper concern: perhaps he is expressing doubts in his own ability to awaken, for instance.

With or without explanation, however, the koan student is advised to throw away the setup and simply engage that single word, Mu. As my own teacher John Tarrant observes: Whether the word is Mu or No or the Chinese variant Wu (which some observers point out is somewhat echoic of a dog's bark), one is, of necessity, given insufficient instructions—basically "Just deal with it."

So we throw ourselves into the great matter, allowing the doubt to rise. At some point we may try critical analysis; at another point, the word may become a mantra—chanted, breathed, whispered, yelled. And each time we think we gain some insight, we take it into the interview room where, most probably, our teacher will reject our response.

My own teacher once told me that awakening is always an accident; and I tell my own students this today. There is no obvious causal relationship between nondual insight and anything we might do or not do. But if awakening is an accident, certain practices can help us become accident-prone. Koan practice is effective at this.

If we open ourselves to this great adventure—with due diligence along with our doubt, faith, and energy—eventually it will happen: We are hit by a bus and everything changes. Or, perhaps the bus just grazes us as it passes by. This is the point of most koans. They give us an opportunity to break out of what we thought the world had been all about for us and encounter it anew.

The teacher trained in koan introspection may go on to ask "checking questions," which reveal how nuanced our insight is. In the case of a breakthrough koan, there might be dozens of checking questions—with some teachers, a hundred. As we move through the breakthrough koan into other cases, there are usually several checking questions for each case beyond the central question.

There are a few books to be found that purport to give "answers" to koans. Occasionally, for reasons that completely elude me, people will take other student's "answers" and present them to their teacher in the interview room, as if some formal or official "passing" of a koan were somehow the important thing, and not our own liberation from our own suffering. But it doesn't take too many checking questions to reveal the true quality of a student's insight.

There are a number of ways to categorize koans, and over the years various systems developed to help clarify how one may engage them. Hakuin's system is the most commonly represented in contemporary Western koan studies, although even it has variations. Hakuin suggested there are five types of koan, the Japanese terms for which are *hoshin, kikan, gonsen, nanto,* and *goi jujukin.*

Hoshin means "dharmakaya" (*kaya* is the Sanskrit word for "body"). These koans are concerned with our fundamental insight into nonduality. *Kikan,* or "dynamic action," koans reveal the activity of emptiness. *Gonsen,* or "explication of words," koans are often quite long and involved. Traditionally one is expected to memorize these koans and recite them in front of the teacher before actually engaging in their points.

Nanto koans are "difficult to pass through"—or at least they seem to have been for old Master Hakuin, who alluded to eight such cases. It isn't precisely clear what this designation really means. Sogen Hori quotes one roshi who remarked bluntly that "the nanto koans have no significance beyond the fact that Hakuin found them difficult to pass through." In my notes from teachers in my lineage, there are occasional references to one koan or another being "particularly difficult." However, they were not all the ones that I'd found problematic. I've come to suspect that we who walk this path each find our own nanto koans.

Goi jujukin koans are actually comprised of two sets of koans. In orthodox Japanese Rinzai, the koans one first completes are the ten grave precepts of moral and ethical action. One also usually includes the Three Refuges of Buddha, Dharma, and Sangha and the Three Pure Precepts of ceasing from evil, practicing good, and actualizing good for others. Together with the ten grave precepts, these crown formal study of koan. There can be hundreds of questions derived from the precepts. One then finishes with the Five Ranks, an ancient system of categorizations that recapitulate all that one has encountered over years of koan study. In the Harada-Yasutani curriculum, the order is reversed, culminating in an investigation of the precepts as koans.

In Japan a student of koan Zen also engages a practice of *jakugo,* or "capping phrases." These are literary tags drawn from the range of East Asian cultures and compiled in various books. Having completed the checking questions, one must then find the appropriate phrase to "cap" the case. Capping phrases are largely eliminated in the Harada-Yasutani curriculum. In the few instances where they are retained, the student is usually asked to compose his or her own verse of appreciation. Most of the orthodox Rinzai teachers in the West also drop the use of capping phrases.

The koan curricula of the Harada-Yasutani system (which ultimately derives from Hakuin's disciple Takuju) might be described like this: After encountering a breakthrough koan and up to a hundred checking questions, we would pass through a collection of brief cases that set the form for future practice. These are "in-house" koans, meaning they are unpublished and not for the general public. After this, we'd work through several classic collections, normally the *Gateless Gate,* the *Blue Cliff Record,* the *Book of Equanimity,* and the *Record of Transmitting the Light.*

The first two collections are associated with the historic Linji/Rinzai tradition; the last two are traditional Soto collections and represent the reformist inclinations of the Harada-Yasutani curriculum. While the varying traditions may use slightly different collections, the arc remains the same.

In Japanese Rinzai, according to Sogen Hori, two curricula are associated with the two principal heirs of Hakuin. In the Takuju school, after the breakthrough students begin the *Gateless Gate (Mumonkan),* and move on the *Blue Cliff Record (Hekigan-roku).* The third collection, the *Shumon Kattoshu,* is only recently available in English under the title *Entangling Vines.* Their last formal collection is *Chin'u-shu,* "The Collection of Wings of the Poison Blackbird," which is not to my knowledge currently available in English.

The other principal line of Hakuin's Zen, through his disciple Inzan, uses its own internally generated list of koans, rather than those found in traditional collections. This school's style is considered more direct and immediate, if somewhat "rougher" in approach than within the Takuju style.

The two schools have minor stylistic differences. As I've suggested, the Inzan school is said to be a bit more dynamic, while the Takuju school is said to be a bit more gentle and meticulous. Nevertheless, we can find teachers of either temperament in either tradition. And each school easily recognizes in the work of the other that they're practicing within the same spiritual system.

In Japan, someone who "completes" formal koan study might have been practicing for thirty years or more. Without the capping phrases, the Harada-Yasutani curriculum is often completed in as little as ten years from the "passing" of the breakthrough koan, although usually it takes considerably longer. It appears that the Western Rinzai koan curricula can be passed through in about the same amount of time.

But most people who take up koan study never complete the formal curriculum—and this isn't seen as a problem. Koans are really just invitations to practice. We do koans to deepen and clarify our zazen, to engage the matter of life and death. Truthfully, we never "complete" our koan work. In schools that use a koan introspection curriculum, however, completion of the formal curriculum is often a necessary condition—if not a sufficient one—for becoming a teacher.

Having examined in a little more detail the practices of the mature Zen school, let us return to the stories of the people who helped shape this school when it came from China into Japan.

FOUR

The Japanese Transformation of Zen

*B*UDDHISM IN JAPAN DATES from the middle of the sixth century. Japan's first known encounter with Zen dates from the seventh century, but it isn't until the Kamakura period (1185–1333) that Zen actually takes root as a distinct school in Japan. What happens in the centuries that follow is very important for our purposes, as the personalities and the institutions of Japanese Zen will come to have some of the most direct influence on the shape of Western Zen.

In this chapter we will look at some of these important people, explore the emergence of a new kind of ordination in Japan, and examine the ramifications in Western Zen of differing understandings of priesthood and Dharma transmission.

So let us start by looking at two people whose influence has reached across centuries and oceans and has profoundly influenced the shape the tradition today: the thirteenth-century master Eihei Dogen and the eighteenth-century master Hakuin Ekaku.

Eihei Dogen and the Soto School

Dogen was born in the year 1200, to imperial court nobility. His mother's name is unknown, and there is argument whether his father was the noble Minamoto Michichika or the noble Minamoto Michitomo. At any rate, there is little doubt that he received the best of educations. A literary prodigy, he composed his first poem in Chinese at the age of four. But his early life was also marked by tragedy. His father seems to have died when he was two, his mother when he was seven.

The young Dogen lived with an uncle until the age of twelve, when he entered monastic life. A year later he entered the Tendai monastery at Mount Hiei. Centered outside Kyoto, the Tendai school was deeply involved in the politics of the day, and its disciplines were often particularly marked by intellectualism and an increasing aridity unconnected with authentic spiritual concerns.

Dogen struggled with the dichotomy between the teachings of inherent buddha nature and the necessity of practice. Why—if we are all inherently awakened and innately possessed of buddha nature and thus perfect just as they are—must we engage in Buddhist practices? This question burned in young Dogen's heart.

His first teacher, Koin, recommended Dogen go to Eisai, a Tendai monk who had traveled to China and received Dharma transmission in the Linji Zen lineage. It is unclear whether Dogen actually studied with Eisai, who died around this time, but the young Dogen did spend years with Eisai's principal heir, the monk Myozen.

What he learned was very much a hybrid Zen rooted in Tendai doctrine and mixed with the "esoteric" practices of the Shingon school of Buddhism. Nonetheless Dogen regarded Myozen as a central teacher. Still, he longed for a more traditional form of Zen. In 1223, he and his teacher departed together for China. Myozen died not long thereafter, but Dogen continued his quest.

Fourteen years later, in his treatise *Tenzo Kyokun,* "Instructions to the Cook," Dogen recounted his awakening experience. It was April, and he was still living aboard the ship that had transported him across the Japan Sea. While wandering around the port he met a Zen monk who had come into port to purchase mushrooms. Dogen sensed this was a wise elder and invited him to stay the night on the ship.

The monk replied that he had to get back to the monastery; he was head cook and still had work to do. This surprised the young Dogen, who asked the cook why, as a venerable elder, he didn't devote himself to shikantaza or koan introspection. The old monk laughed and said it was obvious Dogen hadn't yet understood Zen.

The next year they met again when Dogen was living in the monastery of Tientong. Dogen asked the monk his burning question about practice and scriptures. The monk replied, "Scriptures are *one, two, three, four, five;* and practice means nothing is hidden." With this seemingly enigmatic assertion Dogen finally understood the fundamental matter.

During this time he was also particularly impressed with the rigor of Chinese Zen monasticism, so different from the scholastic communities he knew in Japan. More important, on the first of May 1225, Dogen met Tiantong Rujing, the Caodong master who would become his principal teacher.

In the midst of a difficult meditation retreat, one of the monks began to doze off. Rujing noticed this and said to the company: "In Zen, body and mind are cast off. So, why do you fall asleep?" Once again, Dogen tumbled even deeper into realization. His awakening was sufficiently deep and true that Rujing named the young Japanese monk his heir. In 1227, Master Dogen returned to Japan.

At first he stayed at his old monastery, Kenninji, in Kyoto. While there he composed the *Fukanzazengi,* "Universal Recommendations for Zazen." In 1230, he moved to a country retreat, An'yo-in, in Fukakusa. There he wrote the *Bendowa,* "The Whole-Hearted Way," which would become the first fascicle of his magisterial work the *Shobogenzo,* "True Dharma Eye Treasury." Within three years a larger monastery was built for him in the same area, and young students began to hear of him and seek him out.

Most notable of these was Koun Ejo. Ejo was already the

Dharma heir of Dainichi Nonin, a monk who had had his realization approved through an exchange of letters with a Zen teacher in China. Ejo quickly became Dogen's senior disciple. For the next ten years, Dogen focused his life and the life of his community on the practices of zazen, at the same time cultivating a highly developed monastic life.

In 1243, Dogen moved to the far northern coast of Japan. His writing continued and now included polemics against the Rinzai school, and particularly the renowned twelfth-century koan innovator Dahui Zonggao. In his new location, his temple, Eiheiji, gradually grew along with his fame. In 1247, the Shogun Hojo Tokiyori ordered Dogen to visit him in Kamakura. But beyond this brief time in the capital, he was reluctant to leave his monastery. In 1253 his health, never good, began to seriously decline. At the urgings of disciples and friends and accompanied by Ejo, he went to Kyoto for medical treatment. While there, on the twenty-eighth of August, 1253, at the age of fifty-three, the master died.

A towering figure in the formation of Japanese Zen, Dogen ranks as one of the great spiritual figures of world culture. His writings are translated into nearly every European language. His insights—particularly his emphasis on the absolute identity of practice and awakening—now provide a solid foundation for the development of Zen in the West.

It has been observed that the early success of Dogen's school in Japan had less to do with his thinking or writing, and more to do with his remarkable Dharma heirs. But that was just the beginning of his influence. Today Dogen's writings are considered a world spiritual treasure. He is often compared to Thomas Aquinas (though he is not quite so systematic). And there is no doubt that his perspectives have influenced the whole range of Zen in the West.

Dogen's third-generation successor, Keizan Jokin, ranks second only to Dogen himself in the rise of the Soto school's importance in Japan. In fact the Soto school in Japan has two main temples: Eiheiji, founded by Dogen, and Sojiji, founded by Keizan. Keizan was interested in bringing Zen to the people. In particular, his innovation of lay ordination began to bring esoteric practices that had generally been the property of cloistered monastics into the realm of everyday life. Today Soto is the largest of the Zen schools, second only to the Shin (Pure Land) family of Buddhist schools in Japan.

Hakuin Ekaku and the Rinzai School

The other towering spiritual genius of Japanese Zen was Hakuin Ekaku. His influence on the creation of new forms of koan study is as important to Western Zen as Dogen's emphasis on the identity of practice and awakening. While Dogen was a precise and dramatic example of the value of cloistered life, Hakuin spent much of his life wandering. His was a life marked by dramatic encounters and ecstatic experiences. Considered one of Japan's greatest artists and writers, Hakuin's deeply personal autobiographical writings reveal the inner person in a manner highly unusual for his time and culture. Preserved in his own handwriting, they include everything from depression to ecstasy, offering those of us who follow him an accessible and very human view on the walking of this path. (Much of his autobiographical reflection is available in the excellent book *Wild Ivy,* translated by Norman Waddell.)

Hakuin was born in 1685 in a rural village in the Shizuoka district. His father, who belonged to the Samurai class, was adopted into his mother's clan. The family was registered at the local Nichiren temple, a sect devoted to the Lotus Sutra. The young Hakuin was both brilliant and sickly, his thoughts turning to questions of religion from his earliest years. Obsessed with a fear of hell, he again and again asked permission to become a monk. His parents resisted until he was fifteen, when Tanrei Soden, Rinzai abbot of a nearby temple, Shoinji, ordained him as an *unsui.* There he received his monastic name Ekaku.

Because of his teacher's precarious health, the young monk moved to another temple for several years. At the age of nineteen, having read the story of the ninth-century master Yentou's earth-shattering screams as he faced death at the hands of bandits, Hakuin experienced a crisis of faith. He decided to give up monastic life to pursue art, mainly poetry and painting, though he continued to visit temples. And once, while staying with the poet-monk Bao, the abbot of Zuiunji, Hakuin found himself in the monastery's library. Confronted with a collection of Asia's sacred writings, he randomly picked out a book. It was a collection of Zen stories. He took this as a sign and decided to rededicate himself to the quest for awakening.

Taking up the koan Mu, young Ekaku sat with this case, by his own account "night and day," for two years. After a brief visit home, he traveled to Eiganji temple where he listened to a lecture on Dongshan's Five Ranks, by Master Shotetsu. While Hakuin was considering the connection between Mu and the teachings of the Five Ranks, the temple bell rang. It was, as he later wrote, "as if a sheet of ice had been smashed or a jade tower had fallen with a crash." However Shotetsu did not confirm this experience as an awakening—nor, for that matter, did the several other teachers whom he approached. Nonetheless it proved a turning point in Hakuin Ekaku's spiritual life.

In 1708 he traveled to Shoju-an, a hermitage in the village of Shinano in Nagano province, to meet Master Dokyo Etan. In their brief encounter, the master asked several questions, one of which was how the young monk understood Mu. Ekaku replied with his own question: "What place is there where Mu could be attached to anything?" The teacher grabbed his nose and twisted it saying, "There's a place you can attach Mu to." He dismissed the young monk as a "poor hole-dwelling devil," an epithet he would use for Ekaku for a long time. Still, Dokyo allowed him to stay and study.

Another seminal moment in Hakuin's life came some time later. While begging in the village, an old woman came out and beat him senseless with a broom handle. As he regained consciousness, he realized he understood the answer to his koan. He returned to his teacher who listened and laughed—but from that point on, ceased calling him a "poor hole-dwelling devil." Hakuin stayed for eight more months, then, once again, began wandering. After his father's death in 1716, Hakuin returned home and became the resident priest at the little temple of Shoinji. His reputation spread, and soon monks and nuns came to study with him.

A distinctive feature of Hakuin's teaching is his acknowledgment of how wide-ranging one's insights could be. He said of his own life that he had experienced the great awakening eighteen times and had had little insights too numerous to count.

Another distinctive feature is Hakuin's challenge to koan introspection. The shadow-side of koan introspection is how easily it can ossify, resulting in teachers who demand rote responses rather than lively engagement—as seems to have been the case in Hakuin's era. Challenging this, he offered a full-bodied engagement with the questions of koan introspection.

By the time he died at the age of eighty-three, Hakuin had become the premier teacher of koan Zen in Japan. Today all Japanese Rinzai lineages derive through him, as does the reformed Soto koan lineage called Harada-Yasutani. The koan system—as attributed to him and as developed to maturity within his school—is the Japanese legacy and standard for curriculum koan study.

Bodhisattva Ordination, Leadership Reform, and the Role of Zen Clerics in Japan

To understand the presentation of Zen in the West, it's essential to understand the leadership within Japanese Zen and the way it has marked Western institutions. Perhaps the most significant institutional shift in Japanese Buddhism is the introduction of a new vision of ordination.

Throughout Buddhist history and across the Asian continent, monastics ordained in the Vinaya were the traditional holders or—perhaps better—guardians of the Dharma. Formal Buddhist leadership has been held by Vinaya-ordained monks and occasionally, but rarely, nuns.

Only in Japan did the principal means of formal spiritual leadership shift to a new pattern. Japanese Buddhism is led by clerics who hold what is perhaps best called "Bodhisattva ordination." Understanding this shift in ordination patterns among the Japanese is critical for understanding Zen transmission in the West, as Japanese Zen was the first and continues to be the leading stream of Zen practice among Westerners.

I'm using the term *Bodhisattva ordination* to mean the ordination derived from the ten major and forty-eight minor precepts found in the Chinese *Brahmajala Sutra*. This form is recapitulated as the sixteen-precept form in Japanese Soto and its corollary, the ten precepts, in Japanese Rinzai. To most Vinaya monastics, however, those holding Bodhisattva ordination are simply "pious laypeople," who wear the outer forms of monastic ordination without actually *being* monks or nuns.

The evolution of Japanese Bodhisattva ordination is a story of fits and starts, and of politics as well as spiritual innovation. It is a story marked by confusion, conflict, and occasionally self-deception. It is also the story of a remarkable ordination model, one that might well be the best for the continuance of the Dharma forward in Western culture.

By the end of the twelfth century, the monk Eisai, who eventually introduced the Rinzai school to Japan, received Bodhisattva precepts at Mount Hiei. While departing from Chinese practice, these precepts were still considered essentially monastic in any conventional sense of the term. This continued to be the case into the early thirteenth century, when Eisai's successor, Myozen, ordained Dogen, who would found the Soto school in Japan.

With regard to ordination, Dogen's rhetorical position was one of "radical conservatism." However, throughout his life he demonstrated a sense of innovation and pragmatism. And he always demonstrated a willingness to change even the most traditional forms, if doing so served his purpose of establishing a vital tradition of Dharma within the forms of the Zen school in Japan.

As the centuries passed in Japan, various innovations to ordained practice were introduced. The monastic ordination that people first thought of as an exclusively celibate state slowly began to change. As early as the thirteenth century, one of Dogen's contemporaries, the Pure Land Buddhism reformer Shinran, openly married without renouncing his clerical state. And—while no prominent early Zen monastics took this position—from early on, many Zen teachers also challenged the norms of celibate, monastic life.

It shouldn't be particularly surprising that throughout Zen's history in Japan, there are accounts of monks living with women in some form of intimate relationship. Often what we know of this is inferential, found in reports complaining of how hard it was to enforce celibacy among temple priests. This conflict eventually came to a head in the mid-nineteenth century, during the Meiji era. All laws concerning whether monastics could or could not grow their hair, eat meat, and, most importantly, marry were repealed. This was partially inspired by the government's desire to diminish the authority of clerics by letting them become more like laypeople, and partially a simple acknowledgment of the way things really were.

In the first extended English-language study of Bodhisattva ordination, *Neither Monk nor Layman,* Richard Jaffe cites some significant numbers regarding the Soto school, the only Zen school with readily available statistics on such things as numbers of temples and clerics. We know today that there are 14,000 Soto temples in Japan. Of these, only thirty-one are reserved for "strict monastic training."

Given its Japanese history, the Western reading of "monastic" is complicated. Revealing contemporary cultural norms, Jaffe records that in a 1993 survey of Soto laity in Japan, only five percent preferred celibate clerics. Indeed, seventy-three percent stated a preference for married clergy to serve as priests in their temples. He also reports that the statistics are not significantly different for adherents of the Rinzai school.

The bottom line is that today, no matter what school they belong to, the overwhelming majority of Zen clerics in Japan are married. The principal exception is among ordained women, almost all of whom appear to remain celibate following ordination. While there is no formal prohibition against ordained women being married in the Zen schools, few have availed themselves of this possibility.

Today in Japanese Zen, men and women continue to give the whole of their lives to pursue awakening for the benefit of all beings. But few become permanent monastics, professional meditators, or full-time celibate residents of communities dedicated to Zen practice. For the vast majority, the monastic aspect of practice is a period of training, the duration of which differs among schools and lineages.

Those seeking ordination often ultimately become temple priests, taking on roles not very dissimilar to Western parish ministers or priests. The rituals are different—there is no mass or Western-style worship service in Japanese Buddhism—but there is a regular and full liturgical life to which priests attend, and many see the patterns of the liturgical life of Japanese Zen as near-mirrors of its essence.

What to call such people remains an open question. The terms used within the ordained sangha are traditional monastic terms. The incumbent of a temple, celibate or not, is called a *monk;* the term *nun* is generally rejected, at least in contemporary Western Zen. Jaffe suggests that a more neutral term such as *cleric* or *minister* might be better. Preferred usage suggests the term *priest* is well on its way to becoming the normative English term for an ordained Zen practitioner, at least of the Japanese traditions.

While *priest* may be associated with ceremonial functions—which causes many Western Zen practitioners to balk—there is another way to read the term, simply as a "technologist of the spirit." Within the Zen tradition, this would suggest a certain mastery of one or more of the Zen arts of contemplation. If we consider that the word *priest* literally means "elder," from the Latin *presbyter,* a Zen priest would be both a trained technologist of the spirit and an elder within the community.

The real question, of course, is not what Bodhisattva ordination is called, but what it is *for.* As T. Griffith Foulk writes in *Soto School Scriptures for Daily Service and Practice:* "To summarize, the three most important . . . functions of Soto Zen liturgy are the production and dedication of merit, the commemoration of ancestral teachers, and the sanctification of routine activities in the daily lives of Zen practitioners."

I suggest that in the West—while ordination may well include these functions—the broader expectation of those coming to Zen is for the ordained person to be a proficient guide on the way of awakening. There is another peculiarity of Japanese Zen, at least in the Soto school, which is both the largest Zen school in Japan and the most widely represented in the West. It has to do with the Soto understanding of Dharma transmission.

Throughout Zen's history—while Chinese, Korean, and Vietnamese monks and nuns and later Japanese priests were the normative leaders of Zen schools—acknowledgment of awakening itself remained separate from monastic leadership.

In Japanese Rinzai this acknowledgment is called *Inka* or *Inka Shomei,* the "legitimate seal of clearly furnished proof." Conferred on the one being acknowledged, it is the formal recognition of Zen's deepest realization—though, as the story of Huineng first shows, it has nothing to do with ordination. In fact, laypeople may and occasionally do receive Inka, or the seal of awakening.

In Japanese-derived Soto, however, this recognition has always been part of the ceremonies for ordination as an *osho,* or full priest. Many, perhaps most, Soto priests see no distinction between ordination and Dharma transmission. As the Japanese-derived Soto lines dominate Western Zen, this view that ordination and transmission are one and the same is quite common. The rise of lay lineages in the West has led to considerable debate around this topic (which will be explored more later).

The term *full priest* also calls for some examination. Those ordained in the West generally see the rank of osho as the culmination of formal training. Only an osho may ordain others, which is a critical distinction. In Japan, one receives unsui ordination at the beginning of formal ordained practice, and this is often perceived as "novice ordination." But many scholars point out that this "home-leaving" ordination is actually "full ordination." Thus unsui is the ordination most analogous to Vinaya's *bhikkshu* ordinations. This fact is not generally understood among Western Zen clerics.

The lack of common understanding among Zen teachers about the purpose and nature of unsui ordination points to a significant weakness of the proto-institutions of Zen in the West. A conscious separation of formal religious leadership, with its ordinations and trainings, from the acknowledgment of insight, or spiritual mastery on the Zen way, makes a great deal of sense. As Zen matures in the West, these distinctions will hopefully become clearer.

SECTION 2

MODERN TEACHERS AND INSTITUTIONS IN THE WEST

FIVE

The Birth of Western Zen

*I*T IS POSSIBLE THAT a monk named Huishen (or Hushen) together with several other Chinese Buddhist monastics first visited the Americas at the end of the fifth century of the Common Era. Nothing remains of this possible journey but Huishen's account, recorded in Ma Tuan-Lin's *Great Chinese Encyclopedia.* Its descriptions suggest that he and his companions really did range down the West coast of North America as far as today's Mexico. And the details of this account, while often challenged, are at least plausible.

However, there doesn't seem to have been any lasting connection between medieval China and the Americas. Other than a later Chinese anchor discovered off the coast of Santa Barbara, and occasional fanciful speculations about Chinese influence on an isolated Native American word or two, the Chinese Buddhist encounter with the Americas seems even more ephemeral than that of the pre-Columbian Vikings'.

The next Buddhists to come to America were probably among the many Chinese laborers who toiled in the mid-nineteenth century creating the railroads. Persecuted and isolated from the larger culture, they created their own communities and established small temples up and down the West coast. The ruins of several of these can still be seen; a few, in fact, have continued functioning to this day. Unfortunately, for many reasons—not the least of which was racism—there are few accounts of West Coast European-Americans learning about the religions of their Chinese-American neighbors.

Around this time, however, the Chinese were establishing themselves in America. And Buddhist texts first became available in Western languages. Significantly, some people—particularly New Englanders and particularly Unitarian Transcendentalists—were beginning to express interest in the wisdom of Asia. The first English version of a Buddhist scripture was published in the Transcendentalist journal *The Dial* in 1844. This English text was an "anonymous" version of a French translation of a chapter from the *Sadharmapundarika Sutra,* the Lotus Sutra.

Interestingly, this anonymous translation was long attributed to Henry David Thoreau, who undoubtedly did have affinities with Buddhism and perhaps even more so with Taoism. But in fact, the chapter had been translated by Elizabeth Palmer Peabody, one of the more prominent female leaders of the Transcendentalist movement. Thus once again, as one observer wryly noted, "Anonymous" turns out to be a woman.

From the mid-nineteenth century on, a torrent of Buddhist texts showered upon the West. Discovering these ancient texts in translation, many readers found resonances and hints of a new way of being religious. Over the next century, some of them even traveled to the East. But it wasn't until the beginning of the twentieth century that a few of these Westerners returned as acknowledged Zen masters—or that Asian masters came to make their homes in the West.

The stories of the founders of our North American Zen present us with something a bit different than the stories of ancient Zen worthies. The old stories are uncomplicated by flesh-and-blood problems. Old Master Zhaozhou doesn't have a drinking problem. Linji doesn't have affairs with female lay devotees. Dogen doesn't spend undue amounts of time with his young male acolytes. Hakuin

doesn't bounce checks. But our real-life teachers have all these difficulties and more.

Looking at Zen as it emerges in the West, we're confronted with
all the complexities and ambiguities of real life. At the same time,
these foundational stories of authentic Zen masters teach us about
ourselves and what we might become—and in this sense, they're
immensely important.

The truth is that the ancient stories have been polished to be very
meaningful; anything extraneous to those meanings is eliminated.
If we hold that fact in the back of our mind, the old stories can teach
us much. But today's stories also contain elements of the teachings,
for those willing to open their eyes and ears. Couched as they are in
a contemporary idiom, however, foible and failure are part of the
resumé. And this should be a good thing for a tradition that claims
to describe human possibility.

What follows here are some of these modern stories of Zen in
the West. They focus on the founding teachers and the institutions
they established. Arranged roughly by geographical origin and
chronology, they include some of the unique conditions that arose
from the individual teachers' national heritages. Thus we can see
what was brought to the West as well as who actually worked to
create the frame, or frames, in which we now practice. Moreover, in
addition to stories about flesh-and-blood founders, we will begin to
see the ways in which Zen's ancient institutional and cultural heritages play out within a radically new cultural setting.

While some schools dominate—particularly Japanese-derived
Soto and Rinzai and the Korean-derived Kwan Um School—Western Zen is by no means monolithic. Zen is not so much a "way," in
the sense of one collection of practices. It is many different *ways*
devoted to a view of reality that enables us to find a new way of life
marked by vision and compassion. This early history brought
teachers to the West who would deeply mark the shape of the
Dharma, and it also includes some false starts. As we encounter

these ancestral figures we also discover the questions of teaching and authorization and hierarchy beginning to be framed.

Soyen Shaku: First American Ancestor

Our common ancestor in the foundation of Western and particularly American Zen is without a doubt Soyen Shaku. He was born in 1856. He spent three years at Keio University, which was highly unusual for a Zen priest at that time. This was the first of his many experiences outside the norms of Japanese priesthood. An adventurous young man, he traveled to Ceylon to study Theravada monasticism—possibly the first Japanese priest to do so. In 1880, he was named a Dharma successor to Imagita Kosen, abbot of the prominent Rinzai training monastery Engakuji, in Kamakura, and became master of Engakuji when his teacher died.

When he received an invitation to speak at the World Parliament of Religions in Chicago in 1893, most of Soyen Roshi's associates, priests, students, and prominent laypeople discouraged him from attending. America was, after all, uncivilized and unspeakably barbaric. But he was adventurous and asked one of his lay students who spoke English, D.T. Suzuki, to draft his letter of acceptance.

In Chicago he encountered Paul Carus, a compelling figure who, through his writings and publishing ventures, was important in developing a Buddhist presence among North Americans of European descent. Theirs proved to be a fruitful friendship. In 1905, Soyen Roshi returned to the United States at the invitation of Alexander Russell, staying in San Francisco for about nine months.

This was the extent of Soyen Shaku's direct connection to North America. But over the next few years, several of his students came West. These individuals—D.T. Suzuki, Shigetsu Sasaki (known as Sokei-an), and Zuigan Goto—were the first active Zen teachers willing to reach out across ethnic barriers.

After living in America for a few years, Zuigan Goto Roshi returned to Japan where he became master of Daitokuji temple. When the American musician Walter Nowick traveled to Japan, he became Zuigan Goto Roshi's student and eventually his Dharma heir, the first Western Dharma successor in the Rinzai tradition. D.T. Suzuki and Shigetsu Sasaki had a more direct influence on an emerging Western Zen.

D.T. Suzuki, Alan Watts, and a Zen Philosophy

D.T. Suzuki gave our emergent Western Zen its first theoretical basis, and his admirer Alan Watts became the first Western popularizer of Zen.

Teitaro Suzuki was born in 1870 in Kanazawa, a village some two hundred miles north of Tokyo. His father, a member of the Samurai class, worked as a physician and died when young Teitaro was six years old. The family struggled to keep body and soul together. Among other things, Teitaro had taught himself English and became a tutor for other villagers. In 1891, when he went to Tokyo to attend Waseda University, he encountered actual English speakers and realized that whatever he had been teaching, it wasn't English.

He began studying Zen as a layman with Master Kosen at Engakuji. When the master died not long after, he became a student of Soyen Shaku, the new incumbent of the training hall. Under Soyen Shaku Roshi's tutelage he had his first breakthrough experience. While he never ordained, this experience would mark his life spiritually and as a scholar. His teacher gave him the Buddhist name Daisetz which means "great simplicity." In his later years D.T. Suzuki would tell people it meant "great stupidity."

Through arrangements made by Soyen Shaku, D.T. Suzuki arrived in the United States in 1897 to go to work for the Open Court Publishing Company. He and Paul Carus first worked on a translation of the Taoist classic the *Tao Te Ching.* But he also began working on his first English translation of a seminal Buddhist text, Ashvaghosha's *Awakening of Faith in the Mahayana.* This would begin an illustrious career as the first scholarly interpreter of Zen Buddhism to the West.

As the years passed his influence on Western thought would grow ever wider. His translations and essays on Zen would become the basis for the first generation of popular Western interest in Zen Buddhism. D.T. Suzuki was highly sectarian; he never mentioned the Soto sect at all despite the fact it was by far the larger school of Japanese Zen. Only in his later years did he begin to transcend his sectarian perspectives, expressing his gratitude for the Pure Land teachings of the Shin school.

Also he discounted the historical aspects of Zen's development in favor of giving most attention to that ahistorical experience of awakening. This acknowledged, the debt that we Western follow-ers of the Zen way owe to this single person is incalculable. The list of people he directly influenced is quite long, but includes musi-cians, poets, and novelists like John Cage, Allen Ginsberg, Aldous Huxley, Jack Kerouac, and Gary Snyder. Each of these people would in turn introduce aspects of Zen thought into our North American and Western culture.

Notable among Suzuki's admirers and followers was a young Englishman, Alan Watts (1915–1973). While a devoted follower of Suzuki, he himself appears never to have been an actual practitioner of Zen meditation disciplines. Still, his ever popular books on Zen and related subjects were so influential in attracting the first gener-ation of Zen practitioners, Watts really needs to be at least men-tioned. His *Way of Zen,* based almost entirely on Suzuki's work, was for many in the 1960s and '70s the first book many people read on Zen. This was certainly true for me.

I vividly recall the first time I met Alan Watts. I was on the guest staff of the Zen monastery in Oakland led by Roshi Jiyu

Kennett. I was enormously excited to actually meet this famous man, the great interpreter of the Zen way. Wearing my very best robes, I waited for him to show up—and waited and waited. Nearly an hour later, Watts arrived dressed in a kimono, accompanied by a fawning young woman and an equally fawning young man. It was hard not to notice his interest in the young woman who—as a monk, I was embarrassed to observe—seemed not to be wearing any underwear. I was also awkwardly aware that Watts seemed intoxicated.

An erstwhile Episcopal priest, engaging raconteur, and scandalous libertine, Alan Watts was also a prolific author whose books created an inviting sense of Zen-as-pure-experience and a do-what-you-want spirituality. These qualities both profoundly misrepresented Zen and led many people to it. The title of the English edition of Monica Furlong's biography of Watts, *Genuine Fake,* speaks volumes about this intriguing American Zen trickster/ancestor.

There is little more to say in a book of this sort about this interesting eccentric. He deserves his own study—although, frankly, it would be a study largely outside the mainstream of Zen.

To return to the more mainstream Zen way: After his stint at Open Court, D.T. Suzuki traveled for a while in Europe. Returning to Japan, he taught at what is now Gakushuin, a Rinzai university. He then returned to the U.S., married an American, Beatrice Lane, and stayed on for a decade. In 1921 he returned to Japan to become a professor at Otani University and to found, with others, the Eastern Buddhist Society.

Suzuki advocated an *unmediated experience* of Zen. Rick Fields, in his monumental study of Buddhism in the West, *How the Swans Came to the Lake,* quotes Suzuki: "Zen is the ultimate fact of all philosophy, that final psychic fact that takes place when religious consciousness is heightened to extremity. Whether it comes to pass in Buddhists, in Christians, or in philosophers, it is in the last analysis incidental to Zen." Fields adds that "it was this universalization of Zen that made it possible for all kinds of people to see Zen in all kinds of places." This was true, for good and for ill. Thanks to D.T. Suzuki, "Zen" as shorthand for a universal mystical experience became almost normative for Western intellectuals.

In the 1950s, Suzuki again returned again to the U.S. to serve as a visiting professor at Columbia University. When he died in 1966 at the age of 96, he had published a hundred books and articles, twenty-three in English. D.T. Suzuki is arguably the most influential early figure in the development of a Western Zen.

Sokei-an: Zen Poet and Pioneer

Sokei-an was the first koan master to live in America and take on Western students. Yeita Sasaki was born in 1882. His Buddhist name was Shigetsu, "Finger Pointing to the Moon," but he was generally known as Sokei-an, the name given to him with Dharma transmission. His father was a Shinto priest and eventually chief priest of the Omiya shrine. According to his autobiographical account, his mother was his father's concubine, an unusual arrangement, but apparently quite public. She would later leave the Sasaki household and make a name for herself as a singer and dancer. His legal mother, his father's wife, treated him as her own child.

After his father's death, he was apprenticed to the sculptor Koun Takamura. Successful as an artist, Shigestsu found himself obsessing about the passing nature of all things, a disposition that eventually led him to become a lay student of Master Kosen and, following that teacher's death, of Soyen Shaku.

His breakthrough koan was "Before your parents were born, what is your original face?" He struggled with this for several years. Interestingly, he later wrote that he had his awakening experience shortly after reading a passage by Ralph Waldo Emerson. I haven't discovered the turning phrase he found, but this wouldn't be the first or last time that Unitarianism, specifically Transcendentalism, and Buddhism would influence one another.

In 1905, he graduated from the Imperial Academy of Art and was immediately drafted into the army. Fortunately the Russo-Japanese war ended two months later, and he was discharged. He then married his first wife, Tomé. In 1906, shortly after the great earthquake of San Francisco, he and his wife arrived in San Francisco as members of a party of fourteen including Zuigan Goto, to found an "American Zen community." They took up raising strawberries on a farm in Hayward, California. But the fourteen, all intellectuals with university backgrounds, were apparently dismal failures as farmers.

Then, while studying painting at the California Institute of Art, Shigetsu met Nyogen Senzaki (about whom, more later). They would become lifelong friends—and occasionally rivals—as early presenters of the Zen way in the West.

By 1910 everyone in the original party of fourteen, except Shigetsu, returned to Japan. He worked briefly in Oregon before his wife and young child rejoined him in Seattle, where their second child was born. He began contributing articles to Japanese magazines and newspapers, something he would continue to do for the rest of his life. When his wife was pregnant with their third child, she decided she wanted her children to be raised Japanese and so took the children back to Japan.

Shigetsu began wandering in a generally eastward direction, eventually ending up in 1916 in Greenwich Village in New York City. He began translating Asian texts into English, beginning with the poetry of Chinese poet Li Po, while continuing to write for publications in Japan. He also started composing poetry himself.

In 1920, he returned to Japan to continue formal koan study, first with Soyen Shaku and then with one of his Dharma heirs, Sokatsu Shaku. Although he returned to America, he would visit Japan regularly until 1928, when he received Inka from Sokatsu Shaku and the teaching name Sokei-an. While continuing as an artist, writer, and journalist, his attention focused ever more on teaching Zen.

He began giving public talks in New York's Central Park and at the Orientalia Bookstore on East Twelfth Street. He also began giving *sanzen* (also called *dokusan*), one-on-one formal Zen interviews, perhaps the first teacher to do so in North America. While an inspiring speaker, able to draw on the literary traditions of East and West, Sokei-an seemed unable to inspire people to take up traditional formal sitting practice. His students meditated in chairs briefly before his talks, but only a few took up formal, regular sitting. Among those few who did take up practice, some also began formal koan study.

Records suggest that several of these students advanced through as many as seventy cases in the traditional koan curriculum. And independent accounts of former students assert that he gave several students permission to teach, and perhaps even Dharma transmission to one or two. However, there has been no verification of these alleged permissions, and no one claiming these authorizations has thus far been accepted by the larger Zen community of teachers.

It was in New York that Sokei-an also met Ruth Fuller Everett (whose biography follows immediately below). When World War II began, Sokei-an was interned as an enemy alien. This may have exacerbated his already failing health. Through the efforts of his friends and students, Sokei-an was eventually released but suffered a heart attack not long after. In 1944, after his divorce from Tomé, he married Ruth. But he never completely recovered his health and died in May 1945.

An interesting teacher with a wonderful literary style, Sokei-an's renown has largely faded, perhaps because he left no undisputed Dharma heirs. Still, he holds a central place in the evolution of Zen in North America.

Fortunately, Michael Hotz—a member of the First Zen Institute in New York, founded by Sokei-an in 1930, and one of the

Institute's board presidents—has compiled a collection of his writings. Published under the title *Holding the Lotus to the Rock*, it presents in a chronological manner a reconstructed "autobiography." It is a suitable epitaph for the first fully authorized Zen master to live in the West and teach people of both Western and Eastern descent.

Ruth Fuller Sasaki: First American Woman Zen Teacher

Ruth Fuller Sasaki may be the first Westerner to be fully ordained a Rinzai Zen priest, and she is the coauthor of the first detailed examination of koan introspection in the English language—an excellent book still read today.

Ruth Fuller was born in 1883. Details of her early life are scant, but it seems she spent some time studying with the eccentric Hindu spiritual teacher Pierre Bernard, known as Oom the Omnipotent. She may have also studied Sanskrit and Pali during her youth. When she met and married Charles Everett, a successful attorney, Ruth found the economic freedom to move beyond the dilettante spiritual circles that were previously the only ones available to her.

In 1930, at the age of forty-seven, she visited Japan. Here she met D.T. Suzuki, who introduced her to Zen meditation. Two years later she returned to Japan and spent a training period studying with Rinzai master Nanshinken Roshi, in Kyoto.

In 1938, Ruth Everett began studying with Sokei-an in New York City. In the same year, her daughter Eleanor married Alan Watts. One of the more ironic pairings in Zen history, this was one of those curious coincidences that sometimes occur. Watts, as we've seen, would go on to become a popularizer of his own eccentric vision of Zen, while Ruth Everett's path took her toward orthodox Rinzai and eventual ordination as a priest.

The marriage between Everett's daughter and Watts lasted nearly ten years. The revelation that he was having an extramarital affair led to their separation and eventual formal church annulment as well as divorce. Almost nothing has been written about the relationship between Ruth Fuller Everett and Alan Watts, if indeed there was one. He briefly alludes to her in his autobiography; she never explicitly mentions him in any of her writings. However, writer Andrew Rawlinson suggests, intriguingly, that in her introduction to *Zen Dust,* her allusion to "the misinformation being spread about the koan by those professed exponents of Zen in the West who have never studied koans themselves" could easily have been written with her former son-in-law in mind.

Ruth Fuller's husband died in 1940, and four years later she married Sokei-an. At the time Sokei-an was in an internment camp, and some have suggested this marriage was simply a way to get him released from internment. Others, however, suggest it really was a love affair. Whatever the truth of the matter, her second husband died one year after they were married.

In 1949 she moved to Japan and began practicing and studying at Daitokuji, with Zuigan Goto Roshi. While he wanted her to return to America as a missionary, she decided to remain in Japan where she opened a zendo for Westerners in 1956. In 1958 her zendo was recognized as a sub-temple of Daitokuji. At the age of seventy-five she was formally ordained a priest by one of Goto Roshi's successors, Sesso Oda Roshi. Except for some brief visits back to North America, she remained in Japan for the rest of her life, dying in Kyoto in 1967 at the age of eighty-four.

Her book *Zen Dust,* written with Isshu Miura—master of the Rinzai training temple, Koonji, in Hachioji near Tokyo—is currently available as *The Zen Koan.* Although unfortunately lacking the extensive and valuable footnotes, it remains the single most important English-language introduction to koan study in the Japanese manner. As a scholar and authentic practitioner, Ruth Fuller Sasaki also played host to a generation of Zen inquirers: Walter Nowick, Robert Aitken, Philip Kapleau, and Gary Snyder.

Sasaki Sensei's influence, direct and indirect, on the shape of a Western Zen is immense.

Nyogen Senzaki: Zen's Mushroom

Nyogen Senzaki was to the West Coast what Sokei-an was to the East Coast—an authentic Zen teacher welcoming Western students. He exercised considerable influence on several people who would become central figures in modern Western Zen.

When Soyen Shaku Roshi made his second visit to America in 1905, he was accompanied by a young Rinzai priest, Nyogen Senzaki. Not much is known about Senzaki's early years. He was born sometime in the late nineteenth century in Siberia. His mother was Japanese, his father either Chinese or Russian. Orphaned early on, he was taken in by a Japanese priest and adopted by a shipwright named Senzaki. He was later taken under wing by a Soto priest who provided him with an education and, it appears, ordained him an unsui. In later years he would speak of himself as a "mushroom"—having no deep root, no branches, no flowers, and "probably no seeds."

In 1896 he went to Engakuji and became Soyen Shaku's student. This crossing over of sect, which is fairly unusual today, was at that time unheard of. In those days just to transfer from one teacher to another in the same school led some to cut off a finger as a sign of regret. He studied with Soyen Shaku for five years, after which he left the monastery to found a nursery school, inspired by the German innovation of kindergartens. Determining to live simply as a celibate, he tried hard to live as a monk rather than follow the increasingly normative priestly model of Japanese temple life.

It seems he first came to America with Soyen Shaku Roshi, with the idea of raising funds for his nursery school. But he ended up staying on, first as a houseboy at the home of Alexander and Ida Russell, early supporters of Soen Roshi—Ida being possibly the first Westerner to formally practice koan introspection. He later continued doing domestic work for others and, for a while, taught English and Japanese. He then began working in hotels, first as a porter and eventually making his way up to manager. He briefly owned a hotel, but when that failed, he became a cook.

In 1922, Nyogen Senzaki hired a hall and gave his first lecture on Zen. This was the beginning of his "floating Zendo," which he recreated wherever he could hire a hall or cajole a friend or acquaintance into letting him use her or his living room. He led the itinerant group that gathered around him in various places from San Francisco to Los Angeles for the next thirty years—excepting only the war years following 1942, when he was interned with 10,000 other Japanese nationals at Heart Mountain in the Wyoming desert.

Many Californians and others had their first taste of Zen practice and thought under Senzaki Sensei's tutelage. This number included the young Robert Aitken, who would go on to be one of the most respected Zen teachers in the West. A close friend of the great Soen Nakagawa, Senzaki also became a mentor to Eido Shimano, who would go on to become master of the Zen Studies Society in New York City and Dai Bosatsu Zendo in upstate New York. (We learn more about Aitken, Nakagawa, and Shimano below.)

Nyogen Senzaki died in 1958. Knowing that he was dying, he recorded a message to be played at his funeral. In it he said: "Friends in Dhamma, be satisfied with your own heads. Do not put any false heads above your own. Then minute after minute, watch your steps closely. Always keep your head cold and your feet warm. These are my last words to you." But in fact they weren't. He then added: "Thank you very much, everybody, for taking such good care of me for so long. Bye-bye." Aitken Roshi, who was there, says that at the tail end of the tape the last thing one could hear was a small laugh.

In one sense Nyogen Senzaki *was* a mushroom: he left no Dharma heirs. But thanks to his early books on Zen, and all those halls he hired, and his floating Zendo—much of Zen on the West Coast of North America got its start.

Soen Nakagawa's Endless Vow

Through his regular visits, his Dharma heirs, and others he taught, Soen Nakagawa would become one of the most important figures shaping a Western understanding of Rinzai Zen. Soen Nakagawa was born in 1907 in Iwakuni, near Hiroshima. His father was an army doctor, and so the family relocated frequently. While Soen was still very young his father died. His mother, who never remarried, struggled to support the family. Eventually Soen was admitted to Tokyo Imperial University to study Japanese literature. He specialized in poetry, specifically Basho, perhaps Japan's most beloved poet. Basho had studied as a Zen monk, and while he may have never been formally ordained, the Zen spirit clearly pervades his work.

Fascinated by the idea of the literary monk, Soen Nakagawa determined to ordain. In 1931, a year after taking his degree, Soen was ordained an unsui by the Rinzai master Katsube Keigaku Roshi at Kogakuji. He spent considerable time in a mountain retreat at Daibosatsu Mountain in Yamanashi Prefecture.

At this time he published some poetry and diary entries in a magazine called *Fujin Koron,* "Woman's Review." Nyogen Senzaki read these and in 1934 initiated what would become a lifelong correspondence and profound friendship. At about the same time, Soen Nakagawa met the renowned Gempo Yamamoto Roshi, the abbot of Ryutakuji.

Soen's first book of poems, *Shingan,* "Coffin of Poems," was published in 1936. This was followed by three more, the last being in 1985. Continuing his penchant for deep personal practice, not long after being accepted as a student by Gempo Roshi, he returned to Daibosatsu for two years of solitary retreat. He then returned to Ryutakuji and more formal training. In 1950 he succeeded his teacher as master of this renowned training hall.

Senzaki Sensei thought Soen Nakagawa Roshi would be a perfect teacher for the West and spent years trying to lure him to North

America. Soen Roshi first planned to come to America in 1941, but the War intervened. He arrived in the West for the first time in 1949 where he met Nyogen Senzaki, who arranged his first talk at the Los Angeles Theosophical Society.

In 1950, Soen Nakagawa returned to Ryutakuji. Upon Nyogen Senzaki's suggestion, young Robert Aitken made his way there and began studying with him. The next year, Philip Kapleau would stay there for three months before going on to Sogaku Harada Roshi's temple, Hosshinji. Of equal importance, Soen Roshi would visit the United States thirteen times, leading *sesshin,* intensive meditation retreats, on both coasts and spending extensive time with many different students.

Sean Murphy in his *One Bird, One Stone* recounts the following:

> Soen loved to walk around New York City. He'd stare at the lighted skyscrapers, at their tops, he claimed he saw Buddha figures in the lights. "Look at the Buddha," he'd point, "Shining Buddha!" He'd fill the sleeves of his robes with nuts and berries from Central Park or herbs growing in the sidewalk cracks, and add them to his bowl at the next meal. He loved the musical *Fiddler on the Roof,* and when asked a question about why some particular point of ceremony needed to be performed in a certain way, he might burst into song, responding "Tradition…!"

Soen was a creative teacher. Famously, he was known to conduct tea ceremony using Coca-Cola or instant coffee and occasionally using Styrofoam cups. Nothing was off limits if it would help point the way. The writer and Zen teacher Peter Matthiessen's 1975 journal recorded in *Endless Vow: The Zen Path of Soen Nakagawa* describes his experience of this remarkable teacher:

Cleaning the Zendo after evening sitting, I find Soen alone in the shadows at the end of the empty row, in the stillness of zazen. He is the archetypal old monk of the paintings, ancient as death, burning with life. I dust around him. These days his joy in life is dear; he refers gleefully to "the majority," as he calls the dead…Each day he reminds us that, despite all the tumult and delusion of our life, our true nature is always there, like the sun or moon above black wind and clouds. "The sun is shining; the sun is *always* shining. That sun is enlightenment; everything is enlightenment!" He dabbled his fingers in a water bowl. "Do you hear? *That is enlightenment!*"

Apparently, in 1967 while trying to climb a tree, Soen fell and sustained a severe head injury. From that point on, Soen Roshi suffered from continuous pain and occasional bouts of depression. Following his retirement as abbot of Ryutakuji, he spent increasing amounts of time in solitary retreat. Whether this inclination was connected with the pain he suffered, with depression, or simply with ever deepening practice is unknown. He died in 1984—and his death poem summarizes an authentic Zen life.

Mustard blossoms!
There is nothing left
to hurl away.

Soen Nakagawa Roshi's influence in the West and North America is substantive. He was a formative teacher for Robert Aitken as well as for his Dharma heirs, Maurine Stuart and Eido Shimano, all of whom have played significant roles in the formation of North American Zen. Half his ashes are interred at Ryutakuji, half in America. The ripples playing out from his life continue to wash across the West.

Byways and Dead-Ends

In examining the early history of Zen in America, it's not possible to overemphasize the influence of Soyen Shaku on the shape of a future Western Zen. His students D.T. Suzuki, Nyogen Senzaki, and Sokei-an would each in his own way open the gate of the Dharma for us. Suzuki arrived in the West in 1897, Senzaki in 1905, and Sokei-an in 1906. Each presented variations on the Rinzai perspective, and each would leave a lasting mark.

This was not true of all visiting teachers. From the years before the Second World War and into the following two decades, visiting Asian Buddhist spiritual leaders, including several Zen teachers, gave various permissions and authorizations to individuals with an interest in matters Eastern, particularly Buddhism. Unfortunately, most of these Westerners had little or no genuine preparation to teach. However, as we consider them we see those same questions of authorization and hierarchy, of what Zen teaching is really about, beginning to take shape.

Some who thought they had permission to teach simply misunderstood the nature of the initiations they undertook. Christmas Humphries, for instance, the English writer, Theosophist, and early Buddhist leader, apparently confused the *jukai* ceremony, in which he formally received precepts—a ritual perhaps best understood as being like confirmation in Catholicism—with an ordination ceremony, empowering him as a priest. Others were, in fact, made priests or teachers, but too often without any context or support for their practice or teaching potential.

At least two Zen masters, quite prominent in their home countries, sanctioned numbers of teachers and priests while visiting North America. But none of these authorized people seemed to have spent any significant time with these teachers, and the nature of their previous training was almost always unclear. Thus it is difficult to interpret the teachers in these lineages as legitimately representing the Zen tradition.

One of these visiting teachers was the prominent Japanese Rinzai master Asahina Sogen Roshi. The other was the Korean Zen master and prominent scholar, Dr. Kyong-bo Seo. It's hard to fathom the intent of either of these teachers in their authorizations. Apparently they both tended to give permissions to people who were already running small independent centers, sometimes based on a few years in Asia or previous connections with shadowy figures from the first half of the twentieth century.

While beyond the scope of this book, such cases do deserve serious examination. An interesting illustration is typified by M.T. Kirby, who may have been ordained a Pure Land priest in Japan in 1913. He may then have gone on to study Zen at Engakuji. A controversial presence in Hawai'i in the early twentieth century, he was highly polemical and vociferously anti-Christian.

In the San Francisco Bay area immediately following World War II, a number of individuals claimed, and in varying degrees appeared to possess, Zen and other Buddhist initiations and ordinations. These men—as all those I've been able to reference were indeed men—either traveled to Asia or intimately knew people who had. They each led small groups at various times. In their list of qualifications, they occasionally used Zen joined with larger associations such as the Unreformed Buddhist Church and the American Buddhist Order. Included in this group are Jay DuPont, Don Gilbert, Samuel Lewis, Jack MacDonough, Joe Miller, Iru Price, J. Eugene Wagner, and Neville Warwick.

Not, apparently, of this band, but illustrative of this time in Zen's Western formation is Henry Chikuen Kugai Platov. Trained for thirteen years by Sokei-an, he spent additional time in Japan and claimed to be a Dharma heir of Sokei-an. He has left at least one and possibly two Dharma heirs of his own. While there appear to be no references in Sokei-an's files of him giving Dharma transmission to anyone, it is possible that Dr. Platov had some form of Zen teaching authorization.

Without clear documentary evidence, these early pioneers will continue to be footnotes in the history of Zen Dharma in the West. Nevertheless, they and many others devoted years to sharing the Dharma in the West. Although their influence is gradually vanishing, many contemporary teachers owe a great deal to these increasingly forgotten ancestors.

And it's possible to see the feelings that early visiting Asian teachers might have had for some of these people. In a letter written by Dr. Seo, for instance, he describes meeting the idiosyncratic San Francisco–based mystic Murishid Samuel Lewis (mentioned above). Lewis had already been acknowledged as a Sufi master in several lines, in addition to his various Buddhist connections. Dr. Seo was profoundly impressed by Murishid Lewis's insight and gave him Dharma transmission pretty much on the spot. In Murishid Samuel Lewis's interpretation of this, it was simply a broad acknowledgment of insight. And, while he occasionally wore Korean Zen robes, the Sufi teacher never attempted to ordain others or confer authorizations within the Zen lineage. This however was not true of others who had similarly obtained permissions.

Moreover, as the years passed there have been increasing numbers of people who might be called "Dharma orphans." Having undertaken training with various teachers—and for reasons sometimes not of their own choosing—they found themselves in charge of practice centers while lacking full permission to teach and also lacking formal connections with teachers who could finish their training. Thus a partially trained person was left in charge of a group or groups.

This was often because the master died or left the country before the student's training was completed. It could also come about because of irresolvable disputes around issues other than training: for instance, issues arising with a teacher's serious breach of ethics.

It could come about when, too late, it becomes apparent that a student shouldn't have been leading groups. Or, having committed his (again, usually "his") own breach of ethical standards, the student was asked to leave his teacher's organization. Out of this mix arose a number of small centers, which are effectively independent but attempting to maintain a Zen style.

In addition to the teachers with no traditional authorization, surprising numbers of people use the titles *Zen teacher, master, roshi,* and *sensei* without any obvious connections to Zen. Often they obfuscate their Zen connections, raising the very real question whether they have any authentic relationship to the Zen world at all. In my studies I've run across literally dozens of such cases.

When asked, they might simply refuse to talk about where they trained or who gave them Dharma transmission. Or they might go on the offensive and suggest the question shows the inquirer's lack of authentic insight into what Zen is actually about.

Most of these teachers of mysterious origin appear from nowhere, set up shop for a few months or years, and then, following the current of their own karma, disappear. A few establish centers that last for decades. Perhaps the most prominent of such apparently self-declared teachers is the widely read author and meditation teacher Cheri Huber. Huber may have studied briefly with Jay DuPont (mentioned above), but it is not clear that she was authorized by him or anyone else as a Zen teacher.

This area at the margins of Zen is one of confusion and hurt. Hopefully as Zen matures in the West, much of this sort of thing will fall away. Already the lists published on websites of the American Zen Teachers Association and the Soto Zen Buddhist Association are proving helpful to those trying to sort out who fits within the normative stream of Zen and who does not. However, it should be noted that, while as many as eighty percent of authentic teachers in the West belong to one of these two organizations, still a significant number do not.

Soyu Matsuoka and Western Zen's Difficult Birth

A consideration of Soyu Matsuoka, a Japanese Soto Zen teacher who spent the last half of his life in America, reveals many of the difficulties in establishing a Western Zen. Of all the Zen lineages in North America, his is perhaps the most difficult to interpret. Soyu Matsuoka ranks with Nyogen Senzaki and Sokei-an as one of the first teachers to make his home and life work in North America. He also seems to be the first teacher to clearly and unambiguously give Dharma transmission to Western students.

Born near Hiroshima in 1912, Soyu Matsuoka was one of the Zen priests who came to serve Japanese immigrants in the United States. He arrived just in time to be interned during the War. In 1949, Matsuoka Roshi established the Zen Buddhist Temple of Chicago. In 1970 he moved to Long Beach. While at first an official representative of the Soto school, at some point he became estranged from the Japanese organization. The details are clouded but included lawsuits. This estrangement no doubt further complicated things. Over the years, he ordained numerous students—and here is where the problems begin.

In 1996, I met someone who claimed Matsuoka Roshi had designated him a "roshi"—a title traditionally reserved for the most senior Zen teachers—after the student had studied with the old master for three months. I came away feeling I'd met a nice enough person, who was certainly honest and forthright about himself and his formal Zen experience—but who would be considered a beginner, certainly not a senior student and absolutely not a teacher in any Zen organization I am aware of. There appears to have been a number of such authorizations in Matsuoka Roshi's career.

As a result, few teachers in the Zen tradition today, and fewer still in the Soto school within which Matsuoka Roshi taught, accept his heirs as authentic Zen teachers. The charges against the Matsuoka lineage are essentially twofold: first, he did not properly *train* anyone; and second, he did not in fact *ordain* anyone.

Having examined these questions closely, I believe that the question of proper training is part of the larger question of North American Zen, especially in its Soto derivation. What is appropriate training, if not the *sodo* training-hall model, in which an aspirant spends time in a formal monastic situation? (Here I use the term *sodo* to stand for residential monastic training; it should be noted that in Japan training also assumes the monastic actually lives in the training hall, something rarely done in Western training centers.) I can only say that Matsuoka was hardly the only teacher to feel that close proximity to himself for a significant period of time was sufficient to "train" students.

The second question, about what constitutes ordination, is worth exploring in detail. This opens a much larger conversation regarding authorization. Regarding the Matsuoka lineage, Taiun Michael Elliston and Kongo Richard Langlois were indisputably two of Matsuoka Roshi's long-time senior students, and each has established himself, by many standards, as a legitimate Zen—if not properly Soto Zen—teacher.

Langlois Roshi led the Chicago center from 1970 until his death in 1999. While he left several Dharma heirs, none appears to have been designated the "official" successor to head the Chicago organization.

Taiun Elliston Roshi founded the Atlanta Soto Zen Center in 1977, which he continues to lead. As a footnote, it should be mentioned that Elliston Roshi has been working hard to reconcile with the Soto mainstream. It is possible that within a few years, this one branch, at least, of the Matsuoka line will rejoin the normative Soto tradition.

SIX

Chinese, Korean, and Vietnamese
Zen in the West

*A*s I've mentioned, Japanese Zen is the most obvious Zen influence in the West. This is followed closely by the Korean master Seung Sahn's Kwan Um School of Zen. But there are many other national expressions of Zen including Zen schools from China, Korea, and Vietnam. In this chapter we will examine the influences of these countries upon Western Zen.

Hsuan Hua and Chinese Zen Orthodoxy

Master Hsuan Hua is the earliest and perhaps most prominent Chinese Zen teacher in the West. He brought a traditionalist Chinese vision of Zen that has proven resilient even in America. He was born Yushu Bai early in the twentieth century, in Shuangcheng county of Jilin Province. At the age of eleven, he resolved to become a monk. At fifteen he formally took refuge as a lay Buddhist and then continued his formal education. At the age of nineteen, following his mother's death, he shaved his head and was ordained a novice monk in the Vinaya tradition.

He embraced a harsh discipline, including deep study, meditating in the Zen style, eating a single meal a day, and refraining from sleeping lying down. During this time, he had many visions and gradually acquired a reputation for holiness. In 1946, he went on a pilgrimage to Buddhist holy places and met the renowned Master Hsu Yun. The next year he received full ordination in the Vinaya tradition. And in 1948, he received Dharma transmission from Master Hsu Yun.

Hsu Yun, or "Empty Cloud," was the great reviver of the Chinese synthesis of Zen and Pure Land in the nineteenth and twentieth century. If traditional accounts are to be trusted, he lived to be 119 or 120 years old. During his life he traveled widely in Asia, and his influence extended to southeast Asia and Tibet. Among these, Hsuan Hua is possibly his most important successor in the West. It should be noted there are a number of organizations in the West springing from Hsu Yun's lineage. One organization, the Zen Buddhist Order of Hsu Yun, has been particularly devoted to a largely web-based mission.

In 1959, Hsuan Hua's students established in the United States what would become the Dharma Realm Buddhist Association. After a brief visit to Australia in 1962, Hsuan Hua traveled to America where he would make his permanent home. Centering his teaching in San Francisco's Chinatown, he then moved into the Fillmore district and later to Japantown. Finally he settled back in Chinatown, where he established his center in the Tainhou Temple, the oldest Chinese temple in the United States.

Although very much in traditional Chinese style, his teachings were a synthesis of Zen and Pure Land. They also provided a less rational perspective than Westerners had come to expect of Zen teachers. Once, early on, admirers in Seattle invited Hsuan Hua to come and teach there. He responded that if he were to leave San Francisco, the city would be ravaged by an earthquake and suggested they visit him instead.

Emphasizing as he did the miraculous element in his teachings, Hsuan Hua attracted many interested primarily in psychic phenomena. In response, he strongly underscored how such things were secondary to real understanding of the Dharma. In this small fact we can see that, while he made no overt or significant accommodations to Western culture (unlike most Asian teachers mentioned here), even the tradionalist Hsuan Hua did gradually make minor adjustments to meet contemporary needs.

Many people found his rigorous and uncompromising teaching attractive. In 1968, one of his students took the Vinaya novice vows. In the following year four more took the vows. In 1969, all five—three men and two women—traveled to Haihui Monastery in Taiwan, where they received the full Vinaya ordination within the Chinese tradition.

In 1972, he established a formal ordination platform at the Gold Mountain Monastery, which he founded in 1970 after outgrowing the space at Tainhou Temple. There six more Americans—five monks and one nun—took their vows. His teaching continued to be extremely rigorous, and his ordained disciples emulated his style of ascetic disciplines. Eventually over two hundred people, including many Westerners, received formal ordination in the Chinese Vinaya under Master Hsuan Hua's tutelage.

In addition to Gold Mountain Monastery in San Francisco, he established the City of Ten Thousand Buddhas in rural northern California; Gold Wheel Monastery in Los Angeles; Long Beach Monastery; Gold Buddha Monastery in Vancouver, Canada; Gold Summit Monastery in Seattle; Avatamsaka Monastery in Calgary; the Berkeley Buddhist Monastery; and the Institute of World Religions, as well as the International Translation Institute, in Burlingame (California). He also established the Dharma Realm Buddhist University, housed at the City of Ten Thousand Buddhas. During these years, the master traveled widely throughout the West, including South America and Europe. He died in 1995.

Over the years, Master Hsuan Hua attracted a small but diligent Western-born following, some of whom received Dharma transmission. It's hard to say how deeply his direct influence will be felt in North America, but there is no doubt that his indirect influence—through translation programs and other outreach venues—is already extensive.

Master Hsuan Hua was very encouraging of interfaith dialogue, exemplified by his friendship with the Catholic bishop of his hometown. This interfaith emphasis has been carried on by Master Hua's American successor, the Venerable Heng Sure, who now serves as head of the Berkeley Buddhist Monastery. Soon after Heng Sure—a native Ohioan—became a monk under Master Hua, he made a significant pilgrimage with a single companion, taking many months, walking from Los Angeles to Ukiah, stopping to make a full prostration after every two steps. Abbot Heng Sure, in addition to directing practice at the Berkeley monastery, has become a prominent figure in the interfaith movement. This work has focused on Christian/Buddhist dialogue, but also includes conversations between Theravada and Mahayana monastics as well as between Buddhist and Christian monastics.

Sheng-Yen's Chinese Transmission

Master Sheng-yen, in contrast to Master Hsuan Hua, was somewhat willing to accept Western culture. Perhaps consequently, he became the first Chinese master to publicly name Western Dharma heirs who were *not* Vinaya-ordained monastics, a point of considerable importance. Hui-kong Sheng-yen was born near Shanghai in 1931. At the age of thirteen, he entered monastic life at Guang Jiao Monastery in the Wolf Hills of Nantung, and at sixteen, he moved to the monastery's city branch in Shanghai.

During that period, in addition to suffering a Japanese invasion, China was torn apart by civil war. In 1949 Sheng-yen joined the Nationalist Army, serving as a warrant officer. Nevertheless, he maintained a regular meditation practice and visited temples as frequently as possible. While staying at a monastery, Sheng-yen felt he had had his great awakening. After ten years he was released from the army and reentered formal monastic life at the Buddhist Culture Center in Peitou, Taipei. Between 1961 and 1968, he lived in solitary retreat at the Chao Yuan Monastery. In the early 1970s, he studied at the Rissho University in Japan where he earned both a master's and doctorate degree in Buddhist literature.

In 1975 he received Dharma transmission in the Caodong (Soto) line from Master Dong Chu, and in 1978 he received Dharma transmission in the Linji (Rinzai) line from Master Ling Yuan. In 1977 Master Sheng-yen came to America, but he returned to Taiwan to accept first a professorial appointment at the Chinese Culture University, and then the abbacy of Nung Chan Monastery.

A prolific writer, Master Sheng-yen has published more than ninety books, available in most European and Asian languages. In 1993 he gave Dharma transmission to a lay disciple, Dr. John Crook, who now leads the Western Chan Fellowship based in London. Since that time, he has named three more Western lay followers as Dharma heirs, opening a potentially rich vein of traditional Chinese transmission in the West.

Vietnamese Zen Comes West

Buddhism had come to what is now Vietnam by the first century of the Common Era. But a distinctive Vietnamese style probably didn't form until the tenth century. The traditional founder of Vietnamese Zen was an Indian monk, Vinitaruci. Arriving in Vietnam in 560, he was reputed to be an heir of the Third Chinese Ancestor, Sengcan (renowned as the author of the much-celebrated *"Xinxinming"* or "Faith in Mind" poem). Two hundred and fifty years later, Wuyentung, a Chinese monk and Dharma heir of the redoubtable Baizhang, arrived in Vietnam indisputably bringing the Zen school to Southeast Asia. Other Mahayana schools followed.

Like most modern Zen schools on the Asian mainland, Vietnamese Buddhism is eclectic, integrating the traditions of sitting practice and koan introspection together with sutra studies as well as the practices of the Pure Land tradition. Additionally, Vietnamese Buddhism is profoundly marked by its close proximity to and ongoing cultural exchange with its Theravada neighbors, including the Theravadan Khmer minority within its borders. Vietnamese Buddhism has also been marked by indigenous Vietnamese shamanistic religion.

In general, however, Vietnamese Zen has followed the broad outlines of its Chinese inheritance. Its canonical language remains Chinese, and its ordination rituals as well as its tradition of a Zen-style Dharma transmission derive from China. This said, as is the case throughout East Asia, excepting only Japan, Zen practitioners of meditation share the same hall with people reciting Amitabha's name. And most teachers blend Zen and Pure Land seamlessly.

Vietnamese Buddhist practice follows a pattern of daily offices at dawn, noon, and dusk. Lay people may and sometimes, but not usually, do join the monks for this liturgical practice. Historically temples and monasteries were only loosely connected until the formation of the Unified Buddhist Church of Vietnam in the mid-twentieth century. Primarily serving the exile community in France and America, this institution has not reached much beyond its ethnic enclaves. As with all other forms of Zen, we don't know when the first Vietnamese master came to the West. That person probably arrived with the other immigrants and toiled modestly within his or her community.

That said, a few Vietnamese teachers have begun to attract Western students, and one, Thich Nhat Hanh, has become the most famous Zen master in the West.

Thich Thien-An:
The First Vietnamese Patriarch in the West

Thich Thien-An arrived in America in 1966 as a visiting professor at UCLA. *Thich* is a title used by all Vietnamese Buddhist monks and nuns; it roughly translates as "a member of the Buddha's family." When his students learned that in addition to being a scholar he was a Zen monk, they asked him to guide them in Zen meditation. The following year, when the time came for him to return to Vietnam, his students asked him to stay—presenting him with filled-out application forms for permanent residence. That led to the formal establishment of the International Buddhist Meditation Center, the first Vietnamese Zen center dedicated to presenting the Dharma to non-Vietnamese Americans.

Thich Thien-An was uniquely prepared to teach in the West. He was raised in a Buddhist household; in fact, his father eventually became a monk. He was ordained at fourteen; but, critically for his future life, he continued his formal education and eventually received his doctorate at Waseda University, in Japan. After this he returned to Vietnam to teach. Friendly and accessible, he was once described as "a Zen master without a bark."

When Saigon fell to the Communists in 1975, he found himself at the center of the Vietnamese exile community in Los Angeles, and he founded what is generally counted as the first Vietnamese Buddhist temple in the United States. Tragically, he died in 1980 at the age of fifty-four. His successor as head of the International Buddhist Meditation Center is the American-born Bhikshuni Karuna Dharma.

Karuna Dharma was born Joyce Pettingill in Beloit, Washington, to a Baptist family. After earning an undergraduate degree in English she took two master's degrees: one in secondary education, the other in comparative religions. She was one of Thich Thien-An's first students and helped found the International Buddhist

Meditation Center. She received full ordination as a Buddhist nun in 1976.

Thich Nhat Hanh and the "Other" Zen

Thich Nhat Hanh is by almost any standard the most famous Zen master in the West. After the Dalai Lama he is probably the most recognizable Buddhist figure in the world. At the same time his teaching style is so different than that of the other teachers considered in this book that he might be considered the leader of an entirely different school.

There are a number of reasons for this. Most significant is the Vietnamese Zen inheritance, which is itself considerably different from the other East Asian expressions of Zen. Tellingly, it is part of the Vietnamese tradition that their original school of Zen came not through China but India.

While they in fact transmit traditional Chinese lines, Vietnamese Zen has over the centuries grown in distinctive directions. Nhat Hanh (called by his students Thay, which means "master" or "teacher") is himself profoundly experimental, is drawn to a much "softer" style than are most other Zen teachers in the West, and out of this and over the years has adapted a wide variety of techniques in his teaching that are not found in other "Western" Zen schools.

Nhat Hanh, however, rejects assertions he has started a new school of Zen, countering that all he has done is to develop the presentation of the traditions he received in ways relevant to our times as well as for our Western culture. At the heart of his teaching, Nhat Hanh presents what is often called "Socially Engaged" or simply "Engaged Buddhism," a term it seems he coined.

Rooted in classical Buddhism, Engaged Buddhism also emphasizes one's responsibility within the web of human and natural relations. This is a reasonable extension of formal practice, simply bringing it into every other aspect of one's life, and is a general mark of the move westward of Buddhism. (This socially engaged Buddhism will be explored in more detail later.) There are other Buddhist teachers who emphasize a socially engaged discipline, including Robert Aitken, Joanna Macy, and Sulak Sivaraksa. But Nhat Hanh has been the most prominent presenter of this perspective.

Nguyen Xuan Bao (Nhat Hanh's family name before entering the religious life) was born in central Vietnam in 1926. At sixteen he entered Tu Hieu Temple not far from Hue as a novice monk. His first Zen teacher was the Zen master Thanh Quy Chan That. Nguyen Xuan Bao received full ordination in 1949, becoming Thich Nhat Hanh.

In 1956 he became editor of the journal of the "All Vietnam Buddhist Association" which began to thrust him into the forefront of Vietnam's cultural foment. Not long after he founded a press. In 1964 he founded the School of Youth for Social Services, which sought to bring Buddhist peace workers together to aid peasants and others caught in the middle of the long-raging Vietnamese civil war. The American press called this organization the "Little Peace Corps."

This was a seminal period for Thich Nhat Hanh, where his experimental genius began to take shape. His goal was to develop ways of Zen practice that could help a person maintain a spiritual practice while also being fully engaged in society. It's at this time he began to focus on walking meditation and other mindfulness practices that could be used by social workers as they worked to bring relief to the wounded, the hungry, and the homeless.

In 1962 he came to the U.S. where he briefly studied comparative religion at Princeton. He then lectured at Columbia. In 1963 he returned to Vietnam to join its indigenous peace movement. At this time he also helped in the formation of the Unified Buddhist Church of Vietnam. This was a reform movement unifying all schools of Buddhism in Vietnam from the Theravada to the Mahayana.

On the first of May 1966, Thich Nhat Hanh received Dharma

transmission from his teacher Thanh Quy Chan That at the Tu Hieu Temple. He would eventually succeed his teacher as head of Tu Hieu and with that would become patriarch (although he rejected that usage in favor of "elder") of the Tu Hieu school.

In the same year, he formed the Community of Interbeing, which would eventually be called the *Order* of Interbeing. Its first members were six lay women and men involved in the School of Youth for Social Services. The focus for this enterprise was seen as becoming a bastion of understanding, compassion, and non-discrimination at a time when the Vietnamese war was escalating.

Their focus was articulated as the Fourteen Mindfulness Trainings, a detailed reflection on ethics and practice. These trainings include a focus on tolerance, not taking sides, openness, and compassion, which Nhat Hanh teaches as essential to achieving true peace.

The month after he received Dharma transmission he returned to America where at various forums he called for an immediate ceasefire in Vietnam and a negotiated settlement to the war. Not long after these public statements he was informed he would not be allowed to return to Vietnam, or if he did, he would be arrested and charged with treason.

He was granted political asylum and later citizenship by France. For his work at this time Martin Luther King, Jr., nominated him for the 1967 Nobel Peace Prize. The times were tumultuous, and no one was named recipient that year. As no one won the prize, Dr. King announced he had nominated the Vietnamese monk.

In 1973 Thich Nhat Hanh founded a small community named Sweet Potato in central France and retired there for five years, tending a garden, learning bookbinding, and writing. A prodigious author, Nhat Hanh has, as of this writing, published more than seventy-five books, a number of which have become Western and especially American bestsellers. His books have also been translated into at least twenty-five languages. The Korean translation of his book *Anger* has sold more than one million copies.

In 1982 he founded Plum Village near Bordeaux. There he resumed his active peace work, but he also focused ever more on teaching Buddhism and its practices. He began regularly visiting the United States and other European countries, Australia, and Asia, giving teachings on applying Buddhism in daily life. This was the beginning of the major expansion of his teaching.

As already said, there are a number of distinctive approaches to Zen appearing in the West, ranging from the monastic Vinaya tradition of China and Korea, the priestly Zen of Japan, and now the many shapes of lay practice in several traditions that include an emergent lay leadership. In this spirit, and trying to continue the spirit of traditional Zen practice in Vietnam, Thich Nhat Hanh's Zen is even more open and experimental than any other Zen tradition explored in this book. Perhaps most signficant, Nhat Hanh blends traditional forms of mindfulness practice that are usually associated with the Theravada tradition explicitly together with the insights of the Mahayana sutras and the Zen traditions.

As a committed peace worker Nhat Hanh has been deeply involved in and has developed and taught reconciliation as a spiritual discipline. Even during the Vietnam War, he never took sides with the Communists or the Nationalists. Expanding from this, now living in the West with its own forms of violence, he sees his mission to teach people how to listen deeply, to speak lovingly and constructively, and various ways to mend the ruptures of relationship. In this Nhat Hanh has brought his knowledge of traditional Buddhist psychology as well as his insights in Western psychological systems into a coherent presentation.

The Unified Buddhist Church in America (together with the Unified Buddhist Church in France), the institutions that support Nhat Hanh teachings, may include more than half of all Westerners who consider themselves "Zen practitioners." The Community of Mindful Living, the umbrella of affiliated practice groups, lists approximately three hundred separate groups across North America, most in the United States, but also including twenty in Canada and two in Mexico.

The Order of Interbeing is the core organization supporting his teaching, consisting of nuns, monks, and vow-taking lay practitioners. There may be as many as two thousand members of the Order. The monastic part counts more than three hundred nuns and monks. While at this time most of the monastic community are of Vietnamese origin, increasingly monks and nuns are of European and African descent.

Thich Nhat Hanh has also given what he's called "Lamp Transmission," a teaching authorization, starting in 1990. There are now approximately three hundred people with such transmissions. Within the organization they are called Dharmacharyas. They have a limited teaching authority, but are significant figures within Thich Nhat Hanh's organization. Seventy-three North American and European Dharmacharyas are lay teachers.

Regarding the issue of Dharma transmission, Thich Nhat Hanh has said no single student will succeed him. Instead his community of practice will itself be his successor. He is quoted as saying Maitreya, the Buddha of future birth, may be a community of practice rather than an individual. What this actually means will only become apparent over the next decades.

In his first years in the West, Nhat Hanh focused much of his attention on lay practice. In recent years he has shifted his attention to developing the monastic community. Near the end of the twentieth century Thay and a council of nuns and monks revised the Pratimoksha (the Vinaya rules for monastics, including 250 precepts for monks and 348 for nuns), hoping to address contemporary monastic concerns. While there was discussion of the matter, the council chose not to address the contentious issue of separate precepts for nuns and monks at that time.

Today there are five monasteries affiliated with Thich Nhat Hanh's teaching that have become the principal centers for the community he has established. In addition to Plum Village in France, there is Deer Park in California, Maple Forest/Green Mountain in Vermont, and Tu Hieu and Prajna Temple, both in Vietnam. The new, at this writing, Magnolia Village in rural Mississippi shows signs of growing to a point it may become another monastery.

In 2005 Thich Nhat Hanh returned to Vietnam for three months, accompanied by several hundred monks, nuns, and lay students. At this time he visited his home monastery where he was received as the leader/elder of his Zen line. Thousands greeted him at the airports. And, perhaps naturally, at first there were tensions with the Communist authorities who were worried about the teacher's popularity.

One companion on this trip, Abbess Sister Annabel Laity, of the Maple Forest/Green Mountain Zen Monastery in Middlebury, Vermont, wrote how gradually trust was gained: "It was very moving to watch how wounds healed. One party member asked Thay: 'Is it possible to take Refuge in the Three Jewels and still love the Party?' Thay replied: 'Of course, if you take Refuge you will be able to love the Party even better.' A tremendous feeling of relief overcame the audience, and they applauded and laughed."

Over the years Thich Nhat Hanh and his organization have been growing in separate directions from the other Zen teachers and their groups discussed in this book. Still, there can be no doubt that his vision of a socially engaged Buddhism—as well as his willingness to innovate, and to be vulnerable to criticism in order to follow a vision of the Dharma—might heal the world. Indeed, Thich Nhat Hanh has proven to be one of the most important Zen teachers to come West.

Korean Zen Comes West

Buddhism entered the Korean peninsula from China in the fourth century. According to traditional tellings, Zen was first brought to Korea by the monk Pomnang who, in the mid-seventh century, traveled to China and studied with Daye Daoxin, the Fourth Ancestor of Chinese Zen. At the end of the eighth century, Korean monk Toui traveled to China and returned thirty-five years later as a Zen master and Dharma heir of Xitang Zhizang, who had been acknowledged by the renowned master Baizhang. This was the beginning of the Nine Mountain Schools and the flourishing of a Korean Zen.

The greatest figure of Korean Zen is the twelfth-century master Pojo Chinul. Born in 1158 during a period of civil war and social unrest, he was a child of the gentry. At fifteen, he was ordained by the Zen master Chonghwi of Kulsan temple. His initial training was studying sutras, the sacred texts of the Buddhist tradition. In 1182 he completed his formal studies. Then, feeling disgusted with the laxity of the monastic establishment, he made a compact with nine other young monks to dedicate themselves to finding deepest wisdom.

Sometime later he read this passage in the Platform Sutra: "Self-nature of suchness gives rise to thoughts. But even though the six sense-faculties see, hear, sense, and know, it is not tainted by the myriad of images. True nature is constantly free and self-reliant." These words shocked him, as if he had never heard this teaching before. Suddenly he saw the truth of the old writings for himself. And it led to the development of his teaching of "sudden enlightenment, gradual cultivation." Taking up the koan "Mind is Buddha," he continued to train diligently for several more years.

Gradually a community of students grew around him, and the monastery that formed would eventually be named Songgwang-sa, the premier Zen monastery in Korea. Adapting Dahui's approach to koan study, Chinul's teaching was a vigorous and dynamic demonstration of Zen practice. His eclectic approach as a teacher also demonstrated what would become the uniquely Korean form of Zen.

Korean Zen—called in its native language *Son*—is a vital school distinct in flavor from both its Chinese parent and its Japanese and

Vietnamese siblings. Unlike Japanese Zen, it is considerably less interested in liturgical precision as a central part of spiritual discipline. In addition, Korean Zen continues to inhabit the same monasteries as other Korean Buddhist schools, such as those emphasizing sutra study or Pure Land practices.

Being in such close proximity with other schools, it's not surprising that Korean Zen is much more eclectic than Japanese Zen. In Japan there are also the clear divisions of Soto and Rinzai. But, while Korean Zen has a strong tradition of both silent illumination practice and koan introspection, in Korean monasteries as in Chinese monasteries a Zen monk will also be exposed to both these and many other practices, including mantras and sutra study.

Following traditional Vinaya ordination, monastic life turns on two three-month retreats a year, in winter and summer. It is very common for monastics to wander between monasteries during the break periods. Most monastics are given a *hwadu* (*wato* in Japanese or *huatou* in Chinese), a "word head" or "critical phrase." This is a central point of a koan. The most common form of this practice is constant inquiry into the question, "What is this?"

This form of koan work is different than that of Japanese Zen, where one works initially with a "breakthrough koan," like Mu or No, which is meant to push one toward an initial insight into nonduality, after which one follows a curriculum of hundreds of cases. In traditional Korean Zen, there may be occasional check-ins with the teacher, but for the most part the monastic will work with a single case for a lifetime. Rarely would a student take up a second or third case—and even more rarely would a monk take on more cases than that.

Of the Korean monks and masters serving Korean communities in North America few have taken on Western students. One exception, mentioned above, is Dr. Kyong-bo Seo. While visiting the West, he named some Dharma heirs. But these were mostly people trained in other traditions, and none has emerged as a significant figure in contemporary Western Zen.

Kusan Sunim was another visitor from Korea. *Kusan* was his Dharma name. *Sunim* is an honorific similar to the Vietnamese *Thich;* given to both nuns and monks, it designates them as members of the Buddha's family. A successor to the renowned twentieth-century master Hyo Bong, Kusan Sunim was resident Zen master at Songgwang-sa when, in 1972, he traveled briefly to North America. One Westerner accompanied him back and became a monk. Kusan Sunim only returned to North America one more time, but his reputation spread and eventually a number of Westerners would come to study with him in Korea.

Kusan Sunim had been a married farmer when, following a severe illness, he decided to dedicate his life to Dharma. With his wife's permission, he ordained as a monk and began his training. He eventually became one of the most prominent modern Korean Zen masters. In addition to his reputation as a meditation master, Kusan Sunim took a leading role in denominational affairs within the Chogye Order. Perhaps the most famous of his Western students are Martine and Stephen Batchelor, who were both monastics under his tutelage.

Samu Sunim and a Reformed Korean Zen

Samu Sunim was born in occupied Korea in 1941. In 1944 his father, a college instructor, was killed in Manchuria while fighting the Japanese. His mother died when he was eleven, and the orphan found himself homeless. The next few years were marked by hunger and privation. Well schooled in the nature of suffering, in 1956, at the age of fifteen, he became a monk. He was ordained by Master Solbong Sunim at Pomo-sa monastery in Pusan.

When he was drafted into the Korean army, instead of accepting induction, Samu Sunim left the country, moving first briefly to

Japan then to America. He arrived in New York City in 1968, where he formed the Zen Lotus Society (about which, more below). In 1971 he moved to Montreal and then to Toronto, where he undertook a three-year solitary meditation retreat. He then began teaching. While he lacked formal Dharma transmission, he was widely respected for his skill as a teacher and as a passionate worker for Buddhism in North America.

In 1977 he had a visionary experience wherein he felt his old master Solbong Sunim confirmed him as a teacher. Today Samu Sunim is deeply respected in the Zen community, but this nontraditional claim of authorization is not generally accepted.

Eventually Samu Sunim established a second center in Ann Arbor and later a third in Chicago. In 1985, he established a three-year Dharma Student Training Program, later renamed the Maitreya Buddhist Seminary. A distinctive feature of his Dharma is that he ordains his students without expecting them to be celibate. There is precedent for this in the Korean tradition, if not the Chogye Order.

While the overwhelming majority of Korean Zen practitioners, including Samu Sunim, belong to the Chogye sect, there is a minority school, the Taego sect, that allows for noncelibate ordination. The Taego sect is headquartered at Bongwonsa in Seoul. Due to its associations with the Japanese occupation, it suffered great losses in the years since World War II. It is a very interesting school but has no official representatives in North America.

While not leaving the Chogye school, Samu Sunim married a few years ago. This decision has remained controversial. His Zen Lotus Society, later renamed the Buddhist Society for Compassionate Wisdom, has been a center for interreligious dialogue, and has become—after the Kwan Um School of Zen—the major alternative interpretation of Korean Zen in North America.

Samu Sunim's principal heir is Linda Murray, ordained as Haju Sunim. Born in Vancouver in 1944, Linda began sitting with Samu

Sunim in 1976. She was ordained in 1991 and received Dharma transmission from Samu Sunim in 1999. Today Haju Sunim is the resident teacher at the Ann Arbor Temple. Among Samu Sunim's more prominent students, the best known is probably Geri Larken, a graduate of the seminary program, leader of an independent sangha in Detroit, and author of several popular books on Zen.

Seung Sahn's Kwan Um School

Master Seung Sahn is second only to Thich Nhat Hanh in guaranteeing Western Zen will not simply be derived from Japanese Zen. Seung Sahn was born in 1927 in Suen Choen, in what is today North Korea. An ironic twist—in light of his place as one of the great Buddhist missionaries to the West—is that his parents were both Presbyterians. In 1944, during the Japanese occupation, he joined the underground resistance movement. His career as a revolutionary was brief: he was quickly arrested, narrowly escaped the death penalty, and was sentenced to prison.

After the war he began studies in Western philosophy at Dong Guk University. During this time, a friend who had become a Son (Zen) monk gave him a copy of the Diamond Sutra. According to tradition, this is the same text that first inspired Huineng, the Sixth Ancestor of the Chinese transmission. Upon reading it, he determined to become a monk and received the Vinaya precepts in 1948.

In addition to the traditional communal training of Korean monks, he embraced a number of austere personal practices. Most famously near the beginning of his training he did a hundred-day retreat, during which time he reportedly ate only pine needles and chanted and meditated for twenty hours a day.

After a time of extreme pain and raging doubt, he experienced a variety of visions, and near the end of his retreat, he had his great awakening. Recognizing that the Zen tradition is skeptical of private awakening, he climbed down the mountain to seek out a teacher. He found Master Ko Bong, one of the most renowned Korean teachers of that time. Interestingly, Ko Bong expressed disdain for monks, declaring that only laypeople and nuns were manifesting true Bodhi mind. Nonetheless, after a brief testing exchange the old master accepted the young monk as his student.

By most accounts, Seung Sahn wasn't an ideal monk. There is a famous story of the night he stole all the shoes from the nun's wing and placed them in front of the abbot's door. He barely escaped being expelled from the monastery. Soon after this event, however, his awakening was recognized by two masters, Keum Oh and the renowned Ko Bong.

When the Korean War broke out he was drafted into the army and served as a captain. After leaving the army he served as abbot of a temple near Seoul, where he founded an organization for lay practice. He taught briefly at university and for a time served Korean communities in Hong Kong and Japan. While in Japan, he was introduced to Hakuin's style of koan Zen.

Those familiar with his teaching style speculate that at some point he undertook formal koan study with a Japanese Rinzai teacher or teachers. What can be said with certainty is that Master Seung Sahn was interested in curriculum-style koan study and, at some point, began to develop his own loosely held system. This has continued to evolve over the course of his teaching career. In its current form it includes a minimum requirement of successfully engaging twelve koans—and also almost always includes several hundred additional cases, engaged in no obvious or consistent order. His unique style of koan study is now a hallmark of his Kwan Um School.

In 1971 Seung Sahn came to America, settling in Providence, Rhode Island. At first he supported himself repairing washing machines. But gradually students gathered around him, and—through a combination of a fierce commitment to Dharma and a peripatetic lifestyle—he ended up founding sitting groups and Zen centers across the continent and eventually around the world.

Of particular interest for North American Zen, he also introduced a transmission style considerably different from that taught by Japanese Zen teachers. He encouraged people to ordain as Vinaya monks and nuns and developed institutions to support those who embraced the renunciate life. But in naming Dharma successors, he gave no preference to monks and nuns, naming both monastic and lay successors over the years.

In 1988, the Kwan Um School of Zen was rocked by Seung Sahn's admission he had had sexual affairs with several students. This certainly wasn't the first sex scandal in the Zen world. Scholar Stuart Lachs dates the first Western scandals from as early as 1975. I believe I can push that back by several years.

Most prominently, in 1983 the roshi of the San Francisco Zen Center, Richard Baker, lost his abbacy over a sex scandal (copiously written about in *Shoes Outside the Door,* by Michael Downing). In the same year a similar scandal devastated the Zen Center of Los Angeles.

For a while the future direction of Seung Sahn's institution was in doubt, and, as happened in the similarily affected Japanese-derived centers, quite a number of people left. It's not possible to adequately acknowledge the hurt and dismay that followed in the wake of these and similar scandals at other centers. But for most of these centers, with the passing years a more mature organization has gradually emerged, one less dependent on the personality of a single charismatic teacher. In part because of their willingness to address the reality of ethical concerns, the Kwan Um School is now the single largest Zen institution in the West.

Master Sueng Sahn died in 2004, but the organization he founded continues to flourish. At present there are thirty-four centers in North America alone. Barbara Rhodes—Zen Master Seong Hyang—succeeded Master Sueng Sahn as School Zen Master and Guiding Dharma Teacher of the Kwan Um School.

Zen Master Barbara (Bobbie) Rhodes is one of the many women who have moved to the fore as leaders of the Western Zen sangha.

Born in 1948 to a naval family living at the time in Providence, Rhode Island, Bobbie's childhood was peripatetic. She grew up to become a registered nurse and eventually a hospice nurse. Like many in her generation she tried LSD, but determined it promised more than it delivered. She then discovered D.T. Suzuki and decided to try Zen practice, becoming one of master Sueng Sahn's first students in America.

She helped him to found the Providence Zen Center, living there for nearly two decades and serving in most leadership capacities. Barbara Rhodes received Inga (Inka) in 1977 and was given Dharma transmission and named a Zen master in 1992. This ordering of acknowledgments is different from that of the usual Japanese-derived American koan Zen schools, principally the White Plum lineage of Taizan Maezumi and, on smaller scale, my own Boundless Way Zen sangha, where the first acknowledgment is called Dharma transmission and the much rarer final acknowledgment is Inka Shomei.

Today, as mentioned, Zen Master Soen Hyang Barbara Rhodes's formal title is School Zen Master of the Kwan Um School of Zen. As such she is head of the largest Zen community in the West. She lives in Providence with her two daughters and partner. She is also the most prominent Zen teacher living in a same-sex relationship.

The Kwan Um School follows a distinctive pattern of leadership, considerably different from that of Japanese-derived Zen. Like everything else in this study, the shape of Kwan Um's leadership is dynamic; but their current forms reveal basic patterns well worth examining.

Anyone who attends a Kwan Um center may, after doing four days of retreat-style practice, apply to receive the five traditional lay precepts. If, after receiving the five precepts, that person remains active in the practice for two years, she or he may apply to be a candidate for "Dharma teacher." This application must first be approved by the local teacher; if it is approved, it is passed on to the

Zen master in charge of Dharma teachers. If approved—and so far it appears all applications have been approved—the candidate may take the ten precepts, at which time they're designated a Dharma teacher-in-training.

Over the course of the next two years, the Dharma teacher-in-training must attend eight weekend retreats. Beyond this, each local teacher will have formal or informal expectations. These include mastering the forms and learning some of the theory behind Zen practice. Then—again, upon nomination by the local teacher and confirmation by the Zen master in charge of guiding teachers—they may be designated a Dharma teacher.

This title can be confusing in the larger Zen community. Indeed I've spoken with people who mention knowing a "Zen master" who, upon closer questioning, are referring to Kwan Um Dharma teachers. Dharma teachers in the Kwam Um school are people with responsibilities at the center, but they are not teachers in the usual sense of other Zen communities—and certainly not "Zen masters." One Kwan Um Zen master suggested to me that the more appropriate title might be "Dharma leader"—but added that having used the other term for the last twenty-plus years, the school was unlikely to change it any time soon.

Five years after being confirmed a Dharma Teacher, one may be nominated by one's guiding teacher to be a Senior Dharma Teacher. Upon confirmation of the Zen master in charge of Dharma teachers, one takes the sixteen precepts and becomes a Senior Dharma Teacher. This office actually has elements normally reserved for those holding some form of Dharma transmission. They can give Dharma talks, which are also permitted for Dharma teachers—but they can also respond to questions from the audience, which is not allowed for Dharma teachers. They may also hold private interviews with students, although they may not give or comment on koans.

Aside from teaching, another office should be mentioned here. In Korean Zen institutions, teaching and administration are generally separated (as they were, in fact, in ancient China). A center's abbot is more like a head administrator than a spiritual director. Following this tradition, the administrative head of a Kwan Um Zen center is designated "abbot." But unlike the usual use of this title in the other Zen communities explored in this book, a Kwan Um abbot does not necessarily serve in a teaching position. Rather the abbot is charged with temporal responsibilities: paying the rent, meeting other bills, scheduling the calendar, and so on.

One incident regarding abbots hints at the maturation of the Kwan Um School as an institution. I know an abbot of a local Kwan Um center who was "poached" by another center. They flew her out to visit their center. They gave her flowers and explained how much better it would be for the Dharma and everyone concerned if she would leave her current post and become their abbot instead. What I thought I saw in this flagrant attempt of one center to steal another's abbot was actually a beginning: the development of a semi-professional leadership within the community.

In the Kwan Um School, Zen teachers, as they're generally understood in the larger Zen community, hold some form of what is commonly understood as Dharma transmission: either Ji Do Poep Sa Nims ("Guides to the Way," or "Dharma Masters") or Zen Masters. As in other Zen schools, one may not volunteer for these designations. There are, however, broad outlines for acknowledging teachers as one or the other.

Essentially there are three expectations. The first is "completion" of the Kwan Um School's koan curriculum. Most teachers in this school don't like the term "curriculum"; but, as it does resemble the Japanese curriculum model more than normative Korean koan study, it seems to be the appropriate one. Having passed the dozen core koans as well as hundreds of others, the next two expectations are more subjective.

One must demonstrate to the satisfaction of one's guiding teacher a sense of centeredness. It should be obvious the teaching and practice have "taken hold," and that substantive shifts in perspective and spiritual maturity have taken place. Finally, it should become obvious one has a "calling" to teach; in more traditional Buddhist terms, it is obvious that one's Dharma and karma are taking one to teaching.

When a senior Dharma teacher completes the formal aspects of koan work, shows that strong personal center, and demonstrates a strong direction toward teaching, the guiding teacher nominates that individual for Dharma transmission.

While in other Zen schools, consultation with teachers other than one's own is considered optional and in most cases is nominal or *pro forma,* here four other Dharma holders must sign off on the candidate for Dharma transmission. This may vary from a very informal acceptance to formal and sometimes forceful examinations of the nominated teacher.

Should the nominated senior Dharma teacher obtain approval from these five teachers (including the nominating teacher), there may be an additional waiting period. But at some point a ceremony is scheduled. The first part is Dharma combat where the aspiring Ji Do Poep Sa Nim must meet about twenty-five students to the general satisfaction of the guiding Zen Master. This marks the receiving of formal acknowledgment of mastery.

Following this, the new Ji Do Poep Sa Nim is invested with a full *kasa* (in Japanese, *kesa*), the traditional Zen monk's robe, whether lay or ordained, and is presented with a teacher's stick, another traditional symbol of a Zen teacher. Then there is a period of teacher training. During this time the new JDPSN sits with various senior teachers in interviews, observing how they're done. After about six months, the new Ji Do Poep Sa Nim begins to teach independently. In April 2001, a significant marker in the development of the Kwan Um School occurred when the monk Chong Hae Sunim was designated a JDPSN, without ever having experienced formal interviews with Master Seung Sahn.

As with being nominated a JDPSN, there can be no expectation or application to be designated a Zen Master. The pattern has been that, following a period of three to four years, a JDPSN would visit three senior teachers outside of the Kwan Um School. Thus far these have been peers of Master Seung Sahn: most notably, Joshu Sasaki Roshi and Robert Aitken Roshi (about both of whom, more later). Following formal interviews that take some form of "Dharma combat," the JDPSN writes a verbatim, a transcript of the encounter and forwards it to the guiding teacher, to date always Master Seung Sahn.

No one has advanced to this position since 1991, when Seung Sahn's health began to fail several years before his death. The last people to receive full Dharma transmission from Master Seung Sahn were the lay Zen Master Jeff Kitzes and the nun Dae Kwan Sunim.

With Seung Sahn's death, the next few years proved critical in the development of the Kwan Um School. So far it has shown amazing stability. There is a commonly agreed-upon liturgy, and the forms are the same from center to center. Indeed, JDPSN and Zen Masters sign a document agreeing to conform to the school's forms.

Only two Zen Masters have formally separated from the Kwan Um School. Robert Genthner, Zen Master Dae Gak, leads the independent center called Furnace Mountain in rural Kentucky, as well as four other branches in North America and centers in England and Germany. The second is George Bowman, Zen Master Bomun. Bowman guides the Single Flower Sangha, a "floating zendo" in eastern Massachusetts. Significantly, George Bowman has recently given Inga to his senior student David Rynick, the first person to receive acknowledgment as a teacher in the lineage without also belonging to the Kwan Um School.

For many, the less structured but rigorous form of the Kwan Um School is a welcome change from the formalism of Japanese-derived Zen. Its approach is unique—for Western Zen—in that it gives equal status to Vinaya-ordained monks and nuns and lay teachers; and, it makes no functional distinctions between women and men. This is a shining example of what can occur in an emerging Western Zen. Together with the San Francisco Zen Center network, the Kwan Um School is at the forefront of institutions capable of bringing an authentic Zen way into the coming decades.

SEVEN

American Rinzai

HE FIRST ZEN LINEAGE to come West with the specific intent of reaching beyond immigrant populations was the Japanese Rinzai lineage. This began with the arrival of Master Soyen Shaku, who made a presentation at the World Parliament of Religions in Chicago in 1893. The ripples of influence from that trip continue to this day—even though in America, as in Japan, the larger Zen presence in the West continues to be Soto (however, within the American Soto lineages, unlike the Japanese situation, the Harada-Yasutani reform of Soto practices, and thus Rinzai-style koan introspection, is quite prominent).

Nonetheless, "orthodox" Rinzai presence in North America has been historically significant if numerically small. Genki Takabayashi Roshi taught for some years in Seattle, although when he retired his single Seattle center and its priest, Genjo Marinello, transferred to Eido Shimano Roshi. Omori Sogen Roshi, a prominent Japanese master active in right-wing politics, attempted to establish a formal training *sodo* in Hawai'i, but it disbanded following his death in 1994. A number of teachers received Dharma transmission from him or one of his heirs. While some of these teachers are well known in the martial arts community, they are not generally known in the "non-martial" Western Zen mainstream.

Another smaller temple is the Rinzai Zen Temple of California in Los Angeles. It's founder, Sogen Yamakawa Roshi, vists twice a year to lead sesshin. Also, Soko Morinaga Roshi, best known in America through his memoir *Novice to Master: An Ongoing Lesson in the Extent of My Own Stupidity,* has authorized Tom Daijo Minick and Ursula Jarand to establish Daishu-in West in Garberville, California, as a formal Rinzai temple.

Today four Japanese teachers tend to dominate Rinzai training in North America: Joshu Sasaki, Eido Shimano, Shodo Harada, and Keido Fukushima (more on all of these masters follows below).

One of the earliest Western-born Rinzai masters was Walter Nowick, a Julliard-trained pianist who studied with Zuigan Goto Roshi in Japan for sixteen years. Given permission to teach, Nowick returned to America and for a time led a residential center in Maine. In 1982 he retired from active teaching and the community disbanded.

The two most prominent Western Rinzai teachers in American Zen, however, are both women: Maurine Stuart and Roko Sherry Chayat.

Maurine Stuart: Western Zen's Woman Warrior

Maurine Stuart, one of the first female Zen masters in America, was also one of the first to give Zen a Western face. Maurine was born in Saskatchewan, Canada, in 1922. In 1949 she received a music scholarship to study in Paris with renowned conductor Nadia Boulanger, who would later become the first woman to conduct a major symphony in America. While in Paris, Maurine first stumbled across a reference to Zen in a book called *An Introduction to Oriental Thought.* Many years later, when interviewed for a biographical study by Lenore Friedman, Maurine recounted how she wrote in the margins of the book, *"That's it!"*

But it wasn't until 1966—after she had returned to the United

States, settled in New York, married Oscar Freedgood, and had three children—that Maurine began practicing at the Zen Studies Society. After three weeks, she sat her first *sesshin,* Zen's intensive meditation retreat, with Haku'un Yasutani Roshi in upstate New York.

She studied with Yasutani, Soen Nakagawa, and the Zen Studies Society's resident priest Eido Shimano. In 1970 she moved to Newton, Massachusetts, where she opened the Chestnut Hill Zendo. Soon after she joined the Cambridge Buddhist Association and in 1979 became its president. In 1977 she was ordained a priest by Eido Roshi. From that point, she was the Cambridge Buddhist Association's resident teacher.

Eventually she broke with Eido Roshi but continued her training, primarily with Soen Roshi. In 1982, two years before his death, Soen told her to start calling herself "Roshi." This was a controversial event, as he chose not to give her formal Dharma transmission. Consequently she refrained from using traditional Zen phrases such as "Dharma heir" or "lineage holder" when referring to herself—although she did, as requested, use the title *Roshi.* She ordained several priests, but did not designate any successors before her own untimely death from cancer in 1990.

Often called Ma Roshi and Mother Roshi, Maurine Stuart offered an authentically Western perspective on being a Zen practitioner and teacher: gentle, yet rigorous and relentless. This perspective opened the way not only for many women, but also for the many men who found something compelling in Zen—but not in the harshness of Asian forms.

While she left no Dharma heirs, several of her students went on to prominent places in Western Zen. Most notable of these is Roko Chayat Osho, who is addressed elsewhere in this book. Also there is Susan Jion Postal, resident teacher of the Empty Hand Zendo in New York. Originally ordained by Maurine Roshi, she then continued her training with a number of teachers before finally reordaining with Darlene Cohen Sensei in the Shunryu Suzuki Soto lineage.

Joshu Sasaki and Bootcamp Zen

Joshu Sasaki brought a very traditional Japanese form of Rinzai Zen West and devoted the majority of his life to nurturing its institutions—though he has of this writing given "teaching permissions" but not acknowledged any Dharma heirs. Sasaki was born into a farming family in 1907, in Miyagi Prefecture. He was ordained an unsui at the age of fourteen by Joten Soko Miura Roshi, receiving the Dharma name Kyozan. At the age of twenty-one, he was ordained an osho, or full priest. He followed his teacher, who was appointed abbot of Myoshinji, one of the principal training sodo of the Rinzai schools, and stayed there for nineteen years. In 1947 he received Dharma transmission from Joten Soko Miura Roshi.

Joshu Roshi then became abbot of Yotokuin, a post he held until 1953 when he was appointed abbot of Shojuan, a temple founded by Hakuin's teacher Shoju Ronin. He served there for nine years. Meanwhile Dr. Robert Harmon and Gladys Weisbart, both members of the Joshu Zen Temple in Los Angeles, had been campaigning for several years to bring a Rinzai teacher to California. Daiko Furukawa Roshi, who succeeded Joten Soko Miura as head of Myoshinji, decided Joshu Sasaki would be a suitable candidate. He formally requested Joshu Roshi take up the offer.

In 1962, Sasaki traveled to the West to found a Zen center in Los Angeles to address the needs of the non-Japanese community. He arrived in America carrying a Bible in one sleeve—sleeves often serving as pockets in a Zen monk's traveling robes—and a Japanese-English dictionary in the other.

The new sangha's first zendo was in the house Sasaki had rented. It then moved to larger spaces in members' homes. In 1968 the fledgling sangha purchased its first property, in South Central Los Angeles, which they named Cimarron Zen Center. Three years later, the community purchased property in the San Gabriel Mountains east of Los Angeles. Named the Mount Baldy Zen Center, it has gained an international reputation for rigorous practice. In 1974 the sangha, now incorporated as Rinzaiji, established the Bodhi Manda Zen Center in Jemez Springs, New Mexico.

A deeply respected teacher, Joshu Roshi has not been without controversy over his many years of teaching—there have been allegations of improprieties with students. However, this never gave rise to the institutional shakeups that occurred in other founding Zen centers.

While Joshu Roshi has given full Rinzai ordination to about twenty students, all of whom have the title *osho,* he has not given Dharma transmission to anyone. And, as he is well into his tenth decade and has been in the West for some forty years, it is beginning to look like he may never do so. There are various speculations as to why.

Those who have experienced a sesshin (intensive meditation retreat) guided by him and his senior students report it to be exceptionally profound. In these retreats one truly must practice with no thought of gain, because there will surely be none—and this, after all, is the heart of the Zen experience.

In Sean Murphy's *One Bird, One Stone,* there is this recounting of a karate student who was doing a retreat with Roshi at Mount Baldy Zen Center. After struggling with a koan for days and coming up dry,

> …finally during a private interview, he became so frustrated that he let out a great shout and threw a karate punch directly at the teacher, stopping inches from Sasaki's face. Roshi was unmoved. "Right answer," he said, "wrong koan."

While lacking formal Dharma transmission, a number of his oshos have indeed come to be recognized, both within their community and in the larger Western Zen world, as wise guides of various communities. Among these are Jiun Hosen, Bob Mammoser, and Sandy Gentei Stewart. Also of note is George Bowman, the first Dharma heir of Korean master Seung Sahn. Bowman continued his training for many years with Joshu Roshi, and, over the years, his own teaching style was obviously deeply influenced by this continuing connection.

For anyone wishing to experience Japanese-derived Rinzai in North America, attending sesshin at one of the centers led by Joshu Sasaki Roshi is reportedly a most intimate and precious experience of this. And the centers led by his oshos are spoken of as creative and sincere centers of authentic practice. It is important to note that the larger community of Western Zen teachers tends to accept Sasaki Roshi's oshos as authentic teachers. Indeed the oshos were all invited to join the American Zen Teachers Association, the pan-school, Zen teacher's "professional organization," when it first formed.

Eido Shimano and the Establishment of a Rinzai Lineage in America

Eido Shimano was the first teacher to establish an American Rinzai lineage. He was born in 1932, in a district that is today part of Tokyo but was then considered the "countryside." When he was nine, the War began, and his family moved to Chichibu, where his mother's family lived. When he was quite young he began sitting with Kengan Goto, the priest of Empukuji, a small Rinzai temple in Chichibu. Eventually he was ordained an unsui by Goto Osho and given the Dharma name Eido, which combines the first syllables of the names of Rinzai founder Eisai and the Soto founder Dogen.

His formal training began at Heirinji, near Tokyo, where he was given the koan Mu. He stayed for a little more than two years. Then, after the death of the resident teacher Mineo Da Roshi, he met Soen Nakagawa Roshi and traveled to Ryutakuji to formally become Soen Roshi's student.

Eido had been in Ryutakuji just over a year when Nyogen Senzaki made his only visit back to Japan from America. This visit gave rise to at least one interesting anecdote. Worrying that it had been fifty years since Senzaki Sensei last used a *banj* (Japanese-style squat toilet), Soen Roshi made a drawing of a Western style toilet and instructed the carpenter to fashion one. This was an object of amazement to the young monks, as Eido Roshi tells it. While it couldn't be flushed, it at least provided a higher seat for their elderly visitor.

When Senzaki Sensei arrived, Eido found himself attracted to this "elderly man, with his exotic-looking silver hair, his vital voice, his strangely accented Japanese and, most importantly, by the content of his talk." The young monk found himself thinking of America and the work of this old monk. This—together with the fact that Eido spoke a little English and was therefore responsible for visiting foreigners—encouraged his reflections on the Dharma in the West and his possible part in it.

After a few years, and as his practice matured, Soen Roshi asked Eido to serve as Nyogen Senzaki's attendant in America. But before Eido could actually leave Japan, Senzaki Sensei would die.

Two years passed, and in 1960 Soen Roshi again asked young Eido to travel to the West, this time to Honolulu to assist at the Diamond Sangha center established by Anne and Robert Aitken (more about Robert Aitken later). Thereafter began what would be lasting allegations of improprieties against Eido—which ultimately led to a break between Eido's teacher Soen and Robert Aitken, who would continue his studies with Yasutani Roshi and with Yasutani's heir, Koun Yamada Roshi.

Eido returned to Japan, where he met Haku'un Yasutani Roshi. Soen Roshi asked Yasutani Roshi to travel to America with him to lead a series of retreats on both coasts. Young Eido went with them as an attendant and translator. He would later comment that his English at the time was "just about incomprehensible." Nevertheless, he found this a valuable experience, allowing him to learn from two great teachers and to practice with people who were new and fresh to the Dharma.

Eventually, Eido determined to travel to New York and, with his teacher's permission, begin formal teaching—and in 1964 he did just that. The Zen Studies Society in New York had been established by Sokei-an. One of its founders and continuing leaders, Professor Bernard Phillips, chair of the Religion Department at Temple University and editor of Suzuki's *Essentials of Zen Buddhism,* had arranged for Yasutani Roshi's first visits. Eido Shimano was also invited to teach there. He would later join the board and about a year after that become president of the corporation.

Eido continued his training with Soen Roshi and with Yasutani Roshi on their visits to America. In 1972, he received Dharma transmission from Soen Nakagawa Roshi. Today Eido Roshi continues to guide the Zen Studies Society, which consists of two centers: the New York Zendo, Shoboji; and the country center, Dai Bosatsu Zendo, Kongoji, in Livingston Manor, New York. He has named four Dharma heirs (mentioned below), all of whom now guide sanghas of their own.

The Zen Studies Society that he leads and the lineage he has established are likely to be the primary orthodox Rinzai lineage to take firm root in North America. This seems to be the case for two reasons. First, no other Rinzai community seems focused on cultivating Western-born teachers. And second, the teachers Eido Roshi has produced are generally regarded as demonstrating insight and skill in guiding others on the Way.

The three centers led by the Dharma heirs of Eido Roshi are completely independent of the organization Eido Roshi leads: Jiro Andy Afable's Wild Goose Zendo in East Brookfield, Massachusetts; Junpo Denis Kelly's Hollow Bones in Ashland, Oregon; and the Pine Hill Zendo in Katonah, New York, led by Denko John Mortensen. While also considered "independent," Roko Sherry Chayat's Syracuse Zen Center maintains "a spiritual link" to the Zen Studies Society.

Shodo Harada: The Teacher's Teacher

Shodo Harada Roshi is very important to Western Zen but, at this time, does not have a permanent residence in North America. Still he has become a "teacher of teachers." Zen teachers from various North American lineages and traditions regularly go to sit sesshin with him, either at the One Drop Zendo in Tahoma, Washington, or at his training temple in Okayama, Japan.

Shodo Harada was born in 1940 in Nara and began his formal Zen training in 1962 at the Shofukuji sodo in Kobe. His teacher was the renowned Zen master and calligrapher Yamada Mumon Roshi. After studying with his teacher for twenty years, Shodo was given Dharma transmission by Mumon Roshi and installed as abbot of Sogenji, in Okayama. (In the West Shodo Harada Roshi is usually referred to as "Harada Roshi," rather than by his given or Dharma name and title.)

Sogenji is maintained as a monastic community, and all the resident trainees, men and women, are expected to be celibate. But Harada Roshi welcomes married and single people to sit sesshin with him. Among the prominent Western Zen teachers to sit retreats with him are Chozen and Hogen Bays, Kyogen Carlson, Mitra Bishop, and Daniel Terragno.

For a number of years, there have been plans for him to take up permanent residence at the One Drop Zendo, situated on Whidbey Island. Should this happen, it could prove to be a momentous occasion for the establishment of the Rinzai line in North America.

Keido Fukushima: Thirty Years Visiting America

As with Shodo Harada, Keido Fukushima Roshi has not established a residence in the West but has become a very important figure in the establishment of a Western Rinzai. Keido Fukushima was tonsured a Zen monk at the age of fourteen. He first trained with Okada Roshi, head abbot of the Tofukuji branch of Japanese Rinzai. Later he continued his training with Zenkei Shibayama Roshi (renowned in English for his excellent commentary on the *Mumonkan,* or *Gateless Gate,* collection of koans), then head abbot of the Nanzenji school of Rinzai. Fukushima Roshi also has earned a doctorate in Buddhist Studies from Otani University.

Fukushima Roshi first visited America in 1969 serving as attendant to Shibayama Roshi. Later he returned to America and taught for a year at Claremont College. Since 1989 the roshi has made annual visits to America, lecturing at various colleges and universities, as well as leading sesshin in the Little Rock, Arkansas, area.

A number of Americans have traveled to his home temple Tofukuji in Kyoto to study with him there. These include Grace Schireson, a Dharma heir to Mel Weitsman Roshi in the Shunryu Suzuki lineage, and Jeff Shore, a scholar and senior student of Fukushima Roshi, who lived in Kyoto for twenty-five years, and has now been leading retreats in America for the last several years.

Though it cannot be precisely measured, it is clear that Fukushima Roshi exerts a significant influence on American Zen.

Roko Chayat and the Syracuse Zen Center

Roko Chayat was the first woman to lead a major Western Rinzai temple. Sherry Chayat was born in Brooklyn in 1943. Her father was killed at the tail end of the Second World War, when Sherry was a year and a half old. Her mother, a grade school teacher, remarried when Sherry was four. The couple would have two more children. Her step-father, an artist, was a volatile and harsh taskmaster. Roko Osho would later refer to him as "my first head monk." While a difficult relationship, Roko also speaks of his positive influences on her—particularly his enormous sense of integrity, remarkable creativity, and relentless instance that the children learn to think clearly and for themselves.

The family lived first in New Mexico and then in rural western New Jersey. They had very little money. Young Sherry was frequently ill and inclined to be introspective. Around the age of ten, she discovered the art of sitting still and "inhaling the fragrance of the air and then exhaling vast stillness."

In the eighth grade, Sherry read a book that contained a chapter on Zen. She was shocked to discover a religion that drew on her own childhood discovery. She then determined that when she grew up she'd move to Japan and become a Zen practitioner. Sherry went to Vassar College, majoring in creative writing and painting, with a philosophy minor. She avidly read the works of writers exploring Buddhism and Zen in English—Alan Watts, D.T. Suzuki, Jack Kerouac, Eugen Herrigel, and Karlfried Graf Dürckheim—whom she later would refer to as "my friends."

Sherry went to study art at the New York Studio School for Drawing and Painting. There she met a young scholar, Lou Nordstrom, and before long they married. Sherry had decided she wanted a "Zen wedding" and so had looked in the phone book under Z and found the Zen Studies Society. She went to the center and Eido Shimano answered the door. It was September 1967.

Eido Sensei, as he was then called, agreed to perform the marriage. But Yasutani Roshi was also staying there at the time, and it was he who actually officiated at the wedding. The young couple then began sitting at the Society. Sherry received the Dharma name Roko, which means "sparkling dew." Lou eventually received a one-year appointment at Syracuse University as sabbatical replacement for the famous religious studies scholar Huston Smith. At the end of that year, the couple decided to stay in Syracuse. There they joined a small sitting group that had been founded in 1972 by some university graduate students.

Roko soon became the group's leader, and they began a flurry of programming, with zazen as the base but expanding into various areas. Most notably, there was a conference attended by many of the most prominent Buddhist teachers of the time. Among the presenters was Maurine Stuart, whom Sherry had come to know before leaving New York. Around this time, Sherry and Lou divorced. Lou Nordstrom would later receive Dharma transmission within the White Plum Sangha from Bernard Tetsugen Glassman Roshi (about whom, more later).

The Syracuse sangha decided their next step was to hold a sesshin. In 1984 Roko invited Eido Roshi to lead their inaugural retreat, and he agreed. But shortly before they were to begin, Soen Roshi died and Eido traveled to Japan for the funeral. So Roko invited Maurine Stuart Roshi to come and lead the retreat. This led to a five-year collaboration, during which time Roko was both a student of the roshi and a colleague, in her capacity as the resident leader of the sangha.

Roko's son Jesse, who was born in 1981, quickly formed a particularly close relationship with Maurine, doubly marking the closeness of these two pioneering women of American Zen. In 1985 Maurine ordained Roko a priest. When Maurine died in 1990, Roko resumed her studies with Eido Roshi. Because of irregularities in Maurine's Dharma transmission, Eido Roshi reordained Roko in 1991.

At some point tired of renting spaces, Roko's second husband, artist Andy Hassinger, suggested they renovate the attic of their home as a zendo—which they did. The group continued at that location until 1996, when they purchased their current property. They raised a large sum of money to renovate it, then had a devastating fire and raised *more* money—finally achieving their renovations.

In 1992 Eido Roshi authorized Roko as Dharma teacher, during the annual Rohatsu sesshin (the particularly vigorous sesshin celebrating the awakening of the Buddha) held at Dai Bosatsu. In 1996 she was installed as abbot of the Zen Center of Syracuse. In 1998 Roko Osho received Dharma transmission from Eido Roshi, becoming the first American woman to receive official Rinzai Dharma transmission.

Today Roko Osho is a widely respected teacher and guide, and The Zen Center of Syracuse is one of the oldest continuing Zen centers in North America. Functioning as a Zen training center, cultural institute, and center of a growing community, it is becoming an example for other centers throughout the West.

EIGHT

American Soto

I N MAY OF 1922, Hosen Isobe established the first Soto Zen temple in the West—if one counts Honolulu as the West. In July he came to Los Angeles and established a second temple. This second temple was ephemeral, lasting a month shy of four years. Nonetheless, it led directly to the formation of the Zenshuji Soto Mission in Los Angeles, which, in 1926, became the institutional foundation of Japanese Soto Zen on continental America.

Serving there for eight years, Hosen Isobe then moved to San Francisco, where, in 1934, he established the Sokoji Soto Mission. Various people of European and African descent visited these temple, and some stayed on to study—precisely how many is not known, but certainly in increasing numbers. The debt that the West owes to Hosen Isobe Sensei, this unfortunately largely unknown priest, is as incalculable as the debt we owe to the more widely known Rinzai Zen master Soyen Shaku.

In May 1953 in Hawai'i, Rosai Takashima Roshi gave formal Dharma transmission to Ernest Shinkaku Hunt, making him the first Westerner that I can document to be ordained a full Soto Zen priest. It was five years before the next significant ordination: the first full Rinzai ordination of Ruth Fuller Sasaki, Zen scholar and widow of the late Sokei-an, by Oda Roshi at Daitokuji in Japan.

As in Japan, Soto remains the larger Zen presence in the West—though two distinct streams of Western Soto Zen rather quickly emerged: one serving largely Japanese immigrant populations and their children; the other directed toward people of European and, to a much smaller degree, African descent.

Japanese Soto Zen is the only Asian Zen tradition to formally send missionaries and establish Zen centers in the West. Mostly these centers have been aimed at the immigrant community, but nearly all have been receptive to Western converts. The North American branch of the Soto school lists just fewer than fifty temples maintaining an affiliation with the Japanese-based sect (and they are under the purview of the Soto Bishop of North America, Genko Akiba). Of these fifty temples, fewer than fifteen serve congregants predominantly of Japanese descent.

Shohaku Okumura Roshi has devoted much time and energy to bridging the gaps between these groups. Currently director of the Soto Zen Buddhism International Center in San Francisco, and senior teacher of the Sanshin Zen Community in Bloomington, Indiana, he identifies these two groups as "temple" and "center" Zen, respectively. And—while I agree with Wako Kato Sensei that they, in fact, represent one single stream—there are significant distinctions that need to be noted.

In addition to the older and better-established lineages listed below, there are increasing examples of Western teachers within the Soto tradition who are individual representatives of Japanese lineages. Most prominently, there is Eido Frances Carney, who guides the Olympia Zen Center in Washington state. A Dharma heir in the lineage of the eighteenth-century poet-priest, Ryokan, Carney Roshi is a prominent leader of the Soto Zen Buddhist Association. Then there is Patricia Dai-En Bennage, who studied in Japan for twenty-three years and has arguably the most formal traditional training of any Zen priest in the West. Bennage Roshi serves as abbess of Mount Equity Zendo in central Pennsylvania.

Also of note is Anzan Hoshin, who guides the White Wind Zen Community in Ottawa. His writings, archived on the Web, have become standard references for many Zen students.

If one includes the Harada-Yasutani koan reform tradition within the Soto listing, its numbers swell even more. (Taizan Maezumi's White Plum lineage, the largest group in the Harada-Yasutani lineage in the West, is treated in this book separately, yet is also fully a part of the Soto tradition and could just as easily have been listed in this section.) As already mentioned, Japanese Sotoshu has a long-established formal branch in North America, with many Soto Zen priests connected to it. Perhaps even more interesting, however, is the beginning of an independent North American Zen institution, the nascent Soto Zen Buddhist Association.

This organization is an attempt to draw the various independent lineages together for mutual support, and for the creation of educational and training resources as well as commonly acceptable ministerial/professional standards. Its mission presents a compelling vision. But it is too early to tell if it will have broad enough interest and support among a notoriously independent-minded group of clerics to continue.

Just as Soto Zen is the most common form of Zen in North America, the San Francisco Zen Center network is the largest of the Soto lineages in North America. Together with the Kwan Um School of Zen in the Korean tradition, these two institutions have grown sufficiently in size and complexity to warrant close attention as possible prototypes of a North American Zen.

As one wag asserted, these centers are now old enough and have gotten their scandals out of the way early enough to be able to attend to the matters that actually count. Certainly, the compelling institutions evolving out of these two lineages suggest ways that Zen really may take root in the West. The founding teacher of the San Francisco Zen Center is Shunryu Suzuki Roshi.

Shunryu Suzuki, Beginner's Mind, and SFZC

Shunryu Suzuki is American Zen's first star, and considered by some to be Western Zen's first saint—and the founder of one of the premier Zen institutions in the West.

He was born at Shoganji temple in Tsuchisawa village, near the city of Hiratsuka in Kanagawa prefecture in 1904. He was a child of the newly emerged married-priest system. His father, Sogaku Suzuki, an incumbent at the temple, came from a farming family. His mother, Yoné Shima, one of the first spouses allowed to live in the temple, was from one of the earliest priestly families. There were no family quarters in such traditional temples, so they all slept in the Buddha hall.

In 1916 young Shunryu went to Zounin temple in the town of Mori, to the north of Hiratsuka. Here he began studying Zen with Sogaku's adoptive elder son So'on Suzuki. The next year So'on ordained Shunryu an unsui, giving him the Buddhist name Shogaku, meaning "auspicious peak." In 1925 he began formal training at Shizuoka-shi, under Dojun Kato Roshi. The following year he received Dharma transmission from So'on.

Over the next few years he continued his academic studies at Komazawa University, while also being formally installed as abbot of Zounin. In 1930, Suzuki Roshi completed his *Zuise* ceremony (the "abbot-for-a-day" ceremony at one of the Soto school's head temples—arguably the highest authorization in the Soto school). Later that year he earned his degree in Buddhist and Zen philosophy, with a minor in English. His graduate thesis was a study of Dogen's masterwork, the *Shobogenzo*. He graduated second in his class.

Suzuki Roshi then spent a year at Eiheiji and another six months at Sojiji before resuming his responsibilities at Zounin. After a brief first marriage, he married Chie Muramatsu, who in 1952 was devastatingly murdered by a troubled monk staying at the temple. In 1956, Suzuki Roshi was invited to travel to San Francisco to become assistant priest at Sokoji temple. He was sorely tempted, but the time wasn't right and he declined. In 1958 he remarried, this time to an old friend, kindergarten teacher Mitsu Matsuno.

Finally, in 1959, he accepted an invitation to become priest of Sokoji and left for San Francisco. Over the next few years, people heard of the Zen master living in Japantown and would come to study with him. Suzuki Roshi would reply that he didn't know much about Zen, but that he sat zazen early every morning and all inquirers were invited to come sit with him. Surprisingly quickly a group of students gathered around him.

The rapid growth of this group, young people who were mainly beatniks and eventually hippies, caused tension with the culturally conservative congregation at Sokoji. This tension continued for years, and before long Suzuki Roshi was effectively leading two different congregations.

In 1962 the Zen Center of San Francisco was formally incorporated. Apparently this was the first time the word "center" was used for a Zen community in North America. The following year, Suzuki Roshi ordained Grahame Petchey as his first unsui. In the same year he gave Dharma transmission to his oldest son, Hoitsu Suzuki, who represented his father at Zounin.

As early as 1961, Grahame Petchey and Philip Wilson, another early priest, came upon Tassajara hot springs. Inland from Big Sur, some 150 miles south of San Francisco, they thought it an ideal spot for a formal sodo, a Zen training monastery. They encouraged Richard Baker, who was quickly becoming Suzuki Roshi's senior student, to visit, which he did with his wife. But things didn't come together until 1966, when Richard brought Suzuki Roshi to visit. At first Roshi worried that Tassajara was too far from San Francisco, but in all other regards it felt perfect.

Dick Baker moved into overdrive. Revealing his amazing organizational skills, he quickly raised $150,000—this in a year when the entire Zen Center budget was $8,000. In 1967, they held their first practice period at Tassajara, and later that year Richard Baker was ordained an unsui there. Two years later, in 1969, the break with Sokoji was completed when the Zen Center acquired its own San Francisco property on Page Street.

In 1970, Suzuki Roshi gave Dharma transmission to Richard Baker. The next year, he formally installed Baker Roshi as head of the Zen Center. That same year, Suzuki Roshi began elaborate preparation to give Dharma transmission to Bill Jakusho Kwong. But on December fourth, Suzuki Roshi died of cancer before he could complete the process.

The next few years under Richard Baker's leadership were times of unprecedented growth. In addition to the City Center and Tassajara, they acquired Green Gulch Farm in Marin County, and began "Greens" in San Francisco, a gourmet vegetarian restaurant. Baker Roshi raised the profile of the center to unprecedented heights. Jerry Brown, then state's governor, would be sighted visiting the City Center.

Building on the experience of monastic cooking at Tassajara (recalling Dogen's emphasis on the *tenzo,* or head cook), Greens Restaurant is widely credited with revolutionizing vegetarian cuisine in America. Similarly the Tassajara Bread Bakery helped revitalize bread baking in the larger culture. These businesses were ultimately unsustainable in their attempts to support a large residential urban center, but for some years they were vital practice places, with all employees also doing daily zazen. Other Zen centers benefited directly from these experiments and continued to follow with modified approaches to create their own Zen businesses. Examples include Bernie Glassman's Greyston Bakery and John Daido Loori's Dharma Communications.

In March 1983, some twelve years after Baker Roshi became abbot of the San Francisco Zen Center complex, his tenure began to fall apart. It became public knowledge that the roshi, who was married, was having an affair with the wife of one of his closest friends and supporters. This was the first of a number of high-profile sex scandals to rock the North American Zen world over the next several years.

The uproar was immediate. It soon became obvious that Baker Roshi had had not one but a series of affairs, usually with students. People felt betrayed. Everything wrong with the Zen Center was hashed and rehashed—and for a while, it really did seem that everything was Dick Baker's fault. He was after all following the Japanese model as the autocratic leader of the center. And perhaps the buck did stop with him. He did what he could to save his position. When it became obvious that this wasn't going to be possible, in 1984 Richard Baker resigned as abbot.

This difficult time is chronicled in painful detail in Michael Downing's study *Shoes Outside the Door: Desire, Devotion, and Excess at San Francisco Zen Center.* This book is both strengthened and weakened by the fact Downing is neither a Buddhist nor a Zen practitioner. It is a highly competent journalistic project that holds a mirror up to the institutional workings of a Zen center. There are distortions in the mirror, of course, but they're the waves of contemporary secular culture.

Baker Roshi continues to teach, guiding sanghas at centers in Crestone, Colorado (along with his heir Dojun Dan Welch Sensei) and in the Black Forest of Germany. After Baker Roshi left his post, the San Francisco Zen Center asked Dainin Katagiri to serve as interim abbot while the board decided what the next step would be for the center complex. Katagiri Roshi served until 1985 and then returned to his own center in Minneapolis.

Tenshin Reb Anderson, who had been ordained unsui by Suzuki Roshi and was, at the time, the only person to receive Dharma transmission from Baker Roshi, served as abbot between 1986 and 1988. At this point the board decided to shift the nature of the abbacy in two significant ways. First, from that point on it would be a *co*-abbacy; second, the terms of office would be limited, with the terms of the two abbots staggered for continuity of leadership. Anderson Roshi would serve as co-abbot until 1995.

Reb Anderson is one of the most prominent of contemporary Western Zen teachers. He first discovered Buddhism in his early teens whle reading *Life* magazine's series on the world's religions. In college he began reading the few books that were becoming available on Zen. And finally, in 1967 at the age of twenty-four, he left graduate school where he was studying psychology and came to San Francisco to begin the formal study of Zen with Shunryu Suzuki.

A scholar of Zen as well as a meditation master, Anderson Roshi is one of the first people to have worked hard to bring Dogen studies West. He has also stretched much of Zen's traditional approach to psychology by drawing upon other ancient Buddhist sources, including Abhidharma and Yogachara teachings, while at the same time being solidly informed regarding Western approaches to the discipline.

As already mentioned Anderson Roshi was Richard Baker's first Dharma heir, and therefore the only teacher in the San Francisco Zen Center community following Baker Roshi's departure to stand in direct succession to Suzuki Roshi's Western transmission. Unfortunately, in the heat that followed Baker Roshi's leaving San Francisco, Baker declared Anderson had not completed everything required for the transmission to be complete and that Anderson should not be considered his Dharma successor. It is unfortunate that Anderson has had to endure what seems an unfounded repudiation, particularly in light of his subsequent reputation as a significant Western Zen teacher.

The first of the new co-abbots was Sojun Mel Weitsman, who had been ordained by Suzuki Roshi in 1969. Born in Southern California in 1929, Mel was an artist, musician, and one of Suzuki's earliest students. In 1984, he had received Dharma transmission from Suzuki Roshi's son Hoitsu. In 1985, he was serving as abbot of the Berkeley Zen Center, an independent affiliate of the SFZC complex, which he had been leading for many years. Weitsman Roshi served as co-abbot of the San Francisco Zen Center between 1988 and 1997 and then returned to Berkeley.

In the late 1960s, shortly before he was ordained an unsui, I began sitting in the original small zendo he led. I vividly recall those days when he was the most senior Zen student I'd yet encountered. Already his simplicity and focus in practice manifested a teaching style that has marked a generation of Zen students.

Over the years the San Francisco Zen Center—or "Zen Center" as it's called by its members—has deepened its practice and embraced a transparency of leadership that stands as a beacon for the Zen world.

The SFZC complex is the largest Soto institution in the West. Among leaders of other North American Zen centers, there may sometimes be a sense of an SFZC "hegemony." But in my observation, they try hard *not* to be the only Soto lineage, and they have proven generous and openhanded in dealing with other Soto communities and with the larger Zen world.

Unlike the Kwan Um School—which dispersed widely from its inception, reflecting the peripatetic nature of its founder—the San Francisco Zen Center complex, until fairly recently, stayed close to the Bay Area. Thus it has grown deep rather than wide. In addition to the three branches of the original Zen Center, SFZC maintains informal but close connections with the Berkeley Zen Center led by Weitsman Roshi, Sonoma Mountain Zen Center led by Jakusho Bill Kwong Roshi, and Kannon Do led by Les Kaye Roshi.

Along with the others already mentioned, arguably the best known of Suzuki Roshi's disciples is Ed Brown, author of the famed *Tassajara Cookbook* and *Tassajara Bread Book*. Brown Sensei continues to teach Zen in cooking workshops based on his extensive tenzo, or head cook, experience, initially at Tassajara but also in the many years since. He received Dharma transmission from Mel

Weitsman Roshi. Other notable priests in the San Francisco Zen lineage are the author David Chadwick and the scholar-priest Taigen Dan Leighton, who is rapidly becoming recognized as an important academic investigating the meaning and traditions of Zen. Another significant Zen Center figure is the writer and translator Andy Ferguson, a significant contributor to the presentation of Zen in the West.

Zenkei Blanche Hartman is one of the premier teachers that the San Francisco Zen Center has produced. Roshi Blanche Hartman was the first woman to serve as a co-abbot of the San Francisco Zen Center, in a term following Reb Anderson and Mel Weitsman. She had already earned a well-deserved reputation as a fierce social justice activist and began sitting with Weitsman Roshi at the Berkeley Zen Center in 1969, frequently visiting the San Francisco center, as well. She was ordained by Baker Roshi in 1977 and received Dharma transmission from Weitsman Roshi in 1988.

In her retirement she has devoted much of her time to guiding students, leading sesshin, and notably exploring the way of *kesa* (a monastic's sacred robe) sewing, being a leader in the revitalization of this ancient Japanese spiritual art. A regular participant in the annual American Zen Teachers Association, Hartman Roshi is seen as a quiet and yet compelling leader exercising her authority through her simple and pure presence, a true heir to Suzuki's Dharma.

Subsequent co-abbesses and abbots of the Zen Center include Jiko Linda Cutts, who began sitting at the San Francisco Zen Center in 1971. She was ordained unsui by Baker Roshi in 1975 and received Dharma transmission from Anderson Roshi in 1996. She was installed as co-abbess in 2000. At this writing the most recent co-abbot is Paul Haller, a native of Belfast, Northern Ireland, who arrived in California in 1974 when he took up residency at Tassajara. He was ordained by Baker Roshi in 1980 and received Dharma transmission from Weitsman Roshi in 1993. He was installed as co-abbot of the Zen Center in 2004.

Slowly other centers have grown. These include Hartford Street Zen Center in San Francisco established by Issan Tommy Dorsey, the first openly gay Zen master in North America and perhaps the world. Hartford Street would eventually be led by the Beat poet and Zen teacher Philip Whalen. Currently there are about ten groups in the Bay Area, several of which achieved the status of full centers, and there are another ten groups in California beyond the Bay Area affiliated formally or informally with the San Francisco Zen Center.

Moving beyond California has been a slower process. Today, if both formal and informal connections are counted, there are about fifteen groups beyond California's borders. Three of these centers are particularly significant, as they all have resident Zen teachers.

The Chapel Hill Zen Center in North Carolina is guided by Taitaku Patricia Phelan. Phelan Sensei was ordained by Richard Baker and received Dharma transmission from Sojun Mel Weitsman Roshi. The Austin Zen Center is led by Seirin Barbara Kohn Sensei, who was ordained by Anderson Roshi and received Dharma transmission from Zenkei Blanche Hartman Roshi. And the Houston Zen Center is led by Setsuan Gaelyn Godwin. Godwin Sensei was ordained an unsui by and then received Dharma transmission from Tenshin Reb Anderson Roshi.

In all three cases, these centers formed independently and then requested the San Francisco Zen Center send them teachers. Phelan Sensei, Kohn Sensei, Godwin Sensei, and their centers represent a dynamic new possibility in Western Zen. They are models of an empowered sangha engaging a fully trained priest to lead them as they explore a creative melding of Japanese and North American understandings of priestly ministry and congregational polity.

Indeed, these arrangements seem to be creating *congregations* as well as *centers* for training. All three groups are quite young, of course, and what shape they will take as they mature is, like so many cases in this volume, yet to be determined. Still, these foundations and those similar to them in other lineages are among the most exciting things happening in contemporary North American Zen.

In the case of the San Francisco Zen Center sangha, their struggle for clarification of purpose has been public and frequently painful. But they have also set an example of a community that has done its work. Related to these challenges, they've produced two telling documents.

The first is a detailed ethical code and policies for implementing that code. This is a dynamic document—possibly overly detailed, but nonetheless a template for North American centers, for ethical codes of conduct and, importantly, for the procedures to follow allegations of various forms of misconduct.

The second document is a reflective paper titled "Being a Priest." It addresses the question, *What is ordination for?*—a question that takes up considerable amounts of time and energy of the current generation of Western Zen teachers. For some, the document "Being a Priest" is controversial; for others, it's an important contribution to the conversation, reflecting a vision of ordination that is at once clear and inviting.

SFZC also publishes documents that explore the arc of residential Zen training: what one can expect, and what is expected of someone wishing to undertake a lifetime of practice, particularly as this would manifest at Zen Center. Published as "Paths and Gates," these worthwhile summaries articulate a leading vision of what a formal Zen life might look like in North America—for this generation and beyond.

They point first to the importance of clarity and the need for agreements and covenants. This is a significant correction of the sometimes unexamined enthusiasm of the founding generation of teachers and students, who threw themselves headlong into the matter, without reflecting on the best course of action for the individuals and communities forming from their attention to practice. Of course things change; but if one starts with a clear sense of purpose, the odds are much improved that one will end up in a satisfactory place. The guide speaks of generosity, dignity, honesty, and respect. Its various sections are divided by time, reflecting the arc of a life. (All of these documents can be found online through the SFZC website, if the reader is interested in details.)

There is an additional element of Zen Center's development that warrants attention: they have created a retirement plan that guarantees room and board after the age of seventy for people who have given extensive life-energy to the Zen Center's program . Precisely how this will take shape will be determined by the financial well-being of the institution as its members move into this age bracket.

Currently the center is focused on shoring up its financial state. It still lacks significant endowments and must rely on continuing income to meet its various obligations. And so there is some anxiety as to how the center can fulfill its obligations to its longtime members. At the same time, this is the only center that has seriously begun to consider what happens when members who have dedicated their lives to the Dharma and particularly to the local sangha can no longer support themselves.

Today the San Francisco Zen Center remains the most significant of the Japanese-derived sanghas in North America. And it appears to be doing what it will take to continue to be a beacon of hope and practice well into the twenty-first century.

Dainin Katagiri and Standing-Upright Zen

With Dainin Katagiri a robust form of Zen finds its way to the American Midwest. Whereas Suzuki Roshi was a child of the priestly tradition raised within a temple, Katagiri Roshi, while also a married priest, very much represented the older understanding of Japanese Zen as a monastic enterprise.

When I first decided to study Zen, I got on a bus in Berkeley and went over to the San Francisco Zen Center. It was still housed at the old Sokoji site, which had formerly been a synagogue. After receiving a brief introduction to practice from Ananda Dalenberg, one of the senior Western priests, I was ushered into my first *dokusan,* or private meeting with the master. It was Dainin Katagiri. He asked how long I'd been practicing Zen. I replied, "About an hour." He then told me, "Keep that mind."

Dainin Katagiri was born in Osaka in 1928 into a Shin (Pure Land) Buddhist family, the youngest of nine children. His eldest sister drowned shortly after he was born, and it was the family belief he was her reincarnation. He shared this belief. His mother died when he was fourteen. During the War, he was drafted into the air force. The years immediately following the War were very rough for the Katagiris: the family restaurant failed, and they came close to starvation.

At eighteen he decided to become a Zen monk and asked an elderly nun to be his teacher. She declined, but introduced him to Daicho Hayashi then living at Taizoin, a small rural temple near the Japan Sea. Upon ordination he was given the name Jikai Dainin, meaning "compassion ocean, great patience." He would later tell his students he didn't like patience and so resisted using that name.

After two years he was sent to Eiheiji. Among his teachers was Hashimoto Eko, whose first instruction to the young monk was, "Sit down. Become Buddha." He stayed for three years at Eiheiji studying with Hashimoto Roshi, after which he returned to Taizoin.

He was then sent to college at Komazawa University. There he encountered his third teacher, Kakudo Yokoi, who introduced him to Tomoe, the woman he would marry. He took a master's degree in Buddhist psychology and returned to Taizoin briefly, before accepting a position with the Sotoshu at the Soto Propagation and Research Institute. In 1963, when a position opened up at Zenshuji in Los Angeles as assistant to the bishop, he applied and was accepted. Not much later Shunryu Suzuki invited him to assist him in San Francisco.

After several years assisting Suzuki Roshi, Katagiri decided it was time to begin teaching independently. So after a brief stay in Monterey, in 1982 he and his family moved to Minneapolis where he established the Minnesota Zen Meditation Center. Except for a brief return to San Francisco to serve as interim abbot between 1984 and '85, he would remain and teach in Minnesota for the rest of his life. Katagiri Roshi died in 1990, leaving a dozen Dharma heirs.

After Katagiri Roshi's death, Shohaku Okumura served as interim head teacher of the Minnesota Zen Meditation Center until the installation of Karen Sunna, one of Katagiri Roshi's Dharma heirs. She was succeeded by her Dharma heir Tim Burkett, a long-time student of both Katagiri and Suzuki Roshi. Burkett became head teacher of the Center on November 1, 2002.

Katagiri Roshi has left behind a number of very interesting Dharma heirs. Steve Hagen serves as head teacher of the Dharma Field Zen Center in Minneapolis, which is increasingly marked by an independent sensibility that parallels Charlotte Joko Beck's teaching. Shoken Wiencoff has established the Ryumonji Zen Monastery near Decorah, Iowa. Teijo Munnich is resident priest at the Zen Center of Asheville, in North Carolina. Dosho Port guides the Wild Fox Zen Monastery outside of the twin cities. Another is Nonin Chowaney who serves as abbot of the Nebraska Zen Center and Heartland Temple in Omaha, Nebraska. Nonin Chowaney Roshi is charmingly and accurately described in David Chadwick's memoir *Thank You and Okay,* where he is given the name "Norman." As with Chowaney Roshi, many of Katagiri Roshi's heirs practiced extensively in Japanese monasteries.

Kobun Chino Otagawa: The Reluctant Zen Master

Kobun Chino, a deeply respected teacher, challenged many of the conventions of training and authorization in Western Zen. As such he is a signal figure, offering what nearly all accept as an authentic Zen, but in radical departure from the accepted conventions. His teaching and the wide respect he held among Zen practitioners challenged many assumptions about what it means to be "Zen."

He was born in 1938, a child of the Soto temple system. His childhood was marked by the War, and his family often went hungry. Shortly after the war ended, when things were improving for many, his father died. Fortunately he was adopted into another temple family, who gave him the family name Chino. His adoptive father Chino Roshi ordained him unsui at the age of twelve.

Kobun attended Kyoto University, earning a master's degree in Mahayana Buddhist studies. He then spent the next three years at Eiheiji. He was invited by Shunryu Suzuki to come to America as his assistant. Despite the opposition of his adoptive father who was also his Zen teacher, he accepted the invitation.

His airfare was paid by students of Suzuki Roshi who lived in Los Altos, on the peninsula south of San Francisco. They had hoped Kobun would establish a center there. He ended up spending the first couple of years helping the fledgling Tassajara sodo get started. Shortly after Suzuki Roshi's death, however, he did go to Los Altos and begin teaching independently. The Haiku Zen Center grew. Before long it was incorporated under the name Bodhi, and a country retreat was soon added to the complex.

In these years, Kobun was vastly more accessible than most Japanese teachers. People came and went through his house in much the same way people in an earlier generation would walk in and out of their Protestant minister's parsonage. The stresses of this weighed heavily on his marriage, and eventually his wife took their children and left.

Chino Roshi—because he preferred to be called Kobun, his students wanting to show respect often referred to him as "Kobun Roshi"—then moved to Taos. Here he began developing one more center in the ever growing, if always loose, network of sanghas associated with his teaching. He also began teaching frequently at Naropa University, the second independent and accredited school (after the Institute for Buddhist Studies) in North America with a Buddhist orientation.

In the mid-1990s, he returned to California to settle in Santa Cruz. He decided for a time to dramatically reduce his teaching in order to focus on his responsibilities as a father. He also reclaimed his birth-family name Otagowa. In 2001 he accepted an academic appointment at Naropa University and resumed a rigorous teaching schedule.

In July 2002, while in Switzerland, Kobun Roshi's daughter Maya seems to have fallen off the dock at the lake they were visiting. Kobun Chino Roshi drowned trying to save her.

He leaves behind a fascinating legacy. He was not very interested in the forms of tradition. Carol Gallup, who wrote a beautiful reflection on Kobun Roshi's life, "Remembering Kobun," observed that he "taught tangentially, seemingly by accident." But there is no doubt he was a powerful teacher, marking many lives—including many beyond his formal students. His was a way of manifesting, of seeing the rhythms of an authentic life. As a teacher he would emphasize that "You go into retreat to come out. Your practice is for the benefit of others."

Kobun Chino Otagowa Roshi left six Dharma heirs who guide communities in Switzerland, California, and New Mexico. The best known is probably Angie Boissevain, who led the Jikoji retreat center in the Santa Cruz Mountains for many years. While Chino Roshi's informal and inviting style created some institutional difficulties, particularly around expected forms of training, there is no doubt his influence will continue to be felt in the Western Zen world for some time to come.

Kodo Sawaki and Zen without Toys

With the teaching of Kodo Sawaki we encounter challenges to the orthodoxies of Japanese Zen, where Soto masters minimize and sometimes reject many of the norms of the Japanese inheritance, calling practitioners to a single-minded focus on the practice of shikantaza. While Kodo Sawaki's direct influence is relatively minor in the West, he's had indirect influence both through lineages that have been influenced by his teachings as well as translations of his writings that have slowly gathered a strong following.

When I arrived in Wisconsin to begin serving my first Unitarian Universalist congregation, I saw there was a Zen center in Milwaukee. I called up the resident priest, Tozen Akiyama, and arranged to make a brief visit. The rather surprising feature of this encounter for me was that he introduced himself by his given name, Tozen, without titles or formalities. He was the first Japanese teacher I'd met who not only didn't stand on ceremony, he actively rejected it. He also teased about how my ordination date preceded his and how I should therefore accept his deference. I was definitely not used to a Japanese Zen teacher kidding—especially about what most consider a very serious subject.

This was my introduction to the teaching influence of Kodo Sawaki. While not Tozen Akiyama's teacher, Kodo Sawaki's influence on him and others noted in this section is substantial. Sawaki Roshi was born in 1880. His early life was marked by tragedy. Orphaned at seven, he was adopted by an uncle who also died. He was then raised by a professional gambler.

At the age of sixteen he entered Eiheiji and the next year was ordained a novice priest by Kodo Sawada. He traveled widely, visiting and studying with different teachers, acquiring the nickname

"Homeless Kodo." In 1949 he became abbot of Antaiji temple, which, at the time, was located near Kyoto. Eventually he was appointed a professor of Zen literature at Komazawa University, where he taught until 1963. He died in 1965 revered as a reformer of the Zen way, emphasizing the primacy of zazen in Zen practice.

His primary successor was Kosho Uchiyama, known best in English for his classic work, *Opening the Hand of Thought.* Uchiyama Roshi was born in 1912. In 1937 he received a master's degree in Western philosophy. In 1941 he was ordained by Kodo Sawaki. When his teacher died, he succeeded him as abbot of Antaiji.

Following in the spirit of his teacher, rather than have an elaborate funeral ceremony, Uchiyama Roshi led a memorial sesshin that lasted forty-nine days. This also inaugurated what has come to be thought of as the Antaiji-style "sesshin without toys": no Dharma talks, no sutra recitation, none of the famous and sometimes notorious Zen "awakening stick" (or in some circles, "warning stick"), no work periods—just zazen, eating, more zazen, and very little sleeping. This inclination marks other teachers in Sawaki's sphere of influence, such as Tozen Akiyama, Antaiji-trained or not.

Other teachers significantly marked by Homeless Kodo's teaching now live and teach in the West. They include Isshu Fujita, who until recently guided the Pioneer Valley Zendo in Charlemont, in western Massachusetts. Tozen Akiyama and Shohaku Okumura are probably the most important teachers in this line: Tozen through both his active teaching and his Dharma heirs, and Okumura Roshi as a spiritual director and a tireless worker bridging the gap between Japanese and non-Japanese practice communities.

In fact, as with several teachers touched upon in this section, Tozen Akiyama is not directly in Homeless Kodo's line. Tozen Akiyama began training with one of Sawaki Roshi's Dharma heirs, Tosui Oto Roshi. However Oto Roshi died before Tozen could complete his training, and so he continued with Reiyu

Tamiya who was in a line related to Sawaki Roshi. Tozen's style is most frequently compared to the style he inherited through his first teacher from Sawaki Roshi.

After leading the Zen center in Milwaukee for a number of years, Tozen moved to Anchorage where he continues to teach his bare-bones style of Zen. Also importantly, he has named several successors. They include Tonen Sara O'Conner, who now guides the center in Milwaukee, and Jisho Warner, who has gained a reputation in North American Zen circles as an editor and writer as well as a spiritual director, serving as resident priest of the Stone Creek Zen Center in Sebastopol, California. Jisho Warner also currently serves as president of the Soto Zen Buddhist Association.

Possibly the leading figure in the direct line of this lineage in North America is Shohaku Okumura. Born in 1948, Okumura Roshi earned his academic degree in Zen Buddhism at Komazawa University. He was ordained by Uchiyama Roshi in 1970. In 1975 he came to the United States, serving at the Pioneer Valley Zendo until 1981. Okumura Roshi returned to Japan for a few years where he concentrated on translating the writings of Dogen and Uchiyama.

He then returned to the United States to serve as abbot of the Minnesota Zen Meditation Center following the death of Katagiri Roshi. From there he accepted the position of director of the Soto Zen Education Center—now renamed the Soto Zen Buddhism International Center—headquartered in San Francisco. Okamura Roshi currently leads the Sanshin Zen Community located in Bloomington, Indiana.

Antaiji and its radical style of relentless devotion to zazen continues to have an indirect influence on Western Zen. Recently two Western teachers, the iconoclastic Brad Warner and Jundo James Cohen each returned from Japan to the United States, Warner to California and Cohen to Florida. Both are Dharma heirs of Gudo Nishijima, who though himself an heir of Renpo Niwa, sometime abbot of Eiheiji, first studied for fifteen years with Kodo Sawaki.

The influences of Niwa Roshi's first teacher are obvious in the approach to Zen of both these teachers.

Jiyu Kennett, Shasta Abbey, and Monasticism Reclaimed

Jiyu Kennett was the first female Soto Zen master in the West. While in many ways a controversial figure, Kennett Roshi has established one of the most important Zen lineages in the West. Her teaching career also opens questions of orthodoxy and authority that begin to define the outer limits of what might be described as traditional Zen.

Peggy Theresa Nancy Kennett was born in 1924 in England. Her father, a tailor, was involved in the theosophical Buddhism organized by Christmas Humphries at the London Buddhist Lodge. In the 1950s, as it moved in a more traditional Buddhist direction and out of this was renamed the London Buddhist Society, Peggy joined and eventually took on various leadership responsibilities.

During the war Peggy enlisted in the Royal Navy and worked for naval intelligence, assigned to coding and decoding. After the war she won a scholarship to Durham University and continued her training at Trinity College of Music in London. She supported herself primarily as a church organist. In addition to her connections to the London Buddhist Society, she studied at the London Buddhist Vihara, a Theravada Mission, and undertook a correspondence course of instruction through the Young Men's Buddhist Association in Ceylon.

In 1960 when Chisan Koho Zenji, abbot of Sojiji, traveled to the West and visited the London Buddhist Society, she coordinated his visit. He invited her to come to Japan, and, as soon as she could put her affairs in order, she did so.

For reasons that remain unclear, while on her way to Japan she received novice ordination—in January 1962, while in Malaysia—

from Seck Kim Seng, Linchi abbot of the Cheng Hoon Teng Temple in Malacca. However, as soon as she arrived in Japan, she was formally received as a student by Chisan Koho, with whom she would go on to study extensively. However, since he was also concerned with the administration of a major temple and denominational affairs, in practice her primary teacher was often Suigan Yogo Roshi, one of Chisan Koho's senior associates who would eventually become abbot of Sojiji.

Jiyu Kennett Roshi received Dharma transmission twice, from both Suigan Yogo Roshi and Chisan Koho Roshi. She was then installed as abbess of Unpukuji, in Mie Perfecture. In 1969 she was authorized to start a Zen center in London. On her way home, she stopped at the San Francisco Zen Center to learn more about its enormous success as a Western mission. After assessing the California situation, she decided to stay rather than go on to London. In San Francisco she started a small temple, the Zen Mission Society, in an apartment in Mission Hill.

This was where I first studied with her. My memories of that time continue vividly—particularly of the intimacy of the tiny, new community. I recall, for instance, sitting with the roshi and several other young monastics on chairs and her bed, drinking lobsang suchong tea and watching *Dark Shadows,* a campy vampire soap opera.

My memories of Jiyu Kennett Roshi as a teacher are mixed. She followed in the authoritarian style of her Japanese inheritance. Interpersonally, she was remarkably invasive. Indeed, in my twenties, she pushed me into a marriage with another student that would cause great unhappiness for both of us. On the other hand, she had genuine insight into the boundless realm and also pushed me toward my own deepest experience of the great matter.

She was a complicated person with great wit, keen intellect, and a substantial dark side. Illustrating several of these points, Kyogen Carlson recalls a time at the monastery when it seemed the typical monastic was "thin, pale, and wears glasses":

One day one of the women (Roshi called us "she-monks" and "he-monks") returned after a stint at a branch temple. This was a woman of rather generous proportions, and when she entered Roshi's room, Roshi exclaimed "At last! Finally another woman around here with a decent set of jugs. We've had nothing but skin and bones around here lately."

The Zen Mission Society first moved its temple from San Francisco to Oakland. Finally it established the monastic complex at Mount Shasta in far northern California. It was at Mount Shasta that I was ordained osho and received Dharma transmission from her in 1971. I left the monastery not long after that. Today her organization, now called Shasta Abbey and the Order of Buddhist Contemplatives, has numerous branches around North America and Europe, with the majority in England.

Gradually her organization took a decidedly more monastic approach. This was well after she'd established a temple complex along traditional Japanese lines, where priests and monastics could be and often are married. Thus the shift to mandatory celibacy was very controversial, and a number of priests either left or were expelled. The Oregon Priory, led by two of her married successors, Kyogen Carlson Roshi and Gyokuko Carlson Sensei, separated from Shasta Abbey at that time to form an independent succession. Their Dharma Rain Zen Center is now one of the larger Zen centers in North America.

Kennett Roshi was always controversial, for reasons small and large. She introduced a broadly "Anglican" style, which included substituting a form of Medieval Christian "plain chant" in liturgy and, for several years, having clerics wear Western-style priest's collars. More significant controversies arose following a series of "visions" she experienced in the wake of a severe illness. From this she began offering teachings that were in significant ways at variance from mainstream Zen. This particularly included a complex scheme of stages of awakening and a pronounced theistic cast to some of her writings.

She died from complications due to diabetes in 1996. Since that time, the Order she established seems to have slowly moved back to a more normative Zen Buddhism. Institutionally, however, the community has been more interested in connecting with Chinese rather than Japanese Buddhism. Upon Kennett Roshi's death, leadership of the Order has been divided among several senior teachers.

Daishin Morgan—who was already serving as one of two abbots of the Throssel Hole Buddhist Abbey in England—was joined by Eko Little as abbot of Shasta Abbey. Daizui MacPhillamy was elected head of the Order of Buddhist Contemplatives. Upon his death in 2003, he was succeeded as head by Haryo Young. Today the Order appears to be in a period of transition.

The Order and its branches continue to be a significant Buddhist presence, offering a new vision of monastic life for those practicing within the Japanese inheritance, as well as exploring "congregational" centers for lay practice. In the U.S. and Canada there are ten groups, of which the principal is Shasta Abbey. In Europe there are thirty-seven groups, mostly in England, of which the principal one is Throssel Hole Buddhist Abbey.

Kyogen and Gyokuko Carlson and the Dharma Rain Zen Center

Kyogen and Gyokuko Carlson represent the major non–Shasta Abbey line in succession to the late Jiyu Kennett Roshi. With their leadership, one of the first Soto Zen temples generally understood as nonmonastically centered begins to take shape. Andrea Christine Gass was born at Fort Lewis, Washington, on April 30, 1948. Interestingly, she was, if only briefly, the niece of famous Zen poet Gary Snyder when he eloped with her father's younger sister during their

Reed College days—a marriage that ended quickly. Andrea's father's work in the electronics industry took the family to Portland (Oregon), Kansas City, Dayton, and then back to Portland.

Andrea spent two years at Reed College, but left to marry. She spent the next two years in Sweden studying weaving and wood and metalworking. She returned to the States in 1972 and discovered Zen practice at the San Francisco Zen Center. Andrea began studying with a branch of Shasta Abbey in Portland, entering the monastery in January 1975. She was soon followed at the Abbey by her husband. Twelve months later Andrea was ordained an unsui, receiving the Dharma name Gyokuko. Gyokuko completed Shuso Hossen in 1977 and received Dharma transmission in the same year. Around this time she and her first husband divorced.

Gary Alan Carlson was born in Los Angeles on October 8, 1948. His parents met in the Yukon during military service. His father later worked in the moving and storage business. An only child, he was raised in Orange County, in the Christian Science faith. Gary earned his bachelor's degree at the University of California Berkeley in 1971. In many ways, he came of age at one of the epicenters of the social and political upheavals of the period.

Reading Herrigel's *Zen and the Art of Archery* and *The Method of Zen,* he started seriously contemplating the meaning of his life. Following a profound experience of spaciousness—what he later thought of as an "oceanic feeling"—while in a eucalyptus grove above campus, he determined to pursue the inner life. A year after graduation he entered the monastery at Shasta Abbey. He was ordained an unsui on September 26, 1972, receiving the Dharma name Kyogen.

Kyogen served as *jisha,* or personal attendant, to Roshi Kennett for over nine years. He completed Shuso Hossen in 1974 and received Dharma transmission in the same year. In 1978 after Roshi Kennett introduced Inka as a final certification at Shasta Abbey, Kygoen received Inka and the title Roshi.

In 1982 Gyokuko and Kyogen married. They took over as leaders of both the Portland temple and the Eugene affiliate in the same year. The appointment was originally meant to be temporary, when the visa of the incumbent—a Swiss national—expired. When the former prior resigned, the appointment became permanent.

In 1985 the tensions at Shasta Abbey around issues of center autonomy and new requirements of celibacy for clergy began to focus on the Carlsons and their thriving temple. Rather than accept an ultimatum to divorce if they wished to continue their association with Shasta Abbey, they resigned membership in the Order of Buddhist Contemplatives. They reported the situation to their boards of directors. The temple in Eugene decided to remain affiliated with Shasta Abbey, but the temple in Portland asked the Carlsons to remain and continue as their priests and teachers. This effectively separated the Portland temple from Shasta Abbey.

The former priory changed its name to Dharma Rain Zen Center and, in 1987, purchased a large house. Innovations that had previously been proposed but blocked by the Order were now instituted. A serious religious education program was initiated. Retreats that included elements of psychological work were introduced. Gradually there developed a temple devoted to serving the needs of an ever-increasing lay membership.

Of particular interest is their close friendship and frequent collaboration with Chozen and Hogen Bays, co-abbots of the Great Vow Zen Monastery (about whom and which, more later). They frequently lead retreats together, and their students appear to flow seamlessly from one center to the other. This friendship has enriched the lives of the four people involved and the communities they serve. Demonstrating an open and generous spirit, it also demonstrates how a Western Zen might look.

In addition to the many opportunities for authentic Zen practice, the Dharma Rain Zen Center has cultivated a religious community that serves the same needs as a church or synagogue. They provide a recognizable worship service, and notably they've created a religious education program for their children and youth that promises to help form a new generation of Western Buddhists. With several hundred members, the Dharma Rain Center is today one of the largest Zen centers in North America.

NINE

The Harada-Yasutani and Hybrid Zen in the West

NE OF THE MOST distinctive features of Zen in the West is the emergence of a significant lay presence, particularly the rise of nonordained Zen teachers. There have been lay practitioners acknowledged through the generations as fully awakened. But it seems that only in the twentieth century, and mostly in the West, have nonordained Zen teachers in fact created independent Zen lineages. This is a controversial shift of focus and for the most part a unique feature of Western Zen.

Sogaku Harada and the Foundations of a Lay Zen Lineage

The Japanese Zen master Sogaku Harada represents the most significant shift from the received traditions in Zen's transmission to the West. Harada Roshi is a signal figure in the establishment of Western Zen, and—through his Dharma heirs—he has established what has become the primary current of a lay transmission in Zen authority in the West.

Born in 1870, he rose to become a prominent Soto Zen figure, abbot of Hosshinji, an important Soto monastery, and also served as a professor at the Soto denominational Komazawa University. But he also studied extensively with Rinzai masters, most notably Kogenshitsu Dokutan Sosan Roshi, with whom he completed formal koan study and from whom he received permission to teach, and Unmuken Taigi Sogon Roshi.

Harada decided to reform the koan curriculum he had received to fit his particular teaching needs. First he substituted a Soto collection, Master Keizan's *Denkoroku,* or "Record of Transmitting the Light," for the traditional *Rinzairoku,* the "Record of Master Rinzai." And most significant, he deleted most capping phrases. Originally capping phrases were meant to be appreciations of a koan following its intimate encounter, often in the form of a poem composed by the student.

The capping phrases seem to have contributed to the ossification of koan study, and over the years "correct" responses began to be expected, culled from anthologies of spiritual and literary tags. One presumes there was no such intention behind the development of the use of capping phrases, but it nonetheless was a direct consequence. Further, the use of capping phrases slowed the process of formal koan study down considerably. The intuitive insight required for "answering" koans was one thing, but the sense of how selected fragments of poems and other such literary bits and pieces might fit together, which required a sophisticated understanding of both literature and the deeper philosophical import of the discipline, was something of an entirely different order.

When completed, a koan curriculum that includes capping phrases produces people who had been guided through deep spiritual experiences and at the same time had been forced to relate these experiences to a broad range of spiritual literature. As mentioned earlier, it commonly takes thirty years to complete the traditional Japanese Rinzai koan curriculum. And those who do so are not only profoundly knowledgeable of koan study, but also of the spirit and range of East Asian culture.

Harada Roshi's decision to limit the focus of koan study

eliminated a significant aspect in the preparation of a teacher, and also made koan curriculum more easily transferable across cultures. Indeed, today in the West, the vast majority of those authorized to teach in a koan school teach in this modified form.

There was a second step, as well. While Harada Roshi lived his life as master of a sodo, a formal monastic style training hall, he also authorized as a teacher someone who would reject the sodo system and indeed the whole of the Soto structure in favor of regular zazen and close attention to the koan curriculum as almost the exclusive means of Zen training.

Haku'un Yasutani and Koan Introspection

Haku'un Yasutani founded the first lay Zen line, which quickly spread to the West and is now the source of most Western koan practitioners.

He was born in 1885, and his admirers like to tell a miracle story associated with his birth: His mother had decided her next child would be a priest. To assure this she followed the advice of an elderly nun and swallowed a bead from a *mala,* a Buddhist rosary. When he was born the baby was said to have been clutching the bead in his hand.

The child was given over to temple life at the age of five. His childhood master was a Rinzai priest, Tsuyama Genpo. But at sixteen he was ordained a Soto novice at Denshinji and continued his training under the famous master Nishiari Bokusan. As he was not from a temple family—indeed he was from peasant extraction—he was unlikely to receive an appointment as a temple priest. So instead he attended teacher's college, which led to a ten-year career as a teacher and eventually as a principal. At thirty, he married. He and his wife would have five children.

In 1925, at the age of forty, he returned to active ministry, employed as a traveling lecturer by the Sotoshu. In the same year, he sat his first sesshin with Sogaku Harada Roshi. Two years later, his kensho was acknowledged. Ten years later he completed Harada Roshi's koan curriculum and was given full Dharma transmission in what would over time become a new lineage of Zen, known by his own and his teacher's names: the Harada-Yasutani lineage, mentioned throughout this book.

Haku'un Yasutani decided, however, to devote his time as a teacher of laypeople. In 1954 he established the Sanbo Kyodan, the Order of the Three Treasures, as an independent Zen institution. Over the next thirty years he led over three hundred sesshins, wrote and lectured, and, significantly, in 1962 began a number of visits to North America.

Known as a garrulous figure given to disputation and rhetorical excess in support of his positions, it was nonetheless shocking when in the 1990s excerpts from some of his World War II–era political polemics were translated into English. Most offensive was his use of anti-Semitic shorthand in his attacks on bourgeois democracy.

He made full use of the arguments marshaled by Japan's ally, Nazi Germany, to favor the emperor and an authoritarian state. The actual significance of these writings has been widely debated. Some argue that his apparent anti-Semitic polemic proved he couldn't have experienced awakening.

Others suggest this criticism actually reveals a common misunderstanding of what awakening is—or is not. Awakening, this argument proceeds, is a direct seeing into our original nature, but our actualization will always arise out of our conditioned experience. Zen awakening is about living in the real world, which very much includes our limitations. Ideally these limitations are confronted through the precepts and other Buddhist perspectives, and we engage in an endless process of polishing our character. The good news for all of us is that whatever our shortcomings, they don't stand in the way of awakening. And the most important lesson here is perhaps that awakening is not an end; it's a beginning. Used appropriately each of our awakenings, small and large, can become a gate to an ever deeper, more compassionate life.

Like all things, even awakening can be turned toward ego-driven ends by the unexamined habited-energy of our conditioned lives—and so we must remain ever vigilant, never complacent. Even after awakening—even after *deep* awakening—all of us must always strive to practice the principle of *ahimsa,* nonharming, and never lose sight of the deep not-knowing that Bodhidharma pointed out for us centuries ago.

At bottom, it isn't possible to overstate Yasutani Roshi's influence on the formation of North American Zen. His many students—interestingly in light of his earlier pamphleteering —included Jews and political liberals, most of whom were also anti–Vietnam War activists. Among the many people who studied with him were Eido Shimano, Philip Kapleau, Robert Aitken, and Taizan Maezumi.

The organization that Yasutani Roshi founded, the Sanbo Kyodan, or Society of the Three Treasures, has several official representatives in North America. Ruben Habito, who leads the Maria Kannon Zen Center in Dallas, Texas, is addressed in greater detail below. Elaine MacInnes began studying Zen in 1961. A Catholic nun who worked and taught in the Philippines, she is now retired in Toronto. Roselyn Stone began studying Zen in Japan in 1977 while on sabbatical from the University of Toronto. She was given Dharma transmission by Koun Yamada, Yasutani Roshi's principal heir, in 1985. She teaches in Toronto and Brisbane, Australia. A fourth teacher, Joan Rieck, lives in America but mainly teaches in Europe.

Philip Kapleau: Frontier Zen and the Rochester Lineage

With Philip Kapleau we have the most complicated consideration of authority in Zen. While widely acknowledged as a genuine Zen master, and the source of a significant and widely accepted stream of Western Zen, he in fact lacked formal Dharma transmission from his teacher. Here the contradiction of a generally accepted Zen teacher who has not received the "formal seal" of his teacher has most clearly focused and challenged Western Zen's understanding of legitimate authority.

In August 2003 the American Zen Teachers Association conference was hosted by Kapleau's Rochester Zen Center in Chapin Mill, their country retreat, outside of Rochester. Those of us who were interested were invited to go into Rochester and meet Philip Kapleau Roshi. He was ninety years old and suffering from advanced Parkinson's disease. Most of us understood this could be our last, and for some *only,* chance to meet this old Zen pioneer.

I actually hesitated. He had broken from his teacher Yasutani Roshi many years before. He took to calling himself Roshi and was known in subsequent years to make seemingly self-serving disparaging remarks about other teachers. He also, it seemed to me, gratuitously challenged the technical veracity of the transmission of the lineage from which he had broken—which was a lineage in which I also practiced. But he was also the editor of *Three Pillars of Zen,* a monumentally important book. I cannot fully express how important that single book was in my life; and this has been true for so many others who've taken up the Zen way. So, in the end I went to see him.

Philip Kapleau was living in a small two-room apartment at the center. His Parkinson's was so advanced he could do little more than sit in his recliner and hold hands with each of us who'd made the trip. About ten teachers—Dharma successors in the Soto, Rinzai, Harada-Yasutani, and Korean Chogye traditions—had made the pilgrimage. There was little option, if we wanted to shake Kapleau's hand, but to kneel in front of him and take the initiative. It had clearly not been set up to require such a supplicative posture, but that was inevitably what was called for.

I found tears welling up from deep within me—not just for his physical condition, but for gratitude. This crusty old man was a true founder and absolutely one of the most important figures in bringing the Zen way West. For all his flaws, he was a great man and one of the most important people in my life. I happily knelt, took his hands in mine, and thanked him. I remain grateful for that opportunity.

Philip Kapleau was born in New Haven, Connecticut, in 1912. He served as chief court reporter for the International Military Tribunal at Nuremberg, and later he was also court reporter at the trials in Tokyo. While in Japan he met a number of prominent Zen teachers, including Soen Nakagawa, Sogaku Harada, and Haku'un Yasutani, the founders of the Harada-Yasutani line of koan-studying Soto Zen. After coming back to America he felt profoundly dissatisfied with his life and decided to return to Japan in 1953.

After spending three years at Hosshinji with Harada Roshi, Kapleau became the first Westerner to begin formal study with Haku'un Yasutani. After some twenty sesshins with Yasutani, the roshi confirmed Kapleau's awakening. In 1966, after ten years studying with his teacher, he came home to America and, with Yasutani Roshi's permission, founded the Rochester Zen Center in upstate New York.

There are several accounts of the reasons for his famous break with Yasutani Roshi. The most commonly reported version suggests deep disagreement about appropriate forms for the nascent North American center. Another story is that Kapleau objected to the close association of his teacher to another senior student who Kapleau felt was lax in his ethics.

Philip Kapleau was an aggressive personality who rubbed a number of people the wrong way, including several visiting Japanese teachers. More important, there were the growing tensions between Yasutani Roshi and Philip Kapleau. The specifics are debated but these tensions appear in significant part to have to do with

Kaplau's leadership of his center: his increasingly independent style, his departures in liturgical usage, and his relationships with visiting teachers.

The tensions all came to a head when Yasutani Roshi informed Kapleau that he, Kapleau, would no longer be considered Yasutani's student. At this time Kapleau had completed about half of the Harada-Yasutani koan curriculum, the koans in *The Gateless Gate* and *The Blue Cliff Record*. Could he, in good faith, continue to teach considering his permissions were limited to introducing people to the practices of the Sanbo Kyodan—or "Three Treasures," as the Harada-Yasutani school called itself—to which he no longer belonged? Regardless Kapleau decided to continue as a teacher.

The Three Pillars of Zen was the first book in English to describe authentic Zen training, and it justly became an international bestseller. Kapleau went on to write a number of other books, and his center grew to become one of the most influential Western Zen communities. While seen by many as a difficult personality inclined to unnecessary conflict, he was also a central figure in the establishment of a Western Zen. And there should be little doubt the institution he founded will continue well into the future.

But the Rochester lineage, as it is sometimes called, opens all the questions regarding the nature of Dharma transmission. What does this mean for us today and in the future? Andrew Rawlinson, who spent years studying Western teachers of Eastern religions, makes a pointed comparison of Philip Kapleau and Robert Aitken, as an aid to reflection on the nature of formal transmission—what it might mean, and what it probably doesn't mean. Philip Kapleau spent thirteen years in Japan studying with several teachers. Eventually he received permission to teach but not Dharma transmission, which is the approval to teach independently. Since his split with Yasutani Roshi:

Kapleau has continued to teach, as he is entitled to do, but has also given Dharma transmission to a number of his own students, which, according to the transmission criteria of the Zen tradition, he is not entitled to do. Or at least, these appointments need not be recognized by any other lineage or teacher....In effect, then, Kapleau has created his own Zen lineage.

By contrast, Rawlinson holds up Robert Aitken:

Aitken received Dharma transmission from [Ko'un] Yamada Roshi but he has been far more radical in his attitude to the traditional way of life than Kapleau. He has encouraged Zen (and Buddhist) feminism, for want of a better term, and has actively encouraged gay and lesbian participation in Zen (though he is not gay himself). He is also a committed social activist—he was a co-founder of the Buddhist Peace Fellowship—and sees such commitment as a necessary aspect of Buddhist ethics, which are themselves expressed in the precepts. At the same time he has given Dharma transmission to one of his students who is a Christian priest.

This last action is something for which Aitken has been openly criticized.

As Rawlinson sees it, the difference between these two teachers turns on their understanding of transmission: "In short, for Aitken transmission is a necessary condition (though not a sufficient one) for the tradition to continue; for Kapleau, spiritual qualities hold an equivalent place."

Roshi Kapleau died on the sixth of May, 2004, in the garden of the Rochester Zen Center, surrounded by old and new students. He had suffered from the ravages of Parkinson's disease for years and had long since retired from formal teaching. It is hard to assess yet what Roshi Kapleau's career means for the development of Western Zen. But one thing is certain: despite having teaching authorizations, he ultimately lacked formal Dharma transmission, yet he created a lineage that is largely recognized throughout the Western Zen community. Thus his life and the institution he created forces Western Zen practitioners to carefully consider the nature of Dharma transmission.

Among the most prominent of Kapleau Roshi's heirs are Toni Packer (addressed later), Peter Bodhin Kjolhede (addressed immediately below), and Sunyana Graef, who guides the Vermont Zen Center near Burlington and Casa Zen in Costa Rica.

Bodhin Kjolhede and a Western Lineage

Upon serious consideration, we find that Dharma transmission is a myth, in both senses of the word. It is a large and noble truth—and a lie. Even the great master Hakuin appears to have potentially lacked the technical form of transmission from his teacher Shoju Rojin. Nonetheless *something* is transmitted. There is a shape and a character to Zen. And those normative teachers of it are broadly acknowledged to possess Dharma transmission. In nearly every case, these teachers hold tangible documentation to that effect.

Today, however, we have people in Kapleau Roshi's lineage who are universally accepted as Zen teachers by other Zen teachers, while others with all technical ordinations and certificates, such as those in the Matsuoka line, are *not* accepted by their transmitted peers. Here the way is slippery and curious—but, frankly, I think it's just as it should be.

For example, with Bodhin Peter Kjolhede, Kapleau's successor as head of the Rochester Zen Center, we're seeing one of the first Western lineages manifesting. Of course, this can only be known over time. But Bodhin Kjolhede Roshi is widely recognized as an accomplished teacher and leader in the Western Zen sangha.

Peter Kjolhede was born in Detroit in April 1948. The second-oldest of six, he had five sisters. His father was an executive with General Motors. He earned a degree in psychology from the University of Michigan in Ann Arbor. In November 1970, while visiting two of his sisters who were active in the Rochester Zen Center, Peter took an introductory class. He never looked back. Eventually all but one of the siblings would try Zen practice, and his sister Sonja, who received the Dharma name Sunya, would also receive Dharma transmission from Kapleau Roshi.

Not long after he arrived at the center, Peter was assigned to fix a door. To protect himself from someone opening it on him, he posted a sign on the other side: "Open door gingerly; someone working on other side." Kapleau Roshi appeared to have noticed this: sometime later, when he needed a secretary, he asked for the person who made that sign and knew how to use a semicolon correctly. For the next several years Peter assisted his teacher in a number of writing projects. He received the Dharma name Bodhin from Kapleau Roshi, who ordained him in 1976.

Bodhin gives this example of his teacher's presentation of Dharma outside of zazen and retreat: While staying with the roshi in Tepoztlan, south of Mexico City, Bodhin discovered a scorpion in the middle of the living room. He asked Kapleau Roshi, "Should I kill it?" Roshi replied, "If you can kill it without a trace of malice in your mind, go ahead. If not, you'd better find another way to dispose of it."

We can see in this statement the way that Zen, combined with just a little bit of self-deception or with insufficient reflection, can easily lead to a non-Buddhist path of killing, as it did in samurai Japan. But Bodhin got the scorpion into a glass and deposited it outside in the weeds—as any truly diligent Zen student would have to do.

After twelve years of intensive training, Bodhin received Dharma transmission from his teacher in 1983. In 1986 Bodhin Kjolhede was installed as director of the Rochester Zen Center.

Things continue to change in the Rochester lineage. One of Kapleau Roshi's Dharma successors, Danan Henry, completed the Harada-Yasutani koan curriculum and received Dharma transmission from Robert Aitken after his transmission from Kapleau. Henry Roshi now guides the Denver Zen Center, which blends Kapleau's and Aitken's Zen transmissions.

Mitra Bishop Sensei is another of Kapleau Roshi's heirs. She has spent the last decade studying with the world-renowned Rinzai master, Shodo Harada Roshi (discussed above), while serving as abbess of Mountain Gate in northern New Mexico and spiritual director of the Hidden Valley Zen Center in San Marcos, California.

Kjolhede Roshi has four Dharma heirs: Sevan Ross in Chicago, Sante Poromaa in Stockholm, Gerardo Gally in Mexico City, and Amala Wrightson in Auckland, New Zealand. And other teachers in this line are continuing their training in a variety of ways.

Of possible significance is the fact that to date at least two Zen teachers in the Soto line have offered Bodhin Kjolhede Roshi formal Dharma transmission. Should he ever accept such an offer, it would mark the institutional healing of this significant lineage. However this plays out—whether formally reunited with the Soto line or not—the Rochester lineage is without a doubt one of the most dynamic of the contemporary Western Zen communities. It's the bumble bee that shouldn't be able to fly, but does.

Toni Packer, Krishnamurti, and Zenless Zen

Toni Packer is a Kapleau Roshi heir who has moved to the farther margins of the Zen community. Although she no longer considers herself a Zen Buddhist, she remains a significant spiritual teacher. We can learn a lot about the nature of Zen by considering the margins and the challenges of just about everything brought from Asia to the West—from the forms of Zen, to Dharma transmission, to the purpose of Zen training altogether. Toni Packer's training and teaching career speaks to this range of challenges to what I think can best be termed "normative" Zen.

Toni Packer is without a doubt the most radical of the generally accepted Zen teachers in this volume. Described occasionally as a Zen teacher minus the "Zen" and minus the "teacher," Toni (as she prefers to be addressed) has abandoned all forms that might incline a person to cling to an outside authority. This includes the use of words like *Buddhism* and *Zen*. Indeed, she is the first great Zen "heretic" in the West—and is generally as respected as she is controversial.

Toni was born in Berlin in 1927. Six years later Hitler came to power. The family secret during her childhood was that, while they were nominally Lutheran, her mother was Jewish. Those early years under the Hitler regime were profoundly formative for her, leading to a deep suspicion of authority and all forms of deception.

Eventually the family moved to Switzerland. There in 1950 Toni met and married a young American, Kyle Packer. The couple settled in upstate New York, where Toni earned an undergraduate degree at the State University of New York at Buffalo, followed by some graduate work in psychology.

During this time she discovered Alan Watts, quickly moved on to D.T. Suzuki, and then Philip Kapleau's *Three Pillars of Zen*. As it did for so many young people at that time, Kapleau's book—and the possibility of an actual living Zen—caught her imagination. When she learned that Kapleau had a center in Rochester, only ninety minutes away, she and her husband quickly joined.

By 1970, she was given limited teaching responsibilities. By 1975, she was leading retreats. In 1981, while Kapleau Roshi was on a yearlong sabbatical, she took over the running of the center. By the time the roshi returned, the center was divided over Toni's teaching and particularly the many changes she'd instituted. For example, she had decided to no longer wear the *rakusu,* the small bib-like vestment symbolic of having taken the precepts and refuge in the Zen Buddhist tradition. The roshi supported her; but not long after, she decided she could no longer, in fact, call herself a Buddhist of any sort. And she left the center.

Toni established the Genesee Valley Zen Center. But as she continued stripping away what she saw as "extraneous trappings" and established what would become her longtime home, the Springwater Center for Meditative Inquiry, she'd dropped even the word *Zen.*

Toni was significantly influenced by Jiddu Krishnamurti, a figure who needs to be noticed in any survey of Western Zen. An Indian national, Krishnamurti was born into a Hindu family in 1896. In his childhood he was "discovered" by prominent Theosophists Charles Leadbeter and Annie Besant. Raised to be a world spiritual teacher, the new incarnation of Christ and Maitreya Buddha, he shocked his mentors and sponsors when he came of age by repudiating all titles and association with the Theosophical Society. Instead he spent the rest of his life as a writer, lecturer, independent philosopher, and spiritual teacher. Krishnamurti died in 1986.

Inspired in a distant way by his Theosophical upbringing, but vastly more by Advaita Vedanta, Hinduism's radical nondual philosophy, through which many find connections to Zen, Krishnamurti's teaching style was often considered by his admirers to be like that of a Chinese Zen master. Advocating the absolute autonomy of the individual on her or his path, Krishnamurti offered no prescriptions or nostrums, no practices, and no methods. Instead he relentlessly pointed to direct attention, bare awareness of "what is."

Of the many Western Zen teachers influenced by Krishnamurti, Toni Packer is the most prominent and possibly the most like him in style. It should be noted that, while Krishnamurti had a private regimen that included silent meditation, as a teacher he offered no practices. Toni Packer, however, holds up the possibility of zazen—

simply called "sitting"—as well as silent meditation retreats at her center, where nevertheless there is no form of liturgy and all practice is seen as completely voluntary.

While repudiating any claims to being a teacher and any forms such as Dharma transmission, Toni Packer has at this writing asked six people to "carry on her work." What will become of this non-Zen non-lineage should be very interesting. In both formal and informal ways, there is little doubt that Toni Packer and Krishnamurti remain influential figures in the developing shape of North American Zen.

Taizan Maezumi and the White Plum Sangha

Taizan Maezumi is probably the most important koan master to come West. A Soto priest who also had received Inka in both the Rinzai and Harada-Yasutani lines, his heirs are the most widely distributed koan teachers in the West. As with Master Seung Sahn, with Taizan Maezumi Roshi we can clearly see the difference between the stories of ancient masters and accounts of the real lives of contemporary teachers. In my estimation, Maezumi Roshi is one of the greatest teachers of our time. While I only spoke with him briefly on two occasions and only about technical matters of the Harada-Yasutani lineage, I frankly count him as one of my most significant teachers.

His compassionate engagement with the world; his generous treatment of Robert Aitken, newly anointed as a Zen master but unsure of his abilities; his willingness, even if only after being confronted, to address his own weaknesses, particularly his alcoholism—all these were lessons in how an authentic Zen life might be lived. He is to be deeply admired.

Maezumi Roshi was a skillful teacher, truly a teacher of teachers. He established the White Plum Asanga, eventually renamed the White Plum Sangha, an organization of his Dharma heirs that continues as one of the most important of contemporary Western Zen lineages. As mentioned before, he also suffered from alcoholism, a disease that eventually killed him, and engaged in several inappropriate sexual relationships with students. These two truths sit closely side by side—and, I feel, contain all the difficulties and possibilities of our humanity and the Zen way.

His father was Baian Hakujun Kuroda, a prominent Soto Zen priest and abbot of Koshinji in Otawara City, Tochigi Prefecture. Kuroda Roshi also served officially as "chief advisor" of Sojiji, one of the two head temples of the Soto school in Japan, and was head of the school's internal judicial administration. Maezumi's mother, a temple daughter, was also university educated. Maezumi's name at birth was Hirotaka Kuroda. He was born on February 24, 1931, in Otawara, the third of eight sons, four of whom would become Soto priests.

Like many sons of the temple system he was ordained an unsui as a child, in his case at age eleven, on March 25, 1942. He was given the ordination name Taizan, "Great Mountain." When the last of the males of his mother's family died, he was formally adopted by his maternal grandparents to continue the Maezumi family name. Following Japanese Zen Buddhist conventions for clergy, he began using the Sino-Japanese pronunciation for his given name, changing it from Hirotaka to Hakuyu.

Maezumi began his training at the family temple. He attended the denominational school Komazawa University, earning a degree in 1952 in Japanese and Chinese literature and philosophy. From 1954 to 1956, he trained at Sojiji monastery, one of the two great sodos of the Soto school (Eiheiji being the other one). In 1955 he received Dharma transmission from his father and in the same year performed the Zuise ceremony at both Sojiji and Eiheiji temples, as was the convention.

However, he did not limit his training to mainstream Soto disciplines. While at university, Maezumi lived with and began studying under Koryu Osaka Roshi, a lay Zen master in the Rinzai tradition and an old family friend. He continued this relationship for many years and, in 1973, received the old master's Dharma transmission.

In 1967, Maezumi also met Haku'un Yasutani, the leader of the Sanbo Kyodan, and began formal study with him. In 1970, he completed formal koan study with Yasutani Roshi and received his Dharma transmission as well. He was the first Zen teacher in the West to receive formal Dharma transmission in the Soto, Rinzai, and the Harada-Yasutani lines. While always maintaining close ties to the formal Soto school in Japan, Maezumi Roshi would require his senior students to study the Harada-Yasutani koan curriculum with him, in addition to the more normative forms of Soto Zen training.

Maezumi arrived in California in 1956 to work as a Soto Zen missionary. Except for two years at San Francisco State College studying English, he spent the next decade as a priest at the Zenshuji Soto Mission in Los Angeles. In 1967 he established the Zen Center of Los Angeles, as an independent center for the Western students who were beginning to gather around him. A tireless worker, in 1976 he founded the Kuroda Institute of Transcultural Studies (now called the Kuroda Institute for the Study of Buddhism and Human Values), affiliated with the University of Hawai'i. He also encouraged the formation of the Soto Zen Buddhist Association, the aforementioned organization attempting to draw together the various Soto lineages in North America.

Maezumi Roshi administered the Buddhist precepts to over five hundred people. He ordained sixty-eight priests and gave Dharma transmission to twelve of them. His influence on the shape of Western Zen is incalculable. When Aitken Roshi—who has since become one of the most respected North American Zen masters—was first given permission to teach, he felt uncertain and went to Maezumi Roshi. It is possible that without his gentle guidance, Aitken would not have begun what became an illustrious career as a Zen teacher. There are numerous examples of Maezumi Roshi's teaching style, but one I particularly like has to do with a student who had been a professional dancer.

As recounted in Sean Murphy's *One Bird, One Stone,* the student had badly hurt one of her feet in an accident and was forced to retire from the stage. Embarrassed by her injury, she always kept her foot covered with a sock. In her first interview she asked Maezumi a question about her Zen practice. But he answered, "Never mind that. Tell me about your foot." She was reluctant to talk but he insisted. She told him the story, weeping, and even took off her sock and showed him her foot.

> Maezumi placed his hand silently on her foot. She looked up to find that he was crying too. Their exchanges went on like this for some time. Every time she asked the roshi about her practice, he'd ask about her foot instead, and they'd cry together. "You might think you have suffered terrible karma," Maezumi told her, "But this is not the right way to think. Practice is about learning to turn disadvantage to great advantage." Finally the day came when the student walked into the interview room and began to tell her teacher about her injury, but it summoned no tears from her. "Never mind about that," Maezumi told her. "Let's talk about your practice."

Maezumi Roshi died in 1995. Shortly before his death he decided to create an Inka Shomei ceremony for Bernard Tetsugen Glassman, his senior student (about whom, more below). Through this ceremony he wanted to acknowledge the additional gifts of his lineage, including the Rinzai and Harada-Yasutani lines as a full part of the White Plum transmission. It appears he had been abstemious for some time, but once back in Japan, visiting with his brothers, he became drunk. Returning to the home he was staying in, he climbed into a bath, apparently fell asleep, and drowned.

For our Western Zen to become authentic, rich, and healing, we cannot allow such facts to be obscured. Accordingly, Maezumi's heirs did allow this information to eventually be widely known. Maezumi Roshi left behind his wife Martha Maezumi, three children, and a vital Zen lineage led by his twelve Dharma successors.

The Zen Center of Los Angeles is now led by Wendy Egyoku Nakao. Born in Hawai'i of Japanese and Portuguese parents, Wendy was a librarian in Seattle when she first met Maezumi Roshi. In 1978 she moved to Los Angeles and the center. Roshi Nakao received Dharma transmission and Inka from Glassman Roshi, Maezumi's senior heir. Under her leadership, the center has expanded its mission to be more family-friendly and socially active, creating an important experiment in the development of Western Zen. Significantly, in March 2006, Nakao Roshi gave Dharma transmission to Merle Kodo Boyd, the first African-American woman to receive this authorization.

The Zen Mountain Center was established as a country retreat in the San Jacinto Mountains outside of Los Angeles, during Maezumi Roshi's life. This center is now led by Charles Tenshin Fletcher. An English native, Tenshin began studying with Maezumi Roshi in 1979 and is one of Maezumi Roshi's original Dharma heirs.

The current head of the White Plum Sangha is Maezumi's second Dharma successor, Dennis Gempo Merzel Roshi. Born in 1944, Merzel Roshi holds a master's degree in educational administration. He was ordained an unsui by Maezumi Roshi in 1973 and received Dharma transmission from his teacher in 1980. Merzel Roshi completed Zuise in Japan in 1981. In 1996 he received Inka from Bernie Glassman Roshi, who shortly thereafter transferred leadership of the White Plum Sangha to him.

Bernard Glassman:
American Zen's Peripatetic Master

Bernie Glassman, Taizan Maezumi's first Dharma heir, is one of the more controversial and interesting of the Western Zen teachers. Bernard Glassman was born in Brooklyn, New York, in 1939 of Jewish immigrant parents. His mother was Polish; his father was a printer from Russia. He graduated from the Brooklyn Polytechnic Institute and moved to California to begin working for McDonnell-Douglas as an aeronautical engineer, where his work focused on unmanned missions to Mars. He continued his education, eventually earning a doctorate in applied mathematics from UCLA.

In 1967, inspired (as were so many) by reading Kapleau's *Three Pillars of Zen,* he sought out a Zen teacher in the Los Angeles area and found Maezumi Roshi. Over the years he studied with some of the most famous Zen teachers in the West, but his principal teacher remained Maezumi Roshi, who ordained him an unsui, and gave him Dharma transmission in 1976.

Bernie, as he prefers to be called, returned to New York where he established the Zen Community of New York and began the Greyston Mandala, a network of community development organizations. The most prominent of these is the Greyston Bakery, a four-million-dollar business that trains and employs seventy people. The Mandala also includes the Greyston Family Inn, Greyston Health Services, and the Greyston Garden Project. Peripatetic by nature, Bernie Roshi has since moved on to other projects, most notably what is now called the Peacemaker Circle International.

Glassman is arguably one of the most important figures in the establishment of Western Zen. Famous as a perceptive teacher, he is equally committed to social justice and to bringing Zen into the world. "The Plunge" or "street retreats," for instance, moves sesshin into the streets: participants eat in soup kitchens, and, if they know they're not displacing homeless people, sleep in homeless shelters or, otherwise, sleep in public spaces. Zazen takes place in parks and dokusan in alleys.

Among his controversial moves, he transferred his leadership of the White Plum Sangha to his Dharma brother Merzel Roshi and has formally "disrobed," renouncing priesthood in favor of serving as a lay teacher and leader of what is now called the Zen Peacemaker Family. In 2005 he named Pat Enkyo O'Hara Roshi, abbess of the Village Zendo in New York City, as codirector of the Zen Peacemaker Family. In recent years he has been encouraged by students and others to reordain. Whether he does so or remains a lay teacher there can be little doubt he will remain one of Western Zen's most controversial and compelling teachers.

John Daido Loori and Zen Mountain Monastery

John Daido Loori was born in 1931 in Jersey City. While coming from a working-class background, he was able to attend Monmouth College where he earned a Bachelor of Science degree. Starting in 1947, John spent four years in the navy, serving mostly aboard a destroyer. After that he held a number of jobs, ranging from director of religious education at the Unitarian Church in Middletown, New Jersey, to director of research for Polaks-Frutal Works. Eventually he opened a photography studio in Middletown and began teaching photography at the state university.

John studied Zen with a number of teachers, sitting retreats with Soen Nakagawa Roshi and Eido Shimano Roshi. But in 1976, while leading a workshop on photography at Naropa University he met Maezumi Roshi. Deeply impressed, he followed the teacher back to Los Angeles where he was ordained an unsui.

In 1979, he accompanied Bernie Glassman Roshi when the latter left the Zen Center of Los Angeles to found a center in New York City. The next year Loori left Glassman and moved upstate to Woodstock. Here he started what after several permutations would become the Zen Mountain Monastery. In 1986, while he had not yet formally completed koan study, he received Dharma transmission from Maezumi Roshi. In 1987, Daido Loori Roshi traveled to Japan to perform the Zuise ceremony. He was installed as abbot of the Zen Mountain Monastery in 1989.

As a teacher Loori Roshi has attempted to constantly reform the institutions he inherited. While principally trained in the Harada-Yasutani koan curriculum he has substantially reworked it for his students. He has also tried to create a lifelong residential monastery that can accommodate noncelibate monastics, attempting to face the inherent contradictions of the Japanese inheritance in a forthright manner.

Zen Mountain Monastery has become a cultural and religious center where one may undertake a rigorous version of Japanese-derived Zen, which includes fervent attention to the practice of shikantaza as well as Loori Roshi's expanded version of the Harada-Yasutani koan curriculum. It is, without a doubt, one of the most significant of Western Zen centers.

Chozen and Hogen Bays and Great Vow Zen Monastery

Judith Ann Burgess was born in 1945 in Chicago, on the day America's nuclear bomb was dropped on Nagasaki. Her parents were both students at the University of Chicago, living at the time in a communal house with James Forman, one of the founders of the Congress on Racial Equality. Both parents were fervent social-justice activists. Her father was at the first restaurant sit-in in the South. He became a professor of library science, first teaching at the all-black Talladega College in Alabama, then spending the balance of his teaching career at SUNY–Albany.

Jan, as the family called her, was raised in East Greenbush, a small town outside of Albany—except for two critical years in post-War

Korea, where her father helped to establish a library school at Yonsei University. She credits this experience for establishing her interests in matters Asian, particularly in Buddhism.

She earned her undergraduate degree from Swarthmore and her medical degree, specializing in pediatrics, from the University of California at San Diego. She is a nationally recognized expert on child abuse. After her first marriage failed, she met Laren Hogen Bays whom she later married. She has three children from her first marriage.

Jan was ordained an unsui by Maezumi Roshi in 1979 and given the Dharma name Chozen. In 1983, she received Dharma transmission from Maezumi Roshi. She has continued her training by attending retreats with the Rinzai master Shodo Harada Roshi. She and her husband Hogen moved to Oregon in 1984, where she began working as a supervising pediatrician in an outpatient clinic next to a private hospital.

Jack Lawrence Bays was born in 1949 in Louisville, Kentucky. Through college he was called Larry; after that most of his friends called him Laren. Eventually he would be known primarily by his Dharma name, Hogen. His parents were from rural Virginia and Kentucky and his first home was a trailer. The family worked themselves out of poverty, building a construction firm, Jack Bays, Inc., which is now run by Hogen's sister in McLean, Virginia.

Hogen started at Kentucky College but left at the age of nineteen to go to Kapleau's Rochester Zen Center. From there he went to the National College of Naturopathic Medicine, later working for several years as a naturopath and homeopath. He went on to take a master's degree in psychology at Portland State University and worked for the Oregon Department of Corrections for fifteen years.

He moved to California to study with Maezumi Roshi who ordained him in 1990. Hogen continues his training by regularly attending sesshin with Shodo Harada Roshi. He received Dharma transmission from his spouse Chozen Bays in 2004. This was done following wide consultation with teachers in several traditions, including Zenkei Blanche Hartman, former co-abbess of the San Francisco Zen Center, Gyokuko and Kyogen Carlson, who had watched his emergence as a teacher, and all concurred that this was an appropriate move. Hogen Sensei is widely respected within the Zen community as a wise and compassionate teacher.

Following the shakeup at the Zen Community of Los Angeles, the couple moved permanently to Oregon. At first they weren't interested in forming an official Zen center. But despite their best efforts, a small sitting group eventually gathered around them, and before long it grew to a size requiring formal structures.

They organized as the Zen Community of Oregon and began looking for a site to establish a residential center. Following a first attempt near Corbett, Oregon, they acquired a former elementary school outside Clatskanie, Oregon. Near the Columbia River and about halfway to the Pacific Ocean from Portland, this is now Great Vow Zen Monastery.

Today Great Vow is the center of a network of practice centers in the Pacific Northwest. It provides formal training in the White Plum line of Soto Zen; but it also includes influences both from the Rinzai tradition of Harada Roshi, and from other streams of Soto Zen through the couple's long personal connection to Gyokuko and Kyogen Carlson and the Dharma Rain Zen Center in Portland. This friendship and collaboration is another example of the inviting and generous style that Chozen and Hogen Bays bring to their presentation of the Dharma.

Great Vow is one of the most dynamic of the "new" generation of Zen centers, which attempt to be open and experimental while remaining firmly rooted in the traditions. Like other centers, it struggles with the meaning of ordination in the West, and how best to accommodate an essentially noncelibate monasticism. But the transparency of the process that Chozen and Hogen Bays model in going forward makes it hard to see the future of Great Vow as anything less than a shining beacon for the emerging Western Zen way.

Joan Halifax and Upaya Zen Center

One of Glassman Roshi's most prominent Dharma heirs is Joan Halifax. Joan Halifax was born in 1942 in Hanover, New Hampshire, while her father was studying at Dartmouth College. When she was four, Halifax was stricken with a viral infection that left her functionally blind for the next two years. This would mark the rest of her life. She attended Harriet Sophie Newcomb College at Tulane University, graduating in 1964. During these years she became increasingly involved in the dawning civil rights movement.

She moved to New York where she began working with anthropologist and folklorist Alan Lomax. In 1969, after a year of preparation at the Musée de L'Homme in Paris, Halifax went to Mali to live with and study the Dogen tribe (in such a study as this it probably needs to be noted this is not a reference to the great Japanese Zen master, but a fascinating if not meaning-bearing coincidence). During the 1970s she also continued field work, this time among the Huichols in Mexico. She returned to Florida where she spent the next two years studying and teaching at the University of Miami School of Medicine. Joan Halifax received her doctorate in medical anthropology in 1973 from the Union Graduate School.

In 1972 she married the renowned psychologist and psychedelic investigator Stanislav Grof. Although the marriage did not last, their joint work was exciting and important. Together they worked on early LSD studies in which Halifax was particularly concerned with the psychological and spiritual issues of dying people. Even after the LSD project ended, she continued her interest in working with the dying, eventually becoming one of the most important teachers in the field. In addition she became one of the leading Western authorities on the range and meaning of shamanism, and her classic study *Shamanic Voices* remains required reading in most college-level courses on the subject.

During the 1970s while engaged in her field work among the Huichols in Mexico, Halifax also began seriously studying Buddhism and formally received Buddhist precepts. She worked with many teachers including the Korean master Seung Sahn, who named her a Dharma teacher and the Vietnamese teacher Thich Nhat Hanh, who authorized her as a Dharmacharya (about which, see above); as well as with the Dalai Lama, Khyentse Rinpoche, and Chagdud Tulku in the Tibetan traditions.

In 1979 she established the Ojai Foundation, at which she worked until 1990. Shortly thereafter, she founded the Upaya Zen Center in Santa Fe. She is also a cofounder, with Bernie Glassman, of the Zen Peacemaker community. In 1997 she was ordained a Soto Zen priest, and in 1999 she received Dharma transmission and Inka from Bernard Tetsugen Glassman Roshi.

In many ways Upaya leads the Zen community in developing outreach programs. These include Metta Refuge, which gives respite to people with catastrophic illnesses; the Upaya Prison Project; and the Project on Being with Dying.

Charlotte Joko Beck and Zen as Nothing Special

Charlotte Joko Beck has become a significant figure as a founder of the Ordinary Mind School of Zen. Both she and the community she leads warrant exploration in some detail. The Ordinary Mind School was among the first Zen communities to consciously engage the emotional life and the shadows of the human mind as Zen practice. Joko and her heirs have adapted elements of the vipassana tradition—a relentless inquiry into the contours of the human mind—as unambiguous Zen discipline.

In 1965, when she was in her forties, Charlotte Beck attended a lecture at the First Unitarian Universalist Church of San Diego.

She was struck by the insight of the speaker, Zen teacher Taizan Maezumi—who would become her primary teacher. Charlotte would also study and sit numerous sesshins with Haku'un Yasutani Roshi and Soen Nakagawa Roshi, passing the Mu koan with Soen Roshi.

In 1978, she was ordained and received Dharma transmission from Maezumi Roshi, becoming his third Dharma heir. But in 1983, Joko formally broke with her teacher in the wake of her teacher's improprieties at the Zen Center. She founded the independent San Diego Zen Center, which became the nucleus of the Ordinary Mind School.

While Joko, as she prefers to be known, does have ordained students she, herself, has generally moved away from the Soto school style. She no longer uses her titles and never wears her priest's robes. Liturgical forms in the centers associated with her are minimal.

Her teaching style is particularly interesting as it seems nothing is off the table. She plays down kensho, calling the experience "small intimations." And of Dharma transmission Joko says, "It's no big deal." At the same time, there is clearly a Zen sensibility permeating what she does. One observer says this comes from her relentless nondual perspective, which informs everything she does and all of her teaching.

Barry Magid, one of her Dharma heirs and a practicing psychiatrist in New York, writes: "To me Joko always stressed experiencing the absolute in the midst of the everyday. [S]taying with anger or anxiety wasn't so much a technique for dealing with emotion as a way of seeing emotion itself, resistance itself, as *IT*. Not as obstacles on the path to be worked through and removed, but the path itself." Here we begin to understand what she means by *ordinary mind* and why it became the name of her school.

Some of her students go through the Harada-Yasutani koan curriculum. But completion of formal koan work is not a requirement for Dharma transmission by anyone within the Ordinary

Mind School. Teacher Diane Rizzetto—ordained a Soto priest by Joko and now one of her heirs—moves with her own students between koan introspection and other disciplines such as "labeling" thoughts (borrowed from the Insight Meditation tradition), as seem best for them at the time.

Most of Joko's heirs have undergone traditional Soto forms of ordination and the White Plum style of Dharma transmission. Elihu Genmyo Smith, also an accepted teacher in the White Plum Sangha, follows a slightly modified form of the Soto tradition. But Joko hasn't felt it absolutely necessary to follow the Soto pattern, nor to expect it from her heirs.

As he was nearing the end of his own formal training, Dr. Magid writes, "I felt like a peach she would occasionally sniff and squeeze and one day she said OK, you got it. And that was my transmission 'ceremony.' (Followed by a notice in the newsletter, under the parking instructions, that the Dharma had been transmitted to me....)" However, she recently did give all her Dharma heirs formal Soto lineage papers.

Her Dharma heirs have gone on to found centers of their own across the continent. Among these teachers, the most prominent are probably Diane Eshin Rizzetto who leads the Bay Sangha in Oakland, California; Elihu Genmyo Smith who leads the Prairie Zen Center in Champaign, Illinois; Barry Magid who leads the Ordinary Mind Zendo in New York City; and Elizabeth Hamilton together with her husband Ezra Bayda until recently co-led the Zen Center of San Diego, after the retirement of Joko Beck. Ezra Bayda, through his several widely received books, has perhaps become the second most influential Ordinary Mind teacher after its founder.

Robert Aitken and a Western Lay Lineage

Robert Aitken is, without doubt, one of the most truly venerable elders of the Western Zen way.

Aitken was born in Philadelphia in 1917. When he was five years old, his father accepted an appointment as an ethnologist at the Bishop Museum in Honolulu. Except for a year and a half in California during high school, he was raised entirely in Hawai'i. Before the outbreak of World War II, he spent two and a half years at the University of Hawai'i. Then, taking a break from his university career, Robert took a fateful job in Guam.

In 1941, the day after Pearl Harbor was bombed, he was captured by the invading Japanese Army and spent the entire war in various civilian internment camps in Japan. Fortunately, at some point a guard loaned him a copy of R. H. Blyth's *Zen in English Literature and the Oriental Classics.* Fascinated by the book, Robert reread it so many times the guard became afraid he'd break its spine and so reclaimed it. But through a fateful coincidence he and Blyth himself were transferred to the same camp. Robert took advantage of this opportunity to start the intellectual aspect of what was to become a formidable Zen training.

After the war, Robert returned to Hawai'i and completed his undergraduate degree in English literature. He then moved to California where he met Nyogen Senzaki, the itinerant Zen teacher who was leading his "floating Zendo" in various rented venues up and down the California coast. Senzaki Sensei gave Robert the Dharma name Chotan, which means "Deep Pool," and introduced him to koan study.

He returned to Hawai'i where in 1950 he earned a master's degree in Japanese studies. The year before, Robert had helped put on the East-West Philosopher's Conference, at which he met and began what would be a lifelong friendship with D.T. Suzuki. Also in 1950, he made his first visit to Japan since his time as a prisoner of war. There he began studying with Rinzai master Soen Naka-gawa Roshi.

After traveling for a time between Hawai'i and California, dur-ing which time he married and divorced, Robert landed a job teach-ing at Jiddu Krishnamurti's Happy Valley School in Ojai. There he met Anne Hopkins. They married and traveled together to Japan for their honeymoon. While there, Robert again sat with Soen Roshi and also met Yasutani Roshi. In 1958, when Soen Roshi came to California to preside at Nyogen Senzaki's funeral, Robert served as the teacher's jisha, or attendant.

He had his first intimations of what Zen is about during a sesshin in 1961. But his teacher Soen Roshi was reluctant to confirm it as more than "a little light." His deeper understanding was eventually confirmed by Soen Roshi in 1971, long after he had been successfully engaging in koan study and demonstrating his abilities as a teacher in his own right.

Over time Aitken worked with a number of teachers, but his principal guides were first Yasutani Roshi and then Yasutani's suc-cessor Ko'un Yamada Roshi. In 1974, Yamada Roshi conferred Dharma transmission on Aitken Roshi. Hesitant to accept the responsibility and unsure of himself in many ways, Aitken Roshi traveled to California where he spent some time reviewing koans and deepening his insight with Maezumi Roshi. As mentioned ear-lier, Maezumi Roshi's generosity of spirit launched Aitken Roshi into what would become one of the most widely respected Zen teaching careers in North America.

In 1959 he and Anne established the Kokoan Zendo. This was the nucleus of what would become the Diamond Sangha network, with centers on several Hawai'ian islands and in California, Ari-zona, Texas, Washington State, Germany, Argentina, Australia, and New Zealand. In Australia, working with his senior student and first Dharma heir, John Tarrant, he's built the Diamond Sangha into the largest Zen organization Down Under.

Aitken Roshi has been one of Western Zen's foremost social justice activists. He is a founder, with another of his senior students Nelson Foster—along with Anne Aitken, Thich Nhat Hanh, poet Gary Snyder, deep ecologist Joanna Macy, Insight Meditation teacher Jack Kornfield, Pure Land exponent and priest Al Bloom, and others—of the Buddhist Peace Fellowship. Among the ten plus books written by Aitken Roshi, *Taking the Path of Zen* is a classic and seminal to many starting the Zen way, and his *Mind of Clover* is still considered the best book on Buddhist ethics. These books should surely be read by every beginning Zen student.

Aitken Roshi has now officially retired to an assisted living facility in Kai on O'ahu. The Diamond Sangha network is led by a teacher's circle consisting of his Dharma heirs and their successors. His principal heir is Nelson Foster Roshi, a noted social justice activist, writer, and editor of one of the two most important anthologies of ancient Zen teachings currently available in English, *Roaring Stream: A New Zen Reader*. (The other is Andy Ferguson's *Zen's Chinese Heritage*.) Foster Roshi guides both the Palao Zen Center in Hawai'i, which hosts the principal training activity of the Diamond Sangha network, and Ring of Bone in North San Juan, California.

John Tarrant and the Pacific Zen Institute

John Tarrant Roshi, now guiding an independent sangha called the Pacific Zen Institute, is probably the most prominent of Aitken Roshi's heirs. An Australian national, he was raised in rural Tasmania in a home without indoor plumbing. He was able to get a scholarship and receive his undergraduate degree in literature and human sciences at Australia's National University.

His is a life that makes good copy for the biographical blurb on the back of a book. While in Tasmania working in copper smelters, he wrote poetry on his breaks. He then worked as a fisherman on the Great Barrier Reef; and as a lobbyist for aboriginal rights; and for a while, as amanuensis for Australian poet Judith Wright. Seeking ever greater clarity, John Tarrant would eventually travel to Hawai'i to study Zen and, eventually, become Robert Aitken's first Dharma heir.

Tarrant Roshi brings humor, a keen poetic sense (he is a widely published poet), and a doctorate in psychology and continuing interest in archetypal psychology to his Zen teaching. He is known for pushing the edges of Zen institutions, introducing and dropping liturgical experiments—such as allowing Zen sutras to be set to Cajun tunes or passing out grapes during the service—just to see what happens. Today the Pacific Zen Institute is marked by its willingness to innovate and creatively explore the range of Zen disciplines.

Insofar as I am capable of an objective view of one of my primary teachers, Tarrant Roshi is one of the most exciting of the new generation of teachers, and a very skillful teacher of the koan way. Among his heirs and teachers within the Pacific Zen Institute are Susan Murphy, Joan Sutherland, Daniel Terragno (who chose to realign with the Diamond Sangha), David Weinstein, and myself.

While I also am a Dharma heir within the Soto tradition, it was only with Tarrant Roshi's training and eventually his permission that I felt ready to teach.

The Boundless Way Zen sangha I teach within is very much inspired by the openness taught by Tarrant Roshi. I suspect visitors see his fingerprints all over my work.

Boundless Way has a distinctive characteristic worth noting. Our teacher's council includes me, my own first Dharma successor, Melissa Myozen Blacker who studied first for years in a breakaway branch of the Rochester Zen line, and her husband David Rynick, a Dharma heir of Zen Master George Bowman. Together we're attempting to create a new previously unheard-of focus on a multi-lineage vision for Zen practice.

The most prominent of John Tarrant's Dharma heirs is probably Joan Sutherland, who guides the Open Source Project. While she has a master's degree in Chinese from the University of California at Los Angeles, she originally worked in the field of archaeomythology as an apprentice to Marija Gimbutas. Joan Sutherland's wide-ranging interests include feminist thought, antiviolence and environmental issues, the Western wisdom traditions, and psychology and the arts. Combining these with her mastery of koan introspection, she is a highly innovative and creative teacher.

SECTION 3

THE FUTURE OF ZEN IN THE WEST

TEN

New Directions, New Challenges

*H*AVING EXPLORED SOME of the myths, stories, and people significant in Zen's journey West, this chapter will look at some the new directions Western Zen is going in, and some of the challenges Western Zen will face as it matures into our culture. We also explore in some broad terms issues around morality and enlightenment, teaching and spiritual authority, and varieties of institutional and individual responsibility.

Let's first look at Zen and its relation to two major Western religions.

Christians, Jews, and Zen

Many Christians and Jews have found a significant part of their spiritual lives within the Zen way. But many have been met with confusion and occasionally open hostility by representatives of their faiths of origin. A Christian Zen master in Germany, Benedictine prior Dom Willigis Jager, was formally "silenced" by the then Cardinal Joseph Ratzinger (now Pope Benedict XVI), when he was prefect of the Congregation for the Doctrine of the Faith, which in earlier generations was known as the Office of the Inquisition.

On the Zen side, many question how faithful to the Buddhist

way these dual practitioners can be—particularly those who are not only Christian but also Christian clerics. I'll let Father Jager's comment be the last word here: "Many can argue whether a Christian can validly do or teach Zen or not. The fact is, I am doing it."

While a very small subset of Western Zen, these Christian Zen masters are part of a fascinating and thriving phenomenon. Christians who find Zen interesting and compelling come from many denominations, although most have been Quakers and Roman Catholics and, in recent years, Episcopalians.

The first Christian I can trace to be acknowledged as a Zen master is Hugo Enomiya-Lassale. Lassale was born in Germany in 1898. He joined the Society of Jesus, the Jesuits, and was ordained a priest in 1927. Two years later he was assigned to Japan. Except for occasional visits to Europe, he remained in Japan for the rest of his life, eventually becoming a Japanese citizen. There he met Sogaku Harada and began studying with him. After Harada's death he continued training with Harada's principal heir, Haku'un Yasutani. And after Yasutani's death, he continued with Yasutani's principal heir, Ko'un Yamada, who gave him permission to teach and, in 1980, full Dharma transmission.

For many years Enomiya-Lassale Roshi taught at his Catholic Zendo, Shinmeikutsu, the "Cave of Divine Darkness." Formally dedicated as a retreat center first by the native Japanese Roman Catholic bishop of Hiroshima, and later by the native Japanese archbishop of Tokyo—an impressive imprimatur for what many would consider a heretical institution. Enomiya-Lassale Roshi died in 1990, having introduced a generation of Christian practitioners to Zen and guiding a few who would become teachers themselves.

In North America, a number of Christian Zen teachers have emerged, mostly within the Harada-Yasutani lineage. In fact the sole official representative of the Sanbo Kyodan in the United States is Ruben Habito, a former Jesuit and now professor at Perkins

School of Theology at Southern Methodist University in Dallas, where he also guides the Maria Kannon Zen Center. Having known him for years, I see him as equally manifesting the love of Christ and the wisdom/compassion of the Buddha.

Robert Aitken has named as a teacher a Catholic priest, Patrick Hawk, who is also a monk in the Congregation of the Most Holy Redeemer, or Redemptorists. Bernard Tetsugen Glassman, Taizan Maezumi's first Dharma heir, has named Jesuit priest Robert Jinsen Kennedy as one of his successors. Both Hawk and Kennedy have in turn named their own Dharma heirs; Kennedy, in fact, has at this point named six. And now one of Kennedy Roshi's heirs, Janet Jinne Richardson, has named successors of her own—thus creating what can only be considered a Zen Christian lineage.

The Jewish presence in North American Zen is also rich and equally complicated. In fact the Jewish presence is pervasive throughout Western Buddhism. I know I acquired most of the Yiddish expressions in my vocabulary after entering a Zen monastery. So it shouldn't be surprising that a term for Jewish Buddhist practitioners has emerged: JuBu. This term has met with differing degrees of acceptance among Western Jews who also practice Zen and other types of Buddhism.

Among the many Zen priests and masters who are Jewish by heritage and who incorporate, in varying degrees, acceptance of a dual identity are the remarkable master Bernard Tetsugen Glassman, his Dharma sibling Genpo Dennis Merzel, and Norman Fischer, former abbot of the San Francisco Zen Center. To date one rabbi, Don Singer, has received Dharma transmission from Tetsugen Glassman.

Maria Reis Habito is a Buddhist scholar and Roman Catholic who is also married to the Christian Zen master Ruben Habito. In "On Becoming a Buddhist Christian" in the book *Beside Still Waters: Jews, Christians, and the Way of the Buddha*—perhaps the best collection of essays on the subject in print—she writes:

My encounter with Buddhism and my close connection to my Buddhist teachers, Shih-fu [Master Hsin Tao] and [Ko'un] Yamada Roshi, have not uprooted me from Christian ground. On the contrary, my Buddhist teachers, together with [the Christian Zen master] Father Enomiya-Lassalle, have done everything possible to fertilize these roots and to let them grow stronger and deeper. They have taught me how to water them and how to deal with the weeds. They have taught me how to put the knowledge of God from my head into my heart. My deepest gratitude to all of them.

In his essay "Close Encounters of a Certain Kind," in the same anthology, Maria's husband Ruben Habito observes:

Having been blown by some strange Wind from Cabuyao, Philippines, to Tokyo, Japan, and now to Dallas, Texas, I continue to marvel at the ceaseless unfolding of these four encounters that have graced my life. Incidentally, by a twist of uncanny insight—and perhaps not by chance either—the lineage name given to me by my Zen Teacher, Yamada Ko'un Roshi, is Keiun, which means "Grace Cloud."

I contemplate with gratitude these visits of grace, looking to them for clues to certain kinds of questions posed to me by friends, colleagues, students, or by inquisitive individuals like the editors and would-be readers of this volume: Are you Christian? Are you Buddhist? Are you both Buddhist and Christian? Are you neither?

With that the Zen teacher ends his essay, leaving whatever answers we need to those questions to our private imaginations.

Buddhism, Zen, and Unitarian Universalism

The meeting of Zen Buddhism and Unitarian Universalism is different still. While often categorized as part of the cross-religious Zen/Christian phenomenon, in fact it offers its own unique difficulties and possibilities.

Unitarian Universalism is an old American denomination that spawned the nineteenth-century Transcendentalist movement. This, in turn, had a lot to do with presenting Buddhist and other Eastern religious ideas to Western thinkers in a positive light. As mentioned earlier, it was Unitarianism that gave North America its first Buddhist text in English. The tradition's roots are in New England Congregationalism, but—through a fierce commitment to reason as a spiritual discipline, a concern with the ethical life as being in itself salvific, and with radical resistance to any form of creedalism—Unitarian Universalism in many ways transcends its Christian origins.

Perhaps the fairest summary is to say that somewhere in the first half of the twentieth century, by its own general reckoning, Unitarian Universalism shifted from being a liberal Christian denomination to being a liberal denomination that includes Christians. Actually it is a liberal denomination that includes Christians, Humanists, Theists, Pagans, and Buddhists, among others. Today less than twenty percent of UUs are self-identified as Christian. And while many congregations, particularly in New England, certainly see themselves as fitting broadly within the Protestant Christian stream, the larger majority of contemporary UUs across the continent do not.

It is hard to say how many of today's Western Buddhists are also Unitarian Universalist. A recent survey counted 10,000 people who identify themselves as UU-Buddhists. And the number of Unitarian Universalists who claim some significant Buddhist influence on their thinking and spirituality is much larger. The majority of these are probably "bookstore" or "nightstand" Buddhists: people who may have never attended a Buddhist meditation group and are primarily influenced by the literature. At the same time, there are more than a hundred UU-Buddhist–identified groups across the continent, nestled within UU congregations, which variously combine study with differing forms of practice. Their strongest influences seem to be the teachings of Thich Nhat Hanh and other Engaged Buddhist writers.

Unitarian Universalism's liberal and welcoming environment has been attractive to many Western Buddhists, particularly those with children. The lack of support for the raising of children has been an ongoing problem for a large majority of Western Buddhist sanghas. Various Zen centers have made attempts to address the problem of providing religious education for Zen Buddhist children, but for the most part, however, the response has been "let the UUs do it." This is not an unreasonable response. Unitarian Universalism's broad tolerance and intriguingly similar perspectives to "liberal Buddhists"—an emerging perspective to be explored shortly—has seemed a happy solution for many people.

This certainly was true for me. I now find myself in the interesting position of being both a Unitarian Universalist minister and a Zen Buddhist priest. I am not the only Zen teacher with a formal UU affiliation. Robert Schaibly, a UU minister, was named a Dharmacharya by Thich Nhat Hanh. And there is David Rynick, an active member and past president of the First Unitarian Church in Worcester, Massachusetts, who received Inga from Zen Master George Bowman, as well as my own first Dharma heir, Melissa Blackev, a longtime UU. I am also aware of a number of other serious and senior Zen students, both lay and ordained, within other Zen lineages, who are active Unitarian Universalists. And I wouldn't be surprised if there were several other UU Zen Buddhist teachers joining the list before long.

Questioning Contemporary Zen

Not long after the release of Michael Downing's book, *Shoes Outside the Door: Desire, Devotion, and Excess at San Francisco Zen Center,* I found myself having lunch with a friend who was a Zen Center priest. I jokingly inquired how people were reacting to the detailed exposé of Richard Baker's unraveling abbacy, some twenty years prior. She wasn't amused. Then when Frederick Crews's review of the book in the *New York Review of Books* moved the controversy into the circles of my own non-Zen friends, I found myself being teased—and I must admit, it was much less amusing.

Amusing or not, I think it should be read by every Zen teacher and anyone thinking about Zen practice. In addition to closely examining very real abuses, it reveals what an outsider might see when looking at a Zen center. What this particular outsider saw was a cult-like institution and rampant exploitation of those who had joined.

Of course sex and power aren't the only shortcomings we find in Zen. American Soto Zen priest Brian Victoria's *Zen at War,* followed by his *Zen War Stories* and James Heisig and John Maraldo's *Rude Awakenings: Zen, the Kyoto School, and the Question of Nationalism* are painfully detailed examinations of how Zen Buddhism was co-opted by Japanese ultra-nationalism, in the years prior to and during World War II. Victoria extensively details how priests, who during the war were fanatical, jingoistic, and occasionally anti-Semitic, later became prominent figures in the West. These included, with varying degrees of culpability, D.T. Suzuki, Sogaku Harada, and particularly Haku'un Yasutani.

Heisig and Maraldo show how this co-opting included philosopher D.T. Suzuki, again, among others, and especially the various teachers of the so-called Kyoto School, most notably Keiji Nishitani. The Kyoto school had represented and continues to represent a fertile meeting of Zen insight and Western philosophy, so this revelation has proven to be particularly difficult. In the years after the

War, these different figures would become quite important in the West—in and of themselves, and as cautionary tales for us all.

Victoria's study led to some action in Japan. In 2001 the Myoshinji branch of the Rinzai school, the largest branch of Japanese Rinzai Zen, formally apologized for its part in the War. In the same year Jiun Kubota, at that time head of the Sanbo Kyodan, issued an apology on behalf of its founder Haku'un Yasutani, for the latter's extremist writings during the War. There is no doubt these books were very important in pointing to the ways Zen may be co-opted. In Japan the state co-opted Zen; in the West, the co-opting was more intimate and personal. Recent history suggests it is mostly around personal morality.

Some of the challenges and questions raised here were too much for some Zen students. In a review published in the online *Journal of Buddhist Ethics,* David Loy, scholar, social justice activist, and Zen teacher, observes:

> It is possible that Victoria's books have caused or will cause some Western Zen students to abandon their practice, but there is another alternative. He challenges us to mature in our appropriation of the tradition, especially our understanding of what it means to be enlightened. The anti-intellectual emphasis of Japanese Zen—on an intuition that "transcends" good and evil—works to valorize the prevailing ideology. But is that emphasis more Japanese than Buddhist?
>
> It is easier to see the difference from outside, although American down-to-earth pragmatism shares a similar anti-intellectual bias against abstraction. Perhaps a genuine Buddhist awakening involves, not eliminating concepts but liberating them? ... For enlightened wisdom to manifest most brightly in our benighted times, our meditation practices need to be supplemented with a deeper knowledge and understanding of the past as well as the present world situation.

Continuing the harsh examination of Zen and its Western institutions, longtime Zen practitioner and independent scholar Stuart Lachs has written several essays, which have wide currency on the Web. His 1977 essay "Coming Down from the Zen Clouds: A Critique of the Current State of American Zen," his 1999 essay "Means of Authorization: Establishing Hierarchy in Chan/Zen Buddhism in America," and his 2002 essay "Richard Baker and the Myth of the Zen Roshi" are detailed and thoughtful critiques of Zen in the West.

In that last essay Lachs comments: "The student who enters the 'practice' having read a myth will expect to find the myth, and will think they have found the myth. What they really found is another story of flawed human behavior." This is the difficulty of human consciousness: we do, indeed, tend to find what we're looking for. It takes a serious commitment to authentic practice to leap beyond our expectations—and sadly this seems rarely to happen.

Lachs's observation that Zen is as liable to abuse as any other human endeavor, and that we should always be diligent and responsible for what we accept as well as what we do, is terribly important. And his call for demythologizing Zen is a significant part of that process. For me, this means being ready to be unpleasantly surprised. Zen has much to offer; but what that is can only be found when our fondest hopes and expectations are abandoned.

Lachs does go further to suggest that we don't need the help of teachers, even after they've been taken down a peg or two. He's not alone in his analysis. Treading similar ground is Manfred Steger, who received permission to teach from Robert Aitken, although not the full Dharma transmission, or final formal and public approval of one's insight by one's teacher. Steger separated from Aitken's Diamond Sangha for several reasons, but principal among them was this: Steger felt that Dharma transmission was so vastly overrated that a Western Zen community would be better off without it.

In their intriguing book *Grassroots Zen,* Steger and his spouse, longtime Zen student Perle Besserman, suggest a form of Zen study that is guided by those who've been on the way longer, but without any necessary form of transmission acknowledging some kind of "completion." The website of their Princeton Zen Group spells out a way to accomplish this. The sole formal acknowledgment would be a "Certificate of Completion," which would announce "completion" of various koan collections. It explicitly states that by "renouncing any form of 'religious transmission,' it protects Zen students from arbitrary appointments and helps prevent Zen teachers from indulging in yet another illusion of permanence."

Contemporary Science and Zen

Scientific exploration of meditation is another way our culture is both questioning and exploring Zen and the awakened mind. A book such this one can in no way do justice to the wealth of literature that abounds, but nonetheless there is at least one point I would like to explore in this context. For this I turn to James Austin and his book *Zen and the Brain.*

Austin, professor emeritus of neurology at the University of Colorado Health Sciences Center, provides a comprehensive survey of consciousness studies relating to the insights purported in Zen. Observing how meditation affects the brain physiologically, he suggests that one can see how Zen, over the years, leads to increased clarity and calmness and cultivates simplicity, stability, efficient action, and compassion.

When asked in an interview what the most important thing is to understand about Zen and the brain, Austin replied that he could sum up briefly: "Zen is an agency of character change, one that will point the whole personality in the direction of increasing selflessness and awareness." Even in being stripped down, de-mythologized, and re-packaged as psychology, there is something compelling about the Zen way.

This is certainly my own experience and observation. Our practices, whatever metaphysical superstructure we put on them, actually lead each of us to life-changing experiences. We discover that we genuinely *are* connected beyond even the cellular level. And from that discovery, we find ways of compassionately engaging with the world. We discover that our genuine human inheritance is joy and justice—and a life lived fully in the world, knowing we're intimately related to everyone and everything else.

Monasticism and Scholarship Revisited

Over the centuries, the normative place of Zen practice has been the monastery. If we've only read about Zen, we may find this surprising. But when we move from reading about Zen to actually trying it out, this becomes obvious. Most Zen center schedules follow monastic rhythms, and the monastic terminology used for practice and the clerics who lead most contemporary centers underscore all of this.

In addition to this monastic wash over the practice, we can find a dizzying array of formal opportunities to study Zen Buddhism. Most centers offer classes in ancient Buddhist psychology; classes on a variety of meditation teachings; classes on the sutras, or sacred writings of Buddhism; and study of the koan collections themselves. As we've seen, the tradition "outside words and scriptures" turns out to be closely associated with literary and scholarly engagement.

It's important to acknowledge these two formal aspects of Zen training: its monastic inheritance and the expectation of intellectual engagement. Indeed it's impossible to understand Zen transmission without some sense of the monastic way that fostered and carried it forward.

The Buddha was a monk, a wandering mendicant. His original band of followers consisted of monks and, after a few years, nuns.

Over the forty-five years he taught and led his community, specific circumstances led to the formation of a monastic rule. In the years following his death, slightly different forms of the rule were adapted by different schools. All these various versions of the rule are collected in a volume called the *Vinaya Pitaka,* or "Basket of Discipline." This is the third in the collection of Buddhist sacred writings called the *Tripitaka,* or "Three Baskets." In the *Vinaya Pitaka,* each form, or version, of the rule follows the same pattern of three parts.

The first part, the *Bhikshuvibhanga,* or "Explanation of the Rules for Monks," explores "greater" and "lesser" rules and the various consequences for breaking them, ranging from public confession to expulsion from the monastic sangha. The second part is the *Bhikshunivbhanga,* or "Explanation of the Rules for Nuns." This covers much the same ground, but all its versions have greatly expanded regulations. This built-in sexism has been the subject of much study and comment by modern scholars and practitioners.

The third part, the *Khandaka,* is the most different in the various Buddhist traditions. The Khandaka is concerned with the issues of daily life, including such things as ceremonial etiquette. There is also a summary of the precepts, the *Pratimoksha,* which is recited by monks and nuns at their monthly gathering.

The South Indian monk Dharmagupta, who lived from the end of the sixth through the early seventh century of the Common Era, gives his name to the monastic form of the rule transmitted to China. This became the monastic rule for Chinese Zen. In the West today, it is used by the Kwan Um School of Zen's monastic community. Gradually additional regulations emerged for the Zen schools.

While attributed to and named for the monk Baizhang Huaihai, the great "Zen Rule" is probably not his composition. Whoever the actual author is, this new rule supplemented the Vinaya code and shaped Chinese Zen monastic life with its focus on meditation and physical work. Informed by the enormously practical Chinese approach to spirituality, this new rule focused on living in the world as it is actually encountered.

Japanese Buddhism would take another turn, also critical to the shaping of Zen in the West. With its attention to meditative disciplines, formal Zen training—whether Chinese, Korean, Vietnamese, or Japanese—is most obviously marked by its monastic character.

The sodo, or more precisely, a training center or the monastic place of practice, together with academic preparation and time spent in close proximity to an established teacher are the three necessary elements in the formation of a priest (which I, again, acknowledge may be the best term for ordained leadership within Japanese-derived schools of Zen).

The American Zen teacher Nonin Chowaney writes of his experiences training to be a priest:

I spent three years in training...at Zuioji and Shogoji in Japan and absorbed maybe two-thirds of what Japanese monks absorbed because of language difficulties and, truthfully, my early resistance to the process. I was told that it takes five years to complete all the different aspects of training in the different sections of the monastery (kitchen work, teacher's personal and ceremonial attendant, altar and ceremony set-up, ritual functions and roles, etc.).

Not many monks complete five years, but the point is that it takes time. All of this training goes on within the daily schedule of zazen, services, meals, and work that all of us who've done monastic training are familiar with. And, what's most important is the transformational function of the process. Making a Buddhist monk/priest/practitioner/ teacher is a long, slow, sometimes painful process.

Something mysterious and powerful can be found in a monastic setting. And its variations in the West are central to most people's experience of living Zen. While there may be no traditional sodos in the West in the sense of the monastics actually living in the meditation hall, there is a powerful tradition of strict monastic life that runs a strong current through much of Western Zen. Zen student Laura O'Loughlin describes her life in a North American version of sodo life. It provides a peek into the significance of monastic experience as a signal part of traditional Zen training:

> To live in a Zen community is to enter into a discipline of choicelessness. I live at the mercy of a schedule not of my own design that begins each morning (at the San Francisco Zen Center) at 5:00 A.M. (3:30 A.M. at Tassajara) and often ends after 8:00 P.M. My days are spent primarily in one building, almost every activity done with others. I struggled (and continue to struggle) with the containers of residential practice. Yet, like zazen, these forms have been a source of freedom for me rather than restriction.

A lesser-known element of formal Zen training is the significance given to formal and informal academic study. To people who've read only the more romantic Zen writings or those devoted to its core practice of zazen and relentless introspection, this may seem incongruous. And some, though by no means all, teachers and communities discourage reading when one begins to practice—the rhetoric, again, referring to a tradition "outside words and scriptures."

The truth is Zen is embodied in a rich and compelling literary tradition. Its teachings are often couched in analogy and metaphor, and the tradition has developed a rich language. While it's possible to pick up this language in a less formal way, the wise student reads widely. And increasingly Zen centers are forming study programs to give shape to this important aspect of Zen training.

It's essential for anyone wishing to undertake Zen practice to understand these aspects of Zen life. While we may practice Zen without ever living in a monastery, and we may deepen our understanding without formal academic study, these are the things that have marked the Zen way from its inception. We may indeed find an authentic Zen outside the forms of monastic training—an authentic Zen must be at least as humble and as fully engaging as it is for any monastic.

ELEVEN

The Emergence of a Liberal Buddhism

*T*ODAY, IN THE LIVING Zen practice centers across the
North American continent, the stories of the ancients and
the flesh-and-blood stories of our founders meet in our
hearts and minds. From that meeting, new stories will appear—
some of great value, some not. But it behooves those of us who care
about the health of the Zen way to pay close attention. Those who
find Zen to be one of the great paths to transformation, who see in
it the hope of healing our planet, must attend closely to what is actually going on as Zen takes deeper root in our native soil.

Shifting Perspectives and Assumptions

Wherever it has flourished, Buddhism has always engaged the culture, the times, and the issues—just as it is now doing in the West.
From this, a new perspective is emerging, a perspective of Western
Zen that has traveled a long way from its Asian origins. It exists
alongside, sometimes comfortably, sometimes not so, more traditional visions of Zen for the West.

When the renowned Western Buddhist John Blofeld wrote his
introduction to Stephen Batchelor's 1983 book *Alone with Others: An
Existential Approach to Buddhism,* Blofeld described the book as

"magnificent" and "inspiring." He then added, "The exposition is not intended to be exhaustive, as too much and too varied detail might mar its impact. Hence there are some important omissions such as the operation of karma and the concept of rebirth, both of which are crucial components of the Buddha Dharma."

Fourteen years later Batchelor published his reflections on karma and rebirth in his controversial broadside *Buddhism Without Beliefs*. John Blofeld had died a decade before, so we will never know what he would have thought of this analysis that was, in fact, a radical departure from traditional expositions of the Buddha's Way. It's unlikely the old Buddhist scholar and practitioner would have been happy about it. In this latter book Batchelor asserts:

> The idea of rebirth is meaningful in religious Buddhism only insofar as it provides a vehicle for the key Indian metaphysical doctrine of actions and their results known as "karma." While the Buddha accepted the idea of karma as he accepted that of rebirth, when questioned on the issue he tended to emphasize its psychological rather than its cosmological implications.

Developing this argument, Batchelor presents a modern, rational, and secular vision of Buddhist teachings. A detailed consideration of his understanding of Dharma is beyond the scope of this volume. But he is one of the first to systematically present perspectives held, often unconsciously, by many and possibly most contemporary Western Buddhists.

Here, I suggest, we find the meeting of East and West. Here our underlying Western rational and humanistic perspectives encounter the Dharma: challenging it, being challenged by it, and ultimately synthesizing it. To frame this more helpfully, there is a new Buddhism emerging: a Buddhism clearly continuous with its source and, at the same time, quite different from traditional Asian Buddhism.

Looking closely, we can't ignore the fact that many assumptions held by Western Buddhists differ—sometimes subtly, sometimes radically—from those held by "traditional" Buddhists. Many of these shifting assumptions are of great value—but they *are* shifts and need to be noticed and noted as such. (However, in fact, they are so pervasive among Western Buddhists and popular Western Buddhist writers, it's easy not to notice them.)

What we don't notice about ourselves is the most dangerous part of who we are. For instance, Western Zen communities often make the claim that the Zen teacher transmits an *a*historical path: the once and future way of awakening, teachings unchanged from the time they came from the mouth of the Buddha himself. This can be profoundly misleading.

It is seductive for new movements to see themselves returning to the pure traditions and original teachers, as Donald Lopez observes in his preface to *A Modern Buddhist Bible.* Certainly, many who hold contemporary Buddhist views see themselves—ourselves—as returning to the tenets of an original Buddhism.

Bhikkhu Bodhi—a Western Buddhist monk, renowned English translator of the Buddha's teachings, and critic of both Batchelor's book and the contemporary Buddhist movement—summarizes several tenets of what he calls "Western Buddhism." However, since many of these tenets are in fact held by Buddhists of most traditional schools—including, as some critics suggest, the current Dalai Lama—perhaps Donald Lopez's term "modern Buddhism" is better. There is much truth in the term "modern," particularly if we don't confuse it with "contemporary"; after all, this new Buddhism has roots going back more than a century. But people *do* confuse modern and contemporary. Therefore, I think the most appropriate term to describe this emerging and pervasive perspective is "liberal Buddhism."

The word *liberal* derives from Latin and means, among other things, "free and generous." Thus liberal Buddhism is a Buddhism that contributes most genuinely to freedom and is most generous. But whatever we call it, this new Buddhism has, like every tradition everywhere, both strengths and shadows.

The Secularization of Zen

Bhikkhu Bodhi notes three particular elements marking what I am calling liberal Buddhism. One is a shift from monastic to lay life as the "principal arena of Buddhist practice." Second, there is an "enhanced position of women" in this newer Buddhism. Third, we also find "the emergence of a grass-roots engaged Buddhism aimed at social and political transformation." And underlying all this, Bhikkhu Bodhi suggests, is a fourth characteristic: a pervasive secularization of the Buddha way. This often-missed shift is perhaps the most important of all. Let's look at an example of this trend.

Liberal Buddhism sees Buddhist meditation disciplines and Buddhist teachings, in general, to be "scientific." But this belief—held by both newcomers and elders—is untrue. Scientific method requires that there be a possibility of falsification. And experimental science requires *replicability:* the same practices done the same way should reliably produce the same results.

But never, not even in liberal Buddhism, does one hear that if one does the practices and does not achieve liberation, then Buddhism is somehow "proven" false. Rather, if one does the practices without the promised experiences, most Buddhist teachers will say one has simply not done the practices correctly. And while this may be a form of scientism, it simply isn't science.

The seed of this appeal to science for justification is twofold. What allows this claim to be made is that Buddhism is at heart profoundly empirical. Buddhist insight is based on the experiences of many people over many centuries. Indeed, Buddhist philosophies and psychologies all flow from introspection and examination of those experiences. And empiricism, while not science, is the mother of science. Thus we can see how easily the shift from empirical to scientific might happen.

The second factor driving the appeal to science is the desire of exponents of liberal Buddhism to appear to be up-to-date, current, modern. This impulse had particular appeal in the nineteenth century, when our Buddhist forbears were first asserting their insights as equal to or perhaps better than those offered by Western religions. And it seems as compelling to Buddhists now as it did then.

Appeals to contemporary physics as "proof" of some aspect of Buddhist doctrine is typical of liberal Buddhism. And here, I might add, we find some real shadows: a whole collection of logical fallacies. First among these is the old chestnut, *Appeal to Authority:* the fallacious belief that if a credentialed person says something, it must perforce be true.

There is however a more dangerous effect of unconscious scientism, which is the inclination toward reductionism, another shadow of secularism. Reductionism causes Buddhism to become nothing more than a nostrum for improving one's self-esteem or tennis game, or for getting an edge in business or war. This is not what Zen is about, nor, frankly, is it about relaxation, calmness, achieving less anxiety, or attenuating depression. While it may indeed have salutary effects on all these things, ultimately it is about something else.

Buddhism is a religion. While not particularly concerned with cosmologies and the workings of gods, it is profoundly concerned with the same questions as all religions: how best to address the situations in which we find ourselves here and now. I further assert that Buddhism is quite properly about salvation, from the Latin *salve,* to heal. It makes assertions about the how and why of our hurt and offers us a path to liberation, to wholeness.

And yet, liberal Buddhism, while harboring shadows, has enormous possibilities. Out of its broad inclination to identify with the ideals of science, we find a willingness to see the disciplines studied within scientific institutions. At first this was mostly in the realm of biofeedback studies. But, while these undoubtedly have some value, they tend to be akin to studying a horse by examining its feces. Measurable relaxation or any other outcome is a by-product of Buddhism, not the thing itself.

The continued exploration of assumptions underlying liberal Buddhism, and the positive aspects of its secularization—these are profound shifts in emphasis supporting lay practice. In particular, the contours of Western Zen reveal a shift from Zen *monastery* to Zen *center* as the normative institution. These and other aspects of the liberal Buddhist perspective are compelling for many of us.

For instance, anyone visiting a range of Western Zen centers will find women at every level of leadership. And closely related to that, openly gay and lesbian people are almost uniformly accepted in these centers, often in leadership positions. This is all unheard of in the East. And these are core perspectives of liberal Buddhism.

These new leaders and the perspectives they bring all help to create an even richer, more socially engaged vision of the Dharma than that which we inherited from our traditional teachers. Indeed, while it's calumny to claim Buddhism is "passive" and disengaged from the world, an inclination to withdrawal is indeed the shadow of Buddhism. Thus it is with these social aspects of liberal Buddhism that we in the West have particularly enriched the treasure we've been given.

Another potential problem, aside from the spectre of disengagement, is that Buddhist organizations in East Asia have usually worked with the approval and, in many instances, support of the state. In China, monasteries were often supported by large land grants—including serfs who were little more than slaves. In Japan, the ruling classes quickly saw how Zen, particularly Rinzai Zen, could be adapted to support the needs of the warrior class. This became a mutual relationship. As we now know, in the Second

World War the Zen churches were second to none in their enthusiastic support of the imperialist assertions of emperor and state. On the other hand, in the past, many Buddhist leaders and teachers have seen themselves as moderating the excesses of various rulers, even as others have felt it their patriotic duty to support the nation in times of crisis.

In sum, we must be heedful of a host of Zen's demons as well as its promises as we explore and indeed help create a Western Zen path that we may hope will serve our grandchildren and generations beyond.

TWELVE

Shaping Zen in the West Today

Sanctification of the Ordinary

The most important things in Western Zen are those practices that support the sanctification of the ordinary. Of least concern for Western Zen is the aspect that is, in some of Japanese Zen, considered tantamount: the liturgical creation and dedication of merit. This shift may well reveal the contours of both a monastic and nonmonastic—or more correctly *post*monastic—ordained life in the West.

The shift in Western Zen is the way we order our attention to the disciplines. We sanctify the mundane through zazen and koan study, rituals and chanting, and through our close attention to the details of our lives. This is supported ritually by the commemoration of our ancestral teachers, and, more important, by seeing directly into their way. Seeing that their way is our way, we conform and adapt the tradition and ourselves.

Today in some centers tensions exist between lay and ordained practitioners. Yet it is widely accepted that awakening is as possible for laypeople as it is for monastics. And today in the West we have a number of practice options. We can remain laypeople, fitting our discipline into our busy lives, creating rhythms of meditation and attending retreats when we can. People do awaken in this manner;

I've witnessed it many times. I've watched people grow ever deeper simply as lay practitioners; and I've seen such people become skillful guides on the great way.

I've also seen people embrace both kinds of ordination, Vinaya and bodhisattva, with enormous success. Some, particularly those following the Chogye inheritance, take the 250 precepts of bhikkshu ordination or the 348 precepts of bhikkshuni ordination. Others take the sixteen bodhisattva precepts. For some this means living a celibate life in community or, at least theoretically, as hermits with a close association with a community. For others it means a life of rule, or continuous commitment to a sodo-style life, which also may allow for marriage or other forms of commitment to a partner. But for the majority taking up bodhisattva ordination, it means a period of formal training, probably involving a sodo experience, followed by a life more akin to Western-style ministry than anything else.

Extensive residential training is the principal feature of traditional Japanese-derived Zen training and expected for nearly all ordination candidates. As my ordination teacher, Jiyu Kennett, described it, residential training, whether in its traditional sodo sense where the monastics lived in the meditation hall (such as I experienced early on with Kennett Roshi) or in its more conventional western sense where one lives in a dormitory or even in a semiprivate or private room, but still under close rule is like being a potato thrown into a tub of potatoes. As practitioners rub up against each other, rough spots are worn away.

Eventually this type of training is quite powerful. Anyone who has experienced it can testify that as hard, indeed horrible, as it can sometimes be, it's an amazingly effective spiritual discipline. The training period may last for no more than three months or, more commonly, several years. But in neither case is the learning of liturgical forms the primary point of this experience.

Today a few contemporary ordained teachers express the opinion that the residential experience is no longer necessary at all; others hold that there is simply no ordained life outside the context of the training center or monastic community. Certainly the shape of training and its intent is wildly different among the different schools, and increasingly even within the same lineages. And still creative possibilities continue to present themselves.

A significant aspect of the Soto Zen Buddhist Association is coming to a common understanding of training for North American Soto Zen practitioners. Secondarily, but also of great importance, is the creation of a registry of Soto priests, who are commonly accepted as standing within the same tradition. Here we see the beginnings of a possible "denomination." With the weaving together of disparate Soto lineages, if only at the most tentative edge, something larger is created.

Still, whether registered in a foreign or a native denomination, the support of priests remains problematic. Most North American priests do not and could not rely exclusively on their sanghas for support. A few centers—such as Zen Mountain Monastery in upstate New York, which is attempting to be, by its own new definitions, monastic—expect its priests to reside and work in the monastery and its programs, and thereby support the monastery. Without endowments or any tradition of patronage, how this will continue is one of the many open questions regarding a continuing North American Zen.

Lay Lineages and New Styles of Leadership

In Japan, a lay teacher is affiliated with the larger sect, usually Rinzai, and any clerical needs are always fulfilled by the clergy. In the West—where most Zen organizations are only loosely connected and often without any formal institutional ties beyond their immediate sanghas—these "lay teachers" are called on to fulfill tasks traditionally reserved for clergy. They are, for instance, asked to officiate at traditional rites of passage, perform marriages for their students, improvise naming or other dedication services for the children in their communities, and officiate at funerals. Increasingly they also preside at jukai ceremonies, the formal passing on of the precepts.

The end result is that three kinds of ordained ministers are now emerging in Western Zen. Some are monks and nuns, recognizable as such by anyone East or West. A second group of men and women mistakenly calls themselves monks—but are not monastics in the usual sense, as they are rarely celibate and often work at trades or professions outside their cloisters. Nonetheless, they do function quite legitimately as professional leaders or priests, in the technical etymological sense of "elder." And then there is a third group, mistakenly called "laypeople." These are Zen masters who, like Robert Aitken, also function as de facto clergy in addition to their teaching functions. The only obvious difference between them and their formally ordained counterparts is that they don't shave their heads or wear robes—except, of course, when they do.

Concluding Reflections

I recently attended the American Zen Teachers Association annual conference. The AZTA conference floats around the U.S. and Canada, meeting at centers that are large enough to host a growing number of Western Zen teachers. This time it was held at Great Vow Zen Monastery in Clatskanie, Oregon, overlooking the Columbia River about halfway between Portland and the Pacific Ocean. It was jointly hosted by the Dharma Rain Zen Center in Portland and the Zen Community of Oregon.

About thirty-five native-born Zen teachers attended, representing both the Korean lines and all three of the Japanese lines of Zen that have taken roots in North American soil. I'd been attending this conference for about four years, so I had a number of friends and colleagues in attendance, and I had looked forward to coming.

As with any human gathering, those present were not all best friends. But they were all trying to fulfill the unspoken rule of the gathering: to be respectful and hopeful for each other. The event was shadowed by the fact that a few weeks earlier a respected member of the group had resigned leadership of his sangha after it was revealed he was having an affair with a student. Making this even harder was the fact that both the teacher and the student were married. But I was impressed with how the teachers present were concerned first for the sanghas, and then for their colleague and friend and his paramour, and how he and she might find healing and possible reconciliation.

I was also taken with two other things. First, people whose teachers had feuded and competed over the "best" vision of the Zen way were now close colleagues and often close friends. These teachers had been listening to each other, broadening their own vision, and—as they had in each of the years before—bringing these new perspectives home. These are rich and exciting times for reflecting on the shape of Zen and its possible directions.

I was also struck by the number of young people present, residents of the hosting monastery. On the closing evening of this North American event, we had a low-to-no-talent show. Although created mostly by the teachers, its "glue" was the marimba band composed of Chozen Bays Roshi and a half dozen of those younger members of her monastic community. Watching them make music on ridiculous xylophonic instruments—some of which stood at least five feet high—with pretty much the same attention they were giving to their Zen training was a powerful moment. I saw that there is, indeed, a new generation of Zen practitioners coming along.

On the plane flying home to Boston I found myself reflecting on the people at the AZTA, all of whom I respected and a number of whom I'd come to love. They had given their lives to the Dharma and in doing so most had sacrificed a great deal, certainly in any worldly terms. Thinking about the ancient teachings we've received, and about these people who've given so much to find the truth of the teachings for themselves, and to foster them and present them to a new generation, I felt considerable gratitude and considerable optimism.

Through everything—the years and the hurt and the work and the visioning and the hard, hard practice—we can clearly see that something rare and precious has come to the West. We've been given a rare chance to encounter the Dharma. The ancient and beautiful ways of Zen have met the ancient and beautiful ways of the West. This meeting has been rough: there has been hurt, there has been failure. It has also been beautiful. The shape of the Zen way in North America and the West is conforming to the needs of our time and place. Institutions are developing that might well flourish in our culture. Our teachers and practitioners are blossoming into communities of vision and hope. It may be a fragile bloom, but it is beautiful to behold.

APPENDIX

What to Look For When Looking for a Zen Teacher

BEFORE SEEKING OUT a teacher in the Zen tradition, it would be wise to read a little about all the traditions you sense might help you. If, after a period of reading and questioning, you think Zen might be the path for you, then *continuing* to read about Zen is important.

But more important, if the Zen path sounds right for you, I would suggest you start by taking up the practice of Zen meditation pretty much right now. You can get the basics out of many good books: John Daishin Buksbazen's *Zen Meditation in Plain English* would be a very good way to start, as would Robert Aitken's *Taking the Path of Zen*. A visit to a local Zen group of any flavor can provide some hands-on instruction that can clarify most beginning questions.

You don't have to sign up for anything other than an introductory class, nor, I strongly suggest, should you. Just check things out. If you like the group, perhaps keep going from time to time. But do begin to sit at home regularly. Cultivate a discipline. If after a reasonable amount of time, perhaps six months or so, maybe a year, the practice doesn't feel right, you really don't need to look for a Zen teacher. After all, any real Zen teacher is going to return you over and over again to the practice. If you don't feel a connection to zazen, you can probably find another practice tradition that will be more fruitful.

If, one the other hand, Zen continues to seem to be the best way of addressing the concerns that propel you on the spiritual path, then—and really only then—should you begin to look for a teacher in earnest. At that point, it becomes important for you to sort through the hundreds of teachers and dozens of communities to find one that fits you well. If this book helps with nothing else, I hope it shows how different Zen communities might be, how one could be completely wrong for you and another could be just what you need.

I cannot recommend a seeker join any community led by Zen teachers who will not say who taught them and who gave them permission to teach. Though such people may perhaps be wise beings, the problems that can hide in the shadows of such a stance are just too numerous and too potentially dangerous. If you're in doubt whether a teacher is what she or he says, you can look at the website of the American Zen Teachers Association (www.americanzen-teachers.org). While not a complete list of all authentic Zen teachers in America, it is a list of a large majority of them. If a prospective teacher (or her or his teacher) is not on the list, chances are that person is significantly outside the mainstream of Zen.

Next, consider the possibilities within the authentic Zen paths. Do your inclinations take you toward monastic practice? Are you attracted to the priestly traditions? Or perhaps a lay-led community feels best. Hopefully this book has helped to show what those distinctions mean. Clarifying this can really help in finding the right teacher and the right community.

That said, at the beginning it's hard to know what will be best in your particular situation. Here trusting one's instincts isn't a bad thing, particularly if you're also open to being wrong and have cultivated some sense of humility as you begin to explore unknown territory.

Ask people you respect who have walked a spiritual path for some time whom they might recommend—just like you might if you were looking for a good doctor. Also: most Zen groups now have websites. Read them. And visit. Those things alone will reveal a great deal both about the teacher and the community. I recommend you do this with several communities. Since you're already maintaining a practice, there's no rush to sign on with a teacher. Take your time. Choose carefully.

But please be very clear about this: Zen teachers are not gurus. They—*we*—are not perfect masters. A real Zen teacher is completely, unambiguously, human with a full complement of challenges and shortcomings. Every teacher has flaws. The task is not to find a perfect teacher (you can't) but to find one who, warts and all, can be a good-enough guide on the Zen path. You need to be ready to be surprised.

It's probably not wise to make a decision about the right teacher based mostly on witnessing their public persona. It's really impossible to make a useful judgment of a possible teacher by how they give a Dharma talk, what they say in one magazine interview, or even what they write in a book.

I suggest a different approach: when visiting a teacher or a center examine the teacher's students. Are they simply clones-in-training of the teacher? This is probably not a good thing—after all, Zen is about becoming more fully yourself, not becoming more like your teacher. On the other hand, do the students seem to be people you like, and might like to be with? Can you recognize the values they advocate? Are they independent and engaged in the world? Can they joke about themselves? And, importantly, can they joke about their institution and teacher? And more important still: Do they seem to be genuinely on a path that is freeing them from their suffering?

This step of evaluating the community is an important one and one I strongly urge you not to skip. After all, the community, the sangha is as much the teacher as the person with the title. Often, actually, the community is even more the teacher than the person with the title.

I wish you well in your journey!

ACKNOWLEDGMENTS

I GRATEFULLY ACKNOWLEDGE those sisters and brothers in the Dharma who helped in so many ways with the formation of this book. This list cannot be limited to, but certainly includes Suzanne Allen, Carolyn Atkinson, Doug Bates, Jan Chozen Bays, Laren Hogen Bays, Melissa Myozen Blacker, Gyokuko Carlson, Kyogen Carlson, David Chadwick, Nonin Chowaney, Hugh Curran, Arlene Duelfer, Adam Genkaku Fisher, Norman Zoketsu Fischer, Cushing Giesey, Ruben Habito, Joan Halifax, Blanche Hartman, Alex Holt, Jeff Kitzes, Barbara Seirin Kohn, Stuart Lachs, Victor Sessan Lapuszynski, Barry Magid, Bert Mayo, Rod Meade Sperry, Toshu Neatrour, Edward Oberholtzer, Tonen O'Connor, Doug Phillips, Dosho Port, Judy Roitman, Sevan Ross, David Rynick, Ken Walkama, Jisho Warner, and David Weinstein. I am especially grateful to Richard Seager for his insightful and very helpful comments on multiple drafts of this manuscript.

The communities to which I belong have provided shelter and friendship, as well as too many people to be named who have read parts of the developing manuscript or listened as I worked through various thoughts and provided generous, helpfully critical, and often creative suggestions. These members of the First Unitarian Society in Newton, Massachusetts, and the Boundless Way Zen school have demonstrated over and over again the mysterious and compelling power of sangha. In this regard I need particularly to acknowledge my many guides along the ancient way, especially my core teachers Jiyu Kennett and John Tarrant, each in their own way masters of the Dharma. Endless bows.

Special thanks need to go to two people. First, I need to express my gratitude to my friend and editor Josh Bartok. Without him this book would be a dream. And as everyone who knows me says—and the truth of which I freely acknowledge—without my partner and spouse Jan Seymour-Ford, not only would this book not exist, but I wouldn't be a Zen teacher.

GLOSSARY

Abhidharma from the Sanskrit. Literally "special teaching." An ancient systemization of Buddhist psychology.

Ahimsa from the Sanskrit. Literally "nonharming." A central tenet in Buddhist morality. In recent years, often traditionally associated with vegetarianism and with political pacifism.

American Zen Teachers Association (AZTA) an organization in North America formed to foster dialogue among Zen teachers. A large majority of Western-born Zen teachers in America belong to this organization.

Amitabha/Amitayus/Amida Literally "Boundless Light" or "Immeasurable Life." The Buddha of the Western Paradise. The primary object of devotion within Pure Land Buddhism.

Anatman from the Sanskrit. Literally "not-self" or "no-self." The Buddhist insight that there is no unchanging or eternal, independent self.

Ango from the Japanese. A formal training period of ninety or a hundred days.

Anitya from the Sanskrit. Literally "impermanence." The Buddhist insight that all things and everyone are marked by transitoriness or impermanence.

Arhat from the Sanskrit. (In Pali *Arahat* and in Chinese *Lohan.*) Literally, "a Holy One." Self-realized and no longer bound by the cycles of rebirth. The archetype of Theravada Buddhism.

Avalokiteshvara from the Sanskrit. See Guanyin.

Bhikshu/Bhikshuni from the Sanskrit. Monk/nun. See Vinaya.

Bodhidharma The semi-mythical, semi-historical Indian monk who became the founder of Chinese Zen.

Bodhisattva from the Sanskrit. One who is variously on the path of awakening, one who is awakened, or one who awakens others. Frequently a bodhisattva is an archetype of one aspect of awakening or another. The Bodhisattva is the ideal of the Mahayana school of Buddhism.

Bodhisattva Ordination The unique ordination model used in Japanese Buddhism, in which clerics are ordained. Originally for monks and nuns as commonly understood, but today more commonly also for noncelibate priests guiding local temples and training temples. The major distinction between Bodhisattva-ordained and Vinaya-ordained clerics regards celibacy. All Vinaya-ordained monks and nuns are expected to be celibate. Only a minority of Bodhisattva-ordained clerics maintain celibacy. One observer has made the comparative observation that continental Vinaya ordained monastics more resemble Catholic monks, while Japanese ordained more resemble Anglican clerics. See Vinaya and Osho.

Buddha from the Sanskrit. Literally "one who is awakened." The word commonly refers to the historic Buddha, Siddhartha Gautama, but may also be applied to mythic earlier buddhas, buddhas to come, or to our own essential nature.

Caodong from the Chinese. See Soto School.

Chan from the Chinese. The Zen school in its original Chinese use. The word is derived from Chinese *Channa,* from Sanskrit *Dhyana*, concentration or meditation. A school of Buddhism that emphasizes meditation disciplines, influenced by Chinese Taoism, and as a developed school imported to Japan (as Zen), Korea (as Son), Vietnam (as Thien), and now to the West.

Cleric An ordained person, a monk, nun, minister, or priest.

Daisan from the Japanese. An interview. In the White Plum lineage and others the term used for interviews with junior teachers or teachers who have received Dharma transmission but not Inka Shomei. See Interview.

Dependent Origination See Paticca Samuppada.

Dharma from the Sanskrit. Literally "the Law." In English usage when used without capitalization it usually means a constituent element of reality, a thing. With a capital "D" it usually means the Buddhist way or Buddhist teachings.

Dharmacharya A teacher in the Order of Interbeing established by Thich Nhat Hanh. See Lamp Transmission.

Dharma Combat A public liturgical encounter, sometimes between a teacher and a student, sometimes between senior practitioners. In the Soto school Dharma Combat is the culminating aspect of Shuso Hossen, an intermediate acknowledgment between unsui ordination and Dharma transmission. In the Kwan Um School Dharma Combat is a featured aspect of many rituals including Inga and Dharma transmission.

Dharma Transmission The formal acknowledgment of Zen insight. The recognition on the part of the teacher that the recipient of Dharma transmission is qualified to teach Zen. In Japanese Soto it is often given after three to five years adult preparation, although the recipient may have been originally ordained as a child. In Western Soto Dharma transmission is much less common, frequently after twenty or more years of intensive practice; in Rinzai and Harada-Yasutani, only after completing formal koan study. See Inka Shomei. In either Rinzai or Harada-Yasutani completion of formal koan introspection study is seen as a necessary although not sufficient condition for acknowledgement as a teacher.

Dhyana from the Sanskrit. Literally "concentration" or "absorption." The form of meditation taught in Buddhism, and particularly the Zen schools. See Samadhi.

Dogen Eihei Dogen (1200–1253). Japanese Zen master who introduced the Soto (Caodong) school into Japan. A premier theorist of Zen. His insights into the identity of meditation and awakening has inspired generations of practitioners.

Dokusan from the Japanese. Literally "to go alone" (to see the teacher). See Interview.

Dukkha from the Sanskrit. Literally "suffering, anguish, dis-ease." The unsettled sense of the human condition. The first of the Four Noble Truths.

Dukkha Nirodha from the Sanskrit. The third of the Four Noble Truths. The possibility of dissolution of the anguish of dukkha.

Dukkha Samudaya from the Sanskrit. The second of the Four Noble Truths. The source of human anguish is found in clinging to that which is passing as if it were permanent. .

Eiheiji The Japanese "Monastery of Eternal Peace." Founded by Master Dogen in 1243. Together with Sojiji one of the two principal temples of the Soto school in Japan.

Eko from the Japanese. The dedication that follows a Buddhist service. The transference of merit from the person who created it to others.

Gassho from the Japanese. Literally "palms brought together; hand-to-hand." A mudra or sacred gesture bringing the palms of both hands together in front of the chest, a greeting used in most Buddhist and other South and East Asian traditions.

Guanyin from the Chinese. The Bodhisattva Avalokiteshvara (Kannon or Kanzeon in Japanese, Kwanyin/Guanyin in Chinese, and Kwan Um in Korean), the archetype of compassion in the world.

Hakuin Hakuin Ekaku (1689–1769). The Japanese reformer of koan Zen, the source of both the Rinzai and the Harada-Yasutani schools and the developer of the form of koan introspection principally taught in the West.

Harada-Yasutani A Japanese Zen lineage derived from Soto but incorporating a full koan curriculum, started by Daiun Harada and further developed by Haku'un Yasutani. The main institutional stream is the Sanbo Kyodan (Order or Society of the Three Treasures), but has expressions within mainstream Western Soto, principally the White Plum lineage established by Taizan Maezumi, as well as the lay Zen organization (the Diamond Sangha) founded by Robert Aitken and those organizations derived from the Diamond Sangha including the Pacific Zen Institute, Open Source, and Boundless Way Zen (which also maintains institutional connections to the Western Soto school). A minor Zen school in Japan but the primary source of koan introspection practice in the West.

Inga (Korean) See Inka Shomei.

Inka (Japanese) See Inka Shomei.

Inka Shomei from the Japanese. Literally "the legitimate seal of clearly furnished proof." The formal acknowledgment of mastery in Zen within the Rinzai school. In many Western Zen lines, particularly those with connections to the Harada-Yasutani lineage, a final seal of approval beyond Dharma transmission. Conversely, in the Korean-derived Kwan Um School of Zen the initial acknowledgment is called Inga (a Korean translation of the term), and final acknowledgment is called Dharma transmission.

Interview A traditional aspect of Zen encounter. A meeting between the student and a teacher common to all traditions, less frequently taken up in Soto and more frequently used in Rinzai.

Jisha from the Japanese. The attendant to the teacher.

Jukai from the Japanese. Receiving or taking the precepts. A ceremony similar to Christian confirmation in which an individual declares her or his intention to live by the Buddhist precepts. It has both a more informal sense and a more formal one. The more formal ceremony is sometimes called "lay ordination."

Kanhua Chan from the Chinese. The "Zen that contemplates words." The practice of Zen that emphasizes koan introspection, most closely associated with Rinzai and the Harada-Yasutani lineages of Zen practice.

Kasa from the Korean. See Kesa.

Keisaku from the Japanese. Literally "warning stick." See Kyosaku.

Kensho from the Japanese. To "see directly into one's nature." See Satori.

Kesa from the Japanese. Literally "a rough wool shawl." The traditional robe of the Buddha, and from him the robe of Buddhist monastics. Made in a patchwork pattern, traditionally in a saffron or orange color, although today in many different colors, it has become the significant mark of Buddhist clerics. In Japan the basic color is black, while teachers wear kesas of different colors, most commonly some shade of orange or brown. See Rakusu.

Koan from the Japanese. Literally "public case" as in a legal document. Also an expression of the relative and the absolute, the harmony of boundless emptiness and the phenomenal world. A theme or point in Zen to be made clear.

Kuanyin See Guanyin.

Kwan Um from the Korean. See Guanyin.

Kwan Um School of Zen The mostly Western school of Zen established by the Korean master Seung Sahn. It has many unique characteristics distinguishing it from Japanese-derived Zen schools, and is second only to Thich Nhat Hanh's Unified Buddhist Church in America in size.

Kyosaku from the Japanese. Literally, "waking stick," used in meditation retreats where one is struck on the shoulders by the blade-like wooden stick. In East Asia it has a disciplinary aspect, but is retained in the West because it releases tightened shoulder muscles. Rarely used outside the context of meditation retreats.

Lamp Transmission A form of limited authorization for teachers within the Order of Interbeing led by Thich Nhat Hanh.

Lay Ordination The reception of the Bodhisattva precepts usually accompanied by receiving a rakusu and implicitly or sometimes explicitly assuming a relationship with a teacher. See also Shoken.

Linji Linji Yixuan (died 866). One of the preeminent figures of Zen, generally acknowledged as the source of koan introspection Zen.

Madyamaka from the Sanskrit. Literally the "Middle Way." Contesting with the Yogachara as one of the two primary schools of the emergent Mahayana.

Mahayana from the Sanskrit. Literally "the Great Vehicle" or Great Way. One of the two principle streams of Buddhism (see also Theravada). Often characterized as championing the ideal of the bodhisattva. Zen is a school within the Mahayana.

Maitreya from the Sanskrit. Literally the "loving one." Traditionally the Buddha yet to be born.

Manjushri from the Sanskrit. The bodhisattva or archetype of wisdom. The principal figure on the altar in an Asian Zen monastery or temple. See also Guanyin.

Marga from the Sanskrit. The path. In particular the eightfold path described as the fourth noble truth. The path consists of right or correct or skillful view, resolve, speech, conduct, livelihood, effort, mindfulness and concentration. These can be further reduced as three aspects of the middle way: meditation, morality, and wisdom.

Master usually understood as someone who has received Dharma transmission within a school of Zen. One who has mastered the Zen way.

Metta from the Sanskrit. Meaning compassion, goodwill, loving-kindness. Together with vipassana and shamatha one of the three meditative practices taught in early Buddhism.

Mochao Chan from the Chinese. The "Zen of silent illumination." The practice of Zen that emphasizes "just sitting," most closely associated with the Soto lineages of Zen practice.

Monastic has various meanings in Western Zen. Traditionally this term is used for monks or nuns who have taken Vinaya ordination, and live lives of celibacy under a strict rule. It is also used for noncelibate clergy ordained within the Bodhisattva ordination tradition; although this use for noncelibate clergy appears to be in decline in favor of "priest."

Monk/Nun Someone ordained within the Vinaya tradition. See Bhikkshu/Bhikkshuni, Monastic, and Vinaya.

Okesa from the Japanese. See Kesa.

Order of Interbeing The Tiep Hien Order of monastic and vowed lay practitioners founded by Thich Nhat Hanh. See also Unified Buddhist Church in America.

Ordination Taking vows. In Zen used variously for lay ordination, Vinaya ordination, and Bodhisattva ordination.

Osho from the Japanese. A full priest in the Bodhisattva ordination model, a priest who has received Dharma transmission. See Unsui and Bodhisattva Ordination.

Pali Together with Sanskrit one of the two sacred languages of Buddhism, most closely associated with the Theravada tradition. In this glossary where terms have both Sanskrit and Pali versions, the Sanskrit is used.

Paticca Samuppada from the Sanskrit. Dependent origination. The Buddhist insight that all things are interdependent and interpenetrating. There are several formulas to describe how this works. The simplest is found in the Sanskrit phrase *idam sati ayam bhavati,* "when this exists, that arises." The most common formula is described as having twelve stages: (1) ignorance leads to (2) impulses leads to (3) consciousness leads to (4) "name and form" leads to (5) the six senses (including consciousness) leads to (6) contact with the environment leads to (7) sensations leads to (8) craving leads to (9) clinging leads to (10) becoming leads to (11) birth which leads to (12) old age and death.

Prajanaparamita from the Sanskrit. The "perfection of wisdom." A collection of about forty texts composed roughly from the beginning of the first century before the Common Era through the first century of the Common Era.

Precepts The moral codes of Buddhism. These include the Vinaya vows, 250 precepts for monks and 348 precepts for nuns. Or, the Bodhisattva vows, which might be fifty-eight or sixteen or ten. They may also be the five precepts of traditional lay Buddhism, a vow to refrain from killing, lying, stealing, misusing sexuality, and intoxication, which are often taken together with the refuges within Buddha, Dharma, and Sangha. See Bodhisattva Ordination, Refuge, and Vinaya.

Priest Literally "elder." A term increasingly used in the West by clerics who have received Bodhisattva ordination.

Pure Land One of the principal schools of Mahayana Buddhism. Called Jingtuzong in Chinese and Jodo and Jodo Shinshu in Japanese. Traditionally founded in the late fourth century by Huiyuan. "Faith-oriented," the Pure Land focuses on devotion to Amitabha and out of that devotion rebirth in the Pure Land where liberation is easier to attain.

Rakusu from the Japanese. A biblike vestment worn by both lay practitioners who have received the precepts and priests in Japanese and Korean forms of Buddhism, including the Zen schools. It represents the Kesa, the robe of the Buddha in traditional Buddhism. See Kesa.

Refuge The three refuges are within the Buddha, the Dharma, and the Sangha. "Taking refuge" is sometimes used to mean "becoming" a Buddhist. See Precepts.

Rinzai School from the Japanese. Linji in Chinese. The school of Zen most closely associated with koan study.

Roshi from the Japanese. "Venerable teacher." An honorific for a particularly respected elder or senior teacher. In the West increasingly used as a formal title conferred in most cases by one's teacher, occasionally by one's students or other authority.

Samadhi from the Sanskrit. Literally "concentration" or "absorption." See Dhyana.

Sanskrit Together with Pali one of the two sacred languages of Buddhism. Most closely associated with the Mahayana school. In this glossary where terms have both Sanskrit and Pali versions, the Sanskrit is used.

Sanzen from the Japanese. See Interview.

Satori from the Japanese, ultimately derived from the Sanskrit *satoru,* "to know." The gnostic insight of Zen. See Kensho.

Sensei from the Japanese. Literally "teacher." In Japan a mild honorific for anyone teaching anything. In Western Zen, a title usually reserved for a teacher who has received Dharma transmission.

Sesshin from the Japanese. Literally "to touch the heart-mind." An intensive meditation retreat, most commonly lasting between three and seven days.

Shakyamuni from the Sanskrit. Literally the "Sage of the Shakya Clan." the Buddha of history, Siddhartha Gautama.

Shamantha from the Sanskrit. Literally "dwelling within tranquillity." A practice of concentration. Together with metta and vipassana, one of the three meditative practices taught in early Buddhism. Joined together with vipassana the source practice found in Zen.

Shikantaza from the Japanese. Literally "just sitting." The practice of pure presence that is most commonly associated with the Soto school, but is in fact the base of all Zen disciplines.

Shobogenzo from the Japanese. Literally the "Treasury of the Eye of the True Dharma." The title of several spiritual texts, but most commonly understood as Eihei Dogen's masterwork.

Shoken from the Japanese. "Going to the teacher," a ritual act of covenanting with a spiritual director. In some traditions implicit or even explicit within lay ordination.

Shunyata from the Sanskrit. Literally "emptiness." One of the core insights of Buddhism, that all things and everyone are empty, impermanent, boundless.

Shuso Hossen A rite in Soto Zen where an unsui serves for a period (usually ninety days) as "chief junior" of a meditation hall. It concludes with a ceremony that features Dharma Combat, after which the unsui is considered a "senior" practitioner.

Sodo from the Japanese. Literally the "monk's hall." A Zen training temple or monastery in which one lives and practices. In the West occasionally used for a training hall, whether or not students sleep in the hall.

Sojiji A Japanese temple originally dedicated to the Vinaya school but rededicated by Keizan Jokin as a Zen monastery. Together with Eiheiji one of the two principal temples of the Soto school in Japan.

Son from the Korean. See Chan.

Soto School from the Japanese. (Caodong in Chinese.) The Zen school most closely associated with the practice of shikantaza.

Soto Zen Buddhist Association (SZBA) A professional association of Western priests trained in the Japanese Soto tradition.

Sunim from the Korean. An honorific for a Vinaya ordained Zen monk or nun.

Sutra from the Sanskrit. Literally "thread." The term for spiritual texts attributed to the Buddha.

Tathagata from the Sanskrit. Literally "thus come" or "thus gone." One who has achieved the deepest realization. One of the traditional ten titles of the Buddha.

Tathagata Garbha from the Sanskrit. Literally the "womb of the Buddha." The reality that all are Buddha from the beginning.

Tendai from the Japanese. (Tiantai in Chinese.) An important Mahayana school. In Japan both the Rinzai and Soto schools of Zen were founded by monks originally ordained in the Tendai school.

Tenzo from the Japanese. The head cook in a Zen monastery.

Theravada from the Pali. Literally the "Way of the Elders." One of the two principal schools of Buddhism, most closely associated with the arhat ideal.

Thich from the Vietnamese. An honorific for a Vinaya-ordained Zen monk.

Thien from the Vietnamese. See Chan.

Tokudo from the Japanese. Literally "going beyond." A specific form of ordination. There has been confusion because the term is applied both to *jukai todudo* and *unsui tokudo*. The former is a rite similar to confirmation in the West, where one consciously embraces the Buddha Way. The later is the form of ordination to the monastic or priestly state. See Unsui.

Unified Buddhist Church in America (and France) The umbrella organization that supports the teachings of Thich Nhat Hanh. The largest Zen Buddhist institution in the West. See also Order of Interbeing.

Unsui from the Japanese. Literally "clouds and water." Generally understood to be novice priests or monastics in Japanese Zen. Some scholars and some teachers in the West consider this the baseline ordination as a priest, the rough equivalent to Bhikkshu/Bhikkshuni ordination. See Osho and Bodhisattva Ordination.

Vinaya from the Sanskrit. The code of morality and specifically the traditional precepts for monastic ordination. There are 250 precepts for monks and 348 precepts for nuns.

Vipassana from the Sanskrit. Literally "insight." Together with metta and shamatha one of the three meditative practices taught in early Buddhism. In combination with shamatha, the discipline from which shikantaza developed.

Yogachara from the Sanskrit. Literally "Mind Only." One of the principal schools of the Mahayana. It was the principal contender with the Madhyamika school.

Zazen from the Japanese. Literally "seated Zen" or "sitting Zen." The formal practice of Zen meditation.

Zen from the Japanese. See Chan.

Zenji from the Japanese. Literally "Zen master." An honorific used in some Zen lineages, usually conferred posthumously.

Zuise (also sometimes spelled Zuisse) from the Japanese. A ceremony of acknowledgment of seniority in Japanese Soto Zen. In North America a rite of Dharma Recognition to replace this has been initiated by the Soto Zen Buddhist Association.

NOTES

SECTION ONE

The Founding Stories

I believe the first book on Zen I ever read was Paul Reps's little anthology, *Zen Flesh, Zen Bones*. I was absolutely stunned at this approach to religion so different from my childhood Christian fundamentalism. Not long after that I stumbled upon Alan Watts's introduction to Zen, *The Way of Zen,* which, although I didn't know it at the time, is based almost entirely on the work of D.T. Suzuki. Not long after, I discovered Philip Kapleau's masterwork, *The Three Pillars of Zen.* With Kapleau I was hooked. From that point on I was drawn ever deeper into this strange and compelling spiritual tradition.

Today good surveys of Zen abound. They range from Robert Aitken's classic *Taking the Path of Zen* to Martine Batchelor's wonderful, if often overlooked, *Principles of Zen.* I've even entered the field myself with *In This Very Moment: A Simple Guide to Zen Buddhism.*

I've drawn on many different authors and teachers for this section and those that follow. Probably the standard English language introduction to core Buddhist teachings is Walpola Rahula's *What the Buddha Taught.* I also found H. W. Schumann's *The Historical Buddha* enormously helpful in trying to sort out myth and history in regard to the early formation of Buddhist thought.

Likewise as I tried to find the essential thread of Zen, John R. McRae's *The Northern School and the Formation of Early Ch'an Buddhism* proved to be enormously important. I believe his briefer and more informal reflection *Seeing Through Zen: Encounter, Transformation and Genealogy in Chinese Chan Buddhism* is an absolute must-read for anyone trying to understand the relationship of history and myth in the formation of Zen as a distinct school. I've deeply relied upon McRae's insights. While I drew upon many other sources, beyond McRae, Heinrich Dumoulin's *Zen Buddhism: A History* in two volumes, proved a constant companion and resource for me while researching this book.

Other important contemporary explorations of Buddhist thought I found influencing me must include David Brazier's *The Feeling Buddha*. But for me the signal study of Buddhism from a Western and rationalist perspective is Stephen Batchelor's *Buddhism without Beliefs*. I consider this book together with McRae's *Seeing Through Zen* required reading for any contemporary Western inquirer into the deeper possibilities of Zen Buddhism. I've found Batchelor the most important writer influencing my own thinking on the meeting of Buddhism and Western rationalism, and I owe him endless gratitude.

Some critical primary texts that I drew upon for this section included Bhikkhu Bodhi's *In the Buddha's Words: An Anthology of Discourses from the Pali Canon,* a wonderful anthology of early source texts of teachings attributed to the historical Buddha. It was much more helpful than the larger anthologies I also consulted. Thomas Cleary's *The Flower Ornament Scripture: The Avatamsaka Sutra,* in three volumes, remains the best translation of this critical text in English, without which, I feel, Zen's philosophical foundations cannot be approached. Edward Conze's *Buddhist Wisdom Books, The Large Sutra on Perfect Wisdom: With the Divisions of the Abhisamayalankara,* and *The Shorter Prajnaparamita Texts* proved critical to gaining insight into the Great Wisdom tradition, nearly as important as the *Avatamsaka Sutra*. I was also deeply impressed by more recent translations and commentaries on this tradition, including Red Pine's *The Heart Sutra: The Womb of the Buddhas* and Mu Soeng's *Trust in Mind: The Rebellion of Chinese Zen*. There are several versions of the Lotus Sutra in English, another text that is critical to the development of Zen. I drew upon the Bunno Kato, et al., translation, *The Threefold Lotus Sutra*. Rounding out the primary texts I referenced for this section were Charles Luk's *The Surangama Sutra* and D.T. Suzuki's *The Lankavatara Sutra: A Mahayana Text.*

Ancient Teachers and Nascent Institutions

For this section I continued to draw upon McRae and Dumoulin. The single most important text for this period is the Platform Sutra, available in various translations. I highly recommend Philip B. Yampolsky's translation and commentary, *The Platform Sutra of the Sixth Patriarch: The Text of the Tun-Huang Manuscript*. In addition I found two anthologies of particular use: Andy Ferguson's *Zen's Chinese Heritage: The Masters and Their Teachings* is probably the most important single collection of classic Chinese Zen teachings yet to be put together in English. A close second for me is Nelson Foster and Jack Shoemaker's *The Roaring Stream: A New Zen Reader.* Increasingly collections of teachings of specific teachers are now available such as Ruth Fuller Sasaki's *A Man of Zen: The Recorded Sayings of the Layman P'ang,* Thomas Cleary's *Sayings and Doings of Pai-chang: Ch'an Master of Great Wisdom,* Christopher Cleary's *Swampland Flowers: The Letters and Lectures of Zen Master Ta Hui,* and Taigen Dan Leighton's *Cultivating the Empty Field: The Silent Illumination of Master Hongzhi.*

The Practices of Zen

For most people in the West Zen is a practice. After all the word *zen* itself means meditation. As such the larger part of the literature relating to Zen in English is about its disciplines. I've mentioned Kapleau's seminal *Three Pillars of Zen* and Aitken's *Taking the Path of Zen;* both, so many years after their initial publication, still of use. But they've been joined by newer volumes including John Daishin Buksbazen's very good, simple, and clear *Zen Meditation in Plain English* and the gathering of essential materials from several otherwise long-out-of-print titles, Taizan Maezumi and Bernie Glassman's *On Zen Practice: Body, Breath and Mind.*

Important primary texts that I consulted include *Swampland Flowers: The Letters and Lectures of Zen Master Ta Hui* and *Cultivating the Empty Field: The Silent Illumination of Zen Master Hongzhi.* John Daido Loori has edited two significant anthologies addressing Zen meditation disciplines: *The Art of Just Sitting: Essential Writings on the Zen Practice of Shikantaza* and *Sitting With Koans: Essential Writings on the Practice of Zen Koan Introspection.* Possibly the most important single book on koan introspection is Isshu Miura and Ruth Fuller Sasaki's *Zen Dust: The History of the Koan and Koan Study in Rinzai (Lin-chi) Zen.* D.T. Suzuki's *Essays in Zen Buddhism (Second Series)* is also important. More recent contributions to the literature include the very significant study by Victor Sogen Hori, *Zen Sand: The Book of Capping Phrases for Koan Practice* titled in homage to *Zen Dust.* Perhaps the clearest introduction to koan introspection practice is John Tarrant's *Bring Me the Rhinoceros: And Other Zen Koans to Bring You Joy.*

There are now numerous collections of koans in the English language, several versions with commentaries by Western and Eastern Zen masters. Those I consulted include three now classic versions of the Gateless Gate anthology: Robert Aitken's *The Gateless Barrier: The Wu-men*

Kuan (Mumonkan), Zenkei Shibayama's *The Gateless Barrier: Zen Comments on the Mumonkan,* and Koun Yamada's *The Gateless Gate: The Classic Book of Zen Koans.* Other significant collections are Stefano Mui Barragato's *Zen Light: Unconventional Commentaries on the Denkoroku,* Thomas Cleary and J. C. Cleary's *The Blue Cliff Record,* Thomas Cleary's *Book of Serenity: One Hundred Zen Dialogues,* Thomas Yuho Kirchner's *Entangled Vines: Zen Koans of the Shumon Kattoshu,* and Gerry Shishin Wick's *The Book of Equanimity: Illuminating Classic Zen Koans.*

The Japanese Transformation of Zen

To understand Zen in the West and particularly in North America it is essential to understand how Zen was transformed in Japan. William Bodiford's *Soto Zen in Medieval Japan* is very informative, as is Richard Jaffe's critical study *Neither Monk nor Layman: Clerical Marriage in Modern Japanese Buddhism.* In particular two Japanese thinkers created approaches to Zen that mark all Western Zen directly or indirectly: Eihei Dogen and Hakuin Ekaku. Their writings are available in English translations, most notably the oeuvre of Dogen Zenji that has caught the imagination of the Western scholarly community. I need to underscore that to understand Zen in the West in any depth it is necessary to have some understanding of both these teachers.

As I've suggested, Dogen studies have generated a substantial literature in English. Two very good introductions are Masao Abe's *A Study of Dogen: His Philosophy and Religion* and Hee-Jin Kim's *Eihei Dogen: Mystical Realist.* A first-rate anthology of the master's writings is Kazuaki Tanahashi's *Moon in a Dewdrop: Writings of Zen Master Dogen.* There are also substantial translations with commentary of various specific texts by Dogen. These include Francis Dojun Cook's *How to Raise an Ox: Zen Practice as Taught in Master Dogen's Shobogenzo,* Steven Heine's *Dogen and the Koan Tradition: A Tale of Two Shobogenzo Texts,* and Taigen Daniel Leighton and Shohaku Okumura's *Dogen's Pure Standards for the Zen Community.* There have been several translations of Dogen's masterwork, the Shobogenzo. Currently the only version generally available is Gudo Nishijima and Chodo Cross's four-volume *Master Dogen's Shobogenzo.* Of considerable significance is the recent translation of Dogen's Eihei Koroku by Taigen Dan Leighton and Shohaku Okumura, *Dogen's Extensive Record: A Translation of the Eihei Koroku.*

The literature on Hakuin in English is a bit thinner than that for Dogen. Still there are some very helpful books. Probably the best introduction is either Philip Yampolsky's *The Zen Master Hakuin: Selected Writings* or Norman Waddell's *Essential Teachings of Zen Master Hakuin*. Waddell has also translated other critical Hakuin texts, including *Wild Ivy: The Spiritual Autobiography of Zen Master Hakuin* and *Zen Words for the Heart: Hakuin's Commentary on the Heart Sutra*.

SECTION TWO

The Birth of Western Zen

For possible Zen or at least Buddhist ancient encounters with North America Henriette Mertz's *Pale Ink: Two Ancient Records of Chinese Exploration in America* is quite interesting. Surveys of the historical period should begin with Rick Fields' *How the Swans Came to the Lake: A Narrative History of Buddhism in America*. Fields was the pioneer student of the Buddhist encounter with the West. He was my first inspiration, and his generosity of heart and attention to detail my constant hope for my own work. Later but very important and more traditionally scholarly investigations include Carl T. Jackson's *The Oriental Religions and American Thought: Nineteenth-Century Explorations* and particularly Thomas Tweed's *The American Encounter with Buddhism: 1844–1912: Victorian Culture and the Limits of Dissent*. I also found Louise Hunter's *Buddhism in Hawaii: Its Impact on a Yankee Community* very helpful for several personalities explored here.

More recent studies such as Robert Aitken's *Original Dwelling Place: Zen Buddhist Essays*, Lenore Friedman's *Meetings with Remarkable Women: Buddhist Teachers in America*, Richard Hughes Seager's *Buddhism in America*, Don Morreale's *The Complete Guide to Buddhist America*, Charles S. Prebish and Kenneth K. Tanaka, eds., *The Faces of Buddhism in America*, Helen Tworkov's delightful *Zen in America: Profiles of Five Teachers*, and the absolutely amazing and comprehensive study by Andrew Rawlinson, *The Book of Enlightened Masters: Western Teachers in Eastern Traditions* have been important for me in this study. I also found the collection of anecdotes about Western Zen masters, Sean Murphy's *One Bird, One Stone: 108 American Zen Stories*, a delight to read. I cite Murphy throughout this book.

I also drew upon many sources for individual teachers and other prominent figures in the Western movement of Zen. These include Masao Abe's anthology *A Zen Life: D.T. Suzuki Remembered*, Monica Furlong's *Zen Effects: The Life of Alan Watts*, Elsie Mitchell's *Sun Buddhas, Moon*

Buddhas: A Zen Quest, Nyogen Senzaki, et al., *Namu Dai Bosa: A Transmission of Zen Buddhism to America,* Eido T. Shimano's *Endless Vow: The Zen Path of Soen Nakagawa,* and Alan Watts's *In My Own Way: An Autobiography*—all very helpful. In addition, here and elsewhere I drew upon anecdotes shared directly with me by former students of these and later teachers.

Chinese, Korean, and Vietnamese Zen in the West

For this section I primarily drew upon several volumes mentioned above: most notably *How the Swans Came to the Lake* and *The Faces of Buddhism in America.* For an overview of Chinese Buddhism in the first half of the twentieth century there is little more useful than Holmes Welch's *The Practice of Chinese Buddhism 1900–1950.* Two books by Sheng-yen were particularly helpful in understanding Chinese approaches to Zen and the beginnings of a Western Chan transmission: *Chan Comes West* and *Hoofprints of the Ox.* Robert E. Buswell's *The Zen Monastic Experience* is a compelling description of modern Korean Zen. I was also informed by Kusan Sunim's *The Way of Korean Zen.* Stephen Mitchell's anthology *Dropping Ashes on the Buddha: The Teachings of Zen Master Seung Sahn* remains a Western Zen classic. I found Thich Thien-An's *Buddhism and Zen in Vietnam* and *Zen Philosophy, Zen Practice* very helpful in attempting to understand the shape of Vietnamese Zen. For Thich Nhat Hanh's unique vision of Western Buddhism I recommend *Being Peace* and *Peace Is Every Step: The Path of Mindfulness in Everyday Life. Zen Keys: A Zen Monk Examines the Vietnamese Tradition* is probably his most "Zen" book.

American Rinzai

Once again I need to express my debt to Rick Fields for his pioneering work published as *How the Swans Came to the Lake,* which was critical for this section. I also drew heavily from *One Bird, One Stone* and from Rawlinson's *The Book of Enlightened Masters.* I also found *Namu Dai Bosa: A Transmission of Zen Buddhism to America; Sun Buddhas, Moon Buddhas;* and *Endless Vow* of enormous help. Hosokawa Dogen's *Omori Sogen: The Art of a Zen Master* was particularly helpful in researching this teacher barely known among mainstream Western Zen practitioners, but fairly well-known in martial arts circles. I was particularly taken with Roko Sherry Chayat's delightful study *Subtle Sound: The Zen Teachings of Maurine Stuart* and Michael Hotz's equally compelling *Holding the Lotus to the Rock: The Autobiography of Sokei-an, America's First Zen Master.*

American Soto

As for the previous section, and so much more, I remain indebted to *How the Swans Came to the Lake* and as a close second, *The Book of Enlightened Masters*. *One Bird, One Stone* continues to provide a human face to many of these teachers. I also drew upon Kyogen Carlson's *Zen in the American Grain: Discovering the Teachings at Home*, David Chadwick's magisterial *Crooked Cucumber: The Life and Zen Teaching of Shunryu Suzuki* complemented, corrected, and challenged by Michael Downing's *Shoes Outside the Door: Desire, Devotion, and Excess at San Francisco Zen Center*, Dainin Katagiri's *You Have to Say Something: Manifesting Zen Insight*, Jiyu Kennett's *Zen Is Eternal Life* (originally published as *Selling Water by the River*, and for which I "ghosted" Kennett Roshi's original preface—my first published writing), Jakusho Kwong's *No Beginning, No End: The Intimate Heart of Zen*, Shunryu Suzuki's *Branching Streams Flow in the Darkness*, as well as his now generally acknowledged Western spiritual classic, *Zen Mind, Beginner's Mind: Informal Talks on Zen Meditation and Practice*, and Brad Warner's *Hardcore Zen: Punk Rock, Monster Movies and the Truth about Reality*. I also found Michael Wenger's *Wind Bell: Teachings from the San Francisco Zen Center 1968–2001* very helpful.

The Harada-Yasutani and Hybrid Zen in the West

In this section I rely on *How the Swans Came to the Lake; One Bird, One Stone; The Book of Enlightened Masters;* Robert Aitken's *Encouraging Words: Zen Buddhist Teachings for Western Students;* and Elsie Mitchell's *Sun Buddhas, Moon Buddhas*. There are numerous places I draw upon other books by Aitken, including *The Gateless Barrier: The Wu-men Kuan (Mumonkan), Original Dwelling Place: Zen Buddhist Essays*, and *Taking the Path of Zen*.

I also found Jan Chozen Bays's *Jizo Bodhisattva: Modern Healing and Traditional Buddhist Practice*, Charlotte Joko Beck's *Everyday Zen: Love and Work*, Bernie Glassman's *Infinite Circle: Teachings in Zen*, Daido Loori's *The Eight Gates of Zen: Spiritual Training in an American Zen Monastery*, Taizan Maezumi's *Appreciate Your Life: The Essence of Zen Practice*, Dennis Genpo Merzel's *The Eye Never Sleeps: Striking to the Heart of Zen*, Gerry Shishin Wick's *The Book of Equanimity: Illuminating Classic Zen Koans*, and Toni Packer's *The Work of This Moment* are each illustrative of the Harada/Yasutani approach to Zen training as well as the shifts that have taken place in recent years. David L. Preston's *The Social Organization of Zen Practice: Constructing Transcultural Reality* was of enormous help in examining a developing Western Zen community. Here in particular I also benefited from comments and thoughts of various practitioners and teachers of the tradition.

SECTION 3

I relied on so many for this section. The shape of Zen in Asia as well as in the West has been in considerable flux from the later part of the twentieth century to today. Even before that there was Shoei Ando's suggestive *Zen and American Transcendentalism: An Investigation of One's Self.* Today there are insightful investigations such as Tworkov's *Zen in America,* Charles S. Prebish's *Luminous Passage: The Practice and Study of Buddhism in America,* and Charles S. Prebish and Martin Baumann's *Westward Dharma: Buddhism beyond Asia.* There are critical and cautionary investigations such as Downing's *Shoes Outside the Door,* Bernard Faure's *The Rhetoric of Immediacy: A Cultural Critique of Chan/Zen Buddhism,* James W. Heisig and John C. Maraldo's *Rude Awakenings: Zen, the Kyoto School, and the Question of Nationalism,* Jamie Hubbard and Paul L. Swanson's *Pruning the Bodhi Tree: The Storm over Critical Buddhism,* and Brian Victoria's *Zen at War.*

There are also explorations of the unique aspects of the Zen and Christian encounter in such books as Robert Aitken and David Steindl-Rast's *The Ground We Share: Everyday Practice, Buddhist and Christian,* Marcus Borg's *Jesus and Buddha: The Parallel Sayings,* and Ruben L. F. Habito's profound study, *Living Zen, Loving God.* In addition Harold Kasimow and others put together a sweet and intelligent study that includes Jewish as well as Christian and Buddhist considerations of this meeting in their *Beside Still Waters: Jews, Christians and the Way of the Buddha.*

The psychological implications of Buddhism and Zen have been explored in such volumes as Brazier's *Feeling Buddha,* James H. Austin's *Zen and the Brain: Toward an Understanding of Meditation and Consciousness,* Ellen Birx's *Healing Zen: Awakening to a Life of Wholeness and Compassion While Caring for Yourself and Others,* and Barry Magid's *Ordinary Mind: Exploring the Common Ground of Zen and Psychoanalysis.* I owe much to all these writers.

A literature of Zen memoir has begun to emerge, including the mystery novelist Janwillem van de Wetering's *Afterzen: Experiences of a Zen Student Out on His Ear,* Lawrence Shainberg's *Ambivalent Zen: A Memoir,* Erik Fraser Storlie's *Nothing on My Mind: Berkeley, LSD, Two Zen Masters, and a Life on the Dharma Trail,* and my personal favorite David

Chadwick's *Thank You and OK! An American Zen Failure in Japan*. Also I need to include the intriguing story of growing up within a Zen environment, Ivan Richmond's *Silence and Noise: Growing Up Zen in America,* one of the first of an emerging subset literature of birthright Western Buddhist memoirs.

Among the most interesting aspects of Zen's Westward journey for me is the emergence of an "Engaged Buddhism," a socially concerned Buddhist perspective. I mention in the body of this book how this term was probably coined by Thich Nhat Hanh, who remains one of the signal figures leading Engaged Buddhism. There are an increasing number of Western writers concerned with this emerging phenomenon. These include specifically Zen considerations such as Bernie Glassman's *Bearing Witness: A Zen Master's Lessons in Making Peace* and more generally Buddhist reflections such as Ken Jones's comprehensive study *The New Social Face of Buddhism: A Call to Action,* Christopher S. Queen's *Engaged Buddhism in the West,* and Stephanie Kaza and Kenneth Kraft's exploration of the ecological dimensions of Engaged Buddhism in their *Dharma Rain: Sources of Buddhist Environmentalism.*

Other significant takes on an emerging Western Zen for which I owe an enormous debt in this study include Ezra Bayda's *Being Zen: Bringing Meditation to Life,* Ellen and Charles Birx's delightful *Waking Up Together: Intimate Partnership on the Spiritual Path,* Merrill Collett's *At Home with Dying: A Zen Hospice Approach,* Joan Halifax's *The Fruitful Darkness: Reconnecting with the Body of the Earth,* Diane Eshin Rizzetto's *Waking Up to What You Do: A Zen Practice for Meeting Every Situation with Intelligence and Compassion,* Manfred B. Steger and Perle Besserman's *Grassroots Zen,* and John Tarrant's dense, poetic, and compelling *The Light inside the Dark: Zen, Soul, and the Spiritual Life.*

Another important source throughout this book is the World Wide Web. A good search engine, a knack for search terms, and a highly developed sense for nonsense can lead one to much valuable information about Buddhism and Zen. I hope I've not been misled too often, nor passed on much misinformation from this avenue of research. There are also many traps for the unwary. But then isn't that the story of life? So, for this book as in all matters of real importance, that small reminder: *caveat emptor!*

BIBLIOGRAPHY

Abe, Masao. *A Study of Dogen: His Philosophy and Religion.* Albany, State University of New York Press, 1992.

_____, Editor. *A Zen Life: D.T. Suzuki Remembered.* New York, Weatherhill, 1986.

_____. *Zen and Western Thought.* Honolulu, University of Hawai'i Press, 1985.

Aitken, Robert. *Encouraging Words: Zen Buddhist Teachings for Western Students.* New York, Pantheon Books, 1993.

_____. *The Gateless Barrier: The Wu-men Kuan (Mumonkan).* Berkeley, North Point Press, 1991.

_____. *Original Dwelling Place: Zen Buddhist Essays.* Washington, D.C., Counterpoint, 1997.

_____. *Taking the Path of Zen.* New York, North Point Press, 1982.

Aitken, Robert, and David Steindl-Rast. *The Ground We Share: Everyday Practice, Buddhist and Christian.* Liguori, Triumph Books, 1994.

Ando, Shoei. *Zen and American Transcendentalism: An Investigation of One's Self.* Tokyo, Hokuseido Press, 1970.

Andreasen, Esben. *Popular Buddhism in Japan: Shin Buddhist Religion and Culture.* Honolulu, University of Hawai'i Press, 1998.

Austin, James H. *Zen and the Brain: Toward an Understanding of Meditation and Consciousness.* Cambridge, MIT Press, 1999.

Bankei. Peter Haskel, Translator. *Bankei Zen: Translations from the Record of Bankei.* New York, Grove Press, 1984.

Batchelor, Martine. *Principles of Zen.* London, Thorsons, 1999.

Batchelor, Stephen. *Buddhism without Beliefs: A Contemporary Guide to Awakening.* New York, Riverhead Books, 1997.

_____. *Verses from the Center: A Buddhist Vision of the Sublime*. New York, Riverhead Books, 2000.

Barragato, Stefano Mui. *Zen Light: Unconventional Commentaries on the Denkoroku*. Boston, Charles Tuttle, 1977.

Bayda, Ezra. *Being Zen: Bringing Meditation to Life*. Boston, Shambhala Publications, 2003.

Bayda, Ezra, with Josh Bartok. *Saying Yes to Life (Even the Hard Parts)*. Boston, Wisdom Publications, 2005.

Bays, Jan Chozen. *Jizo Bodhisattva: Modern Healing and Traditional Buddhist Practice*. Boston, Tuttle Publishing, 2002.

Beck, Charlotee Joko. *Everyday Zen: Love and Work*. San Francisco, Harper & Row, 1989.

_____. *Nothing Special: Living Zen*. New York, HarperCollins, 1993.

Besserman, Perle, and Manfred Steger. *Crazy Clouds: Zen Radicals, Rebels and Reformers*. Boston, Shambhala Publications, 1991.

Birx, Ellen. *Healing Zen: Awakening to a Life of Wholeness and Compassion While Caring for Yourself and Others*. New York, Viking Compass, 2002.

Birx, Ellen, and Charles Birx. *Waking Up Together: Intimate Partnership on the Spiritual Path*. Boston, Wisdom Publications, 2005.

Bloom, Alfred. *Shinran's Gospel of Pure Grace*. Tucson, University of Arizona Press, 1965.

Bodhi, Bhikkhu. *In the Buddha's Words: An Anthology of Discourses from the Pāli Canon*. Boston, Wisdom Publications, 2005.

Bodiford, William. *Soto Zen in Medieval Japan*. Honolulu, University of Hawai'i Press, 1993.

Borg, Marcus, Editor. *Jesus and Buddha: The Parallel Sayings*. Berkeley, Ulysses Press, 1997.

Braverman, Arthur. *Living and Dying in Zazen: Five Zen Masters of Modern Japan*. New York, Weatherhill, 2003.

Brazier, David. *The Feeling Buddha*. New York, Fromm International, 1998.

Broughton, Jeffrey L. *The Bodhidharma Anthology: The Earliest Records of Zen*. Berkeley, University of California Press, 1999.

Buksbazen, John Daishin. *Zen Meditation in Plain English*. Boston, Wisdom Publications, 2002.

Buswell, Robert E., Jr. *The Zen Monastic Experience*. Princeton, Princeton University Press, 1992.

Carlson, Kyogen. *Zen in the American Grain: Discovering the Teachings at Home*. Barrytown, Station Hill Press, 1994.

Carter, Robert E. *The Nothingness beyond God: An Introduction to the Philosophy of Nishida Kitaro*. New York, Paragon House, 1989.

Chadwick, David. *Crooked Cucumber: The Life and Zen Teaching of Shunryu Suzuki*. New York, Broadway Books, 1999.

_____. *Thank You and OK! An American Zen Failure in Japan*. New York, Penguin Books, 1994.

Chang, Garma C. C. *The Buddhist Teaching of Totality: The Philosophy of Hwa Yen Buddhism*. University Park, The Pennsylvania State University Press, 1971.

Chayat, Roko Sherry, Editor. *Subtle Sound: The Zen Teachings of Maurine Stuart*. Boston, Shambhala Publications, 1996.

Chih-i. Thomas Cleary, Translator. *Stopping and Seeing: A Comprehensive Course in Buddhist Meditation*. Boston, Shambhala, 1997.

Chung-yuan, Chang. *Original Teachings of Ch'an Buddhism*. New York, Pantheon Books, 1969.

Cleary, Thomas, Translator. *Book of Serenity: One Hundred Zen Dialogues*. Hudson, Lindisfarne Press, 1990.

_____, Translator. *Entry into the Inconceivable: An Introduction to Hua-yen Buddhism*. Honolulu, University of Hawai'i Press, 1983.

_____, Translator. *Secrets of the Blue Cliff Record: Zen Comments by Hakuin and Tenkei*. Boston, Shambhala Publications, 2000.

Cleary, Thomas, and J. C. Cleary, Translators. *The Blue Cliff Record*. Boston, Shambhala, 1977.

Collcutt, Martin. *Five Mountains: The Rinzai Zen Monastic Institution in Medieval Japan*. Cambridge, Harvard University Press, 1981.

Collett, Merrill. *At Home with Dying: A Zen Hospice Approach*. Boston, Shambhala Publications, 1999.

Conze, Edward. *Buddhist Wisdom Books*. London, Allen & Unwin, 1975.

_____, Translator. *The Large Sutra on Perfect Wisdom: With the Divisions of the Abhisamayalankara*. Berkeley, University of California Press, 1975.

_____, Translator. *The Shorter Prajnaparamita Texts*. London, Luzac, 1974.

Cook, Francis Dojun. *How to Raise an Ox: Zen Practice as Taught in Master Dogen's Shobogenzo*. Boston, Wisdom Publications, 2002.

_____. *Hua-yen Buddhism: The Jewel Net of Indra*. University Park, The Pennsylvania State University Press, 1977.

Dogen, Eihei. Taigen Dan Leighton and Shohaku Okumura, Translators. *Dogen's Extensive Record: A Translation of the Eihei Koroku.* Boston, Wisdom Publications, 2004.

_____. Taigen Daniel Leighton and Shohaku Okumura, Translators. *Dogen's Pure Standards for the Zen Community.* Albany, State University of New York Press, 1996.

_____. Gudo Nishijima and Chodo Cross, Translators. *Master Dogen's Shobogenzo,* Four Vols. London, Windbell Publications, 1994, 1996, 1997, 1999.

Dogen, Hosokawa. *Omori Sogen: The Art of a Zen Master.* London, Kegan Paul International, 1999.

Downing, Michael. *Shoes Outside the Door: Desire, Devotion, and Excess at San Francisco Zen Center.* Washington D.C., Counterpoint, 2001.

Dumoulin, Heinrich. *Zen Buddhism: A History,* Two Vols. New York, Macmillan, 1988, 1990.

Faure, Bernard. *Chan Insights and Oversights: An Epistemological Critique of the Chan Tradition.* Princeton, Princeton University Press, 1993.

_____. *The Rhetoric of Immediacy: A Cultural Critique of Chan/Zen Buddhism.* Princeton, Princeton University Press, 1991.

_____. *The Will to Orthodoxy: A Critical Genealogy of Northern Chan Buddhism.* Stanford, Stanford University Press, 1997.

Ferguson, Andy. *Zen's Chinese Heritage: The Masters and Their Teachings.* Boston, Wisdom Publications, 2000.

Fields, Rick. *How the Swans Came to the Lake: A Narrative History of Buddhism in America.* Boston, Shambhala Publications, 1981.

Ford, James Ishmael. *In This Very Moment: A Simple Guide to Zen Buddhism.* Boston, Skinner House Books, 2002.

Foster, Nelson, and Jack Shoemaker. *The Roaring Stream: A New Zen Reader.* Hopewell, New Jersey, Ecco Press, 1996.

Franck, Frederick, Editor. *The Buddha Eye: An Anthology of the Kyoto School.* New York, Crossroads, 1991.

Friedman, Lenore. *Meetings with Remarkable Women: Buddhist Teachers in America.* Boston, Shambhala Publications, 1987.

Furlong, Monica. *Zen Effects: The Life of Alan Watts.* Boston, Houghton Mifflin, 1986.

Glassman, Bernie. *Bearing Witness: A Zen Master's Lessons in Making Peace.* New York, Bell Tower, 1998.

_____. *Infinite Circle: Teachings in Zen.* Boston, Shambhala Publications, 2002.

Gregory, Peter N. *Traditions of Meditation in Chinese Buddhism*. Honolulu, University of Hawai'i Press, 1986.

Groner, Paul. *Saicho: The Establishment of the Japanese Tendai School*. Honolulu, University of Hawai'i Press, 2000.

Habito, Ruben L. F. *Living Zen, Loving God*. Boston, Wisdom Publications, 2004.

Hagen, Steven. *Buddhism Plain and Simple: The Practice of Being Aware, Right Now, Every Day*. Boston, Charles Tuttle, 1997.

Hakuin. Norman Waddell, Translator. *Essential Techings of Zen Master Hakuin*. Boston, Shambhala Publications, 1994.

_____. Norman Waddell, Translator. *Wild Ivy: The Spiritual Autobiography of Zen Master Hakuin*. Boston, Shambhala Publications, 1999.

_____. Philip B. Yampolsky, Translator. *The Zen Master Hakuin: Selected Writings*. New York, Columbia University Press, 1971.

_____. Norman Waddell, Translator. *Zen Words for the Heart: Hakuin's Commentary on the Heart Sutra*. Boston, Shambhala Publications, 1996.

Halifax, Joan. *The Fruitful Darkness: Reconnecting with the Body of the Earth*. San Francisco, HarperSanFrancisco, 1993.

Hanh, Thich Nhat. *Being Peace*. Berkeley, Parallax Press, 1987.

_____. *Peace Is Every Step: The Path of Mindfulness in Everyday Life*. New York, Bantam Books, 1992.

_____. *Zen Keys: A Zen Monk Examines the Vietnamese Tradition*. Garden City, Anchor Books, 1974.

Heine, Steven. *Dogen and the Koan Tradition: A Tale of Two Shobogenzo Texts*. Albany, State University of New York Press, 1994.

Heine, Steven, and Charles S. Prebish. *Buddhism in the Modern World: Adaptations of an Ancient Tradition*. Oxford, Oxford University Press, 2003.

Heine, Steven, and Dale S. Wright, Editors. *The Zen Canon: Understanding the Classic Texts*. Oxford, Oxford University Press, 2004.

_____, Editors. *The Zen Koan: Texts and Contexts in Zen Buddhism*. Oxford, Oxford University Press, 2000.

Hongzhi. Taigen Dan Leighton, Translator. *Cultivating the Empty Field: The Silent Illumination of Zen Master Hongzhi*. Boston, Tuttle Publishing, 2000.

Hori, Victor Sogen. *Zen Sand: The Book of Capping Phrases for Koan Practice*. Honolulu, University of Hawai'i Press, 2003.

Hotz, Michael, Editor. *Holding the Lotus to the Rock: The Autobiography of Sokei-an, America's First Zen Master*. New York, Four Walls Eight Windows, 2003.

Hunter, Louise H. *Buddhism in Hawaii: Its Impact on a Yankee Community.* Honolulu, University of Hawai'i Press, 1971.

Jackson, Carl T. *The Oriental Religions and American Thought: Nineteenth-Century Explorations.* Westport, Greenwood Press, 1981.

Jaffe, Richard. *Neither Monk nor Layman: Clerical Marriage in Modern Japanese Buddhism.* Princeton, Princeton University Press, 2001.

Jones, Ken. *The New Social Face of Buddhism: An Alternative Sociopolitical Perspective.* Boston, Wisdom Publications, 2003.

Kalupahana, David J. *Nagarjuna: The Philosophy of the Middle Way.* Albany, State University of New York Press, 1986.

Kapleau, Philip, Editor. *The Three Pillars of Zen: Twenty-fifth Anniversary Edition.* New York, Anchor Books, 1989.

Kashiwahara, Ysuen, and Koyu Sonoda, *Shapers of Japanese Buddhism.* Tokyo, Kosei Publishing, 1994.

Kasimow, Harold, and others, Editors. *Beside Still Waters: Jews, Christians and the Way of the Buddha.* Boston, Wisdom Publications, 2003.

Kato, Bunno, and others, Translators. *The Threefold Lotus Sutra.* New York, Weatherhill, 1975.

Kaye, Les. *Zen at Work: A Zen Teacher's 30-Year Journey in Corporate America.* New York, Three Rivers Press, 1996.

Kaza, Stephanie, and Kenneth Kraft, Editors. *Dharma Rain: Sources of Buddhist Environmentalism.* Boston, Shambhala Publications, 2000.

Keel, Hee-Sung. *Chinul: The Founder of the Korean Son Tradition.* Berkeley, Berkeley Buddhist Studies Series, 1984.

Keizan. Francis H. Cook, Translator. *The Record of Transmitting the Light: Zen Master Keizan's Denkoroku.* Los Angeles, Center Publications, 1991.

Kennedy, Robert E. *Zen Spirit, Christian Spirit: The Place of Zen in Christian Life.* New York, Continuum, 1995.

Kim, Hee-Jin. *Eihei Dogen: Mystical Realist.* Boston, Wisdom Publications, 2004.

Kirchner, Thomas Yuho, Translator. *Entangled Vines: Zen Koans of the Shumon Kattoshu.* Kyoto, Tenryu-ji Institute for Philosophy and Religion, 2004.

Kusan. *The Way of Korean Zen.* New York, Weatherhill, 1985.

Kwong, Jakusho. *No Beginning, No End: The Intimate Heart of Zen.* New York, Harmony Books, 2003.

Lancaster, Lewis, Editor. *Prajnaparamita and Related Systems: Studies in Honor of Edward Conze.* Berkeley, Berkeley Buddhist Studies Series, 1977.

Lin-chi. Burton Watson, Translator. *The Zen Teachings of Master Lin-chi*. Boston, Shambhala Publications, 1993.

Loori, John Daido. *The Art of Just Sitting: Essential Writings on the Zen Practice of Shikantaza*. Boston, Wisdom Publications, 2002.

_____. *The Eight Gates of Zen: Spiritual Training in an American Zen Monastery*. Mt. Tremper, Dharma Communications, 1992.

_____. *Sitting With Koans: Essential Writings on the Practice of Zen Koan Introspection*. Boston, Wisdom Publications, 2005.

Luk, Charles (Lu K'uan Yu). *The Secrets of Chinese Meditation*. London, Rider & Company, 1964.

_____, Translator. *The Surangama Sutra*. London, Rider & Company, 1966.

McCandless, Ruth S., and Nyogen Senzaki. *Buddhism and Zen*. New York, Philosophical Library, 1953.

McRae, John R. *The Northern School and the Formation of Early Ch'an Buddhism*. Honolulu, University of Hawai'i Press, 1986.

_____. *Seeing Through Zen: Encounter, Transformation and Genealogy in Chinese Chan Buddhism*. Berkeley, University of California Press, 2003.

Maezumi, Taizan. *Appreciate Your Life: The Essence of Zen Practice*. Boston, Shambhala Publications, 2001.

Maezumi, Taizan, and Bernie Glassman. *On Zen Practice: Body, Breath, and Mind*. Boston, Wisdom Publications, 2002.

Magid, Barry. *Ordinary Mind: Exploring the Common Ground of Zen and Psychoanalysis*. Boston, Wisdom Publications, 2002, 2005.

Mertz, Henriette. *Pale Ink: Two Ancient Records of Chinese Exploration in America*. Chicago, Swallow Press, 1972.

Merzel, Dennis Genpo. *The Eye Never Sleeps: Striking to the Heart of Zen*. Boston, Shambhala Publications, 1991.

Mitchell, Elsie. *Sun Buddhas, Moon Buddhas: A Zen Quest*. New York, Weatherhill, 1973.

Miura, Isshu, and Ruth Fuller Sasaki. *Zen Dust: The History of the Koan and Koan Study in Rinzai (Lin-chi) Zen*. New York, Harcourt, Brace & World, 1966.

Muller, A. Charles, Translator. *The Sutra of Perfect Enlightenment: Korean Buddhism's Guide to Meditation*. Albany, State University of New York Press, 1999.

Murphy, Sean. *One Bird, One Stone: 108 American Zen Stories*. New York, Renaissance Books, 2002.

Nakagawa, Soen. *Endless Vow: The Zen Path of Soen Nakagawa*. Boston, Shambhala Publications, 1996.

Packer, Toni. *The Work of This Moment*. Boston, Shambhala Publications, 1990.

Pai-chang, Thomas Cleary, Translator. *Sayings and Doings of Pai-chang: Ch'an Master of Great Wisdom*. Los Angeles, Center Publications, 1978.

Pine, Red, Translator. *The Heart Sutra: The Womb of the Buddhas*. Washington D.C., Shoemaker & Hoard, 2004.

_____, Translator. *The Zen Teachings of Bodhidharma*. New York, North Point Press, 1987.

Prebish, Charles S. *Luminous Passage: The Practice and Study of Buddhism in America*. Berkeley, University of California Press, 1999.

Prebish, Charles S., and Martin Baumann. *Westward Dharma: Buddhism beyond Asia*. Berkeley, University of California Press, 2002.

Prebish, Charles S., and Kenneth K. Tanaka, Editors. *The Faces of Buddhism in America*. Berkeley, University of California Press, 1998.

Preston, David L. *The Social Organization of Zen Practice: Constructing Transcultural Reality*. Cambridge, Cambridge University Press, 1988.

Queen, Christopher S., Editor. *Engaged Buddhism in the West*. Boston, Wisdom Publications, 2000.

Rahula, Walpola. *What the Buddha Taught*. New York, Grover Press, 1974.

Rawlinson, Andrew. *The Book of Enlightened Masters: Western Teachers in Eastern Traditions*. Chicago, Open Court, 1997.

Richmond, Ivan. *Silence and Noise: Growing Up Zen in America*. New York, Atria Books, 2003.

Sahn, Seung. Stephen Mitchell, Editor. *Dropping Ashes on the Buddha: The Teaching of Zen Master Seung Sahn*. New York, Grove Press, 1976.

_____. *Only Don't Know: The Teaching Letters of Zen Master Seung Sahn*. San Francisco, Four Seasons Foundation, 1982.

Sasaki, Ruth Fuller, and others. *A Man of Zen: The Recorded Sayings of the Layman P'ang*. New York, Weatherhill, 1992.

Schumann, H. W., *The Historical Buddha*. London, Arkana, 1989.

Seager, Richard Hughes. *Buddhism in America*. New York, Columbia University Press, 1999.

Sekida, Katsuki. *Zen Training: Metehods and Philosophy*. New York, John Weatherhill, 1975.

Senzaki, Nyogen, and others. *Namu Dai Bosa: A Transmission of Zen Buddhism to America*. New York, Zen Studies Society, 1976.

Shainberg, Lawrence. *Ambivalent Zen: A Memoir.* New York, Pantheon Books, 1995.

Shaku, Soyen. *Zen for Americans: Including the Sutra of Forty-two Chapters.* La Salle, Open Court, 1974.

Sheng-yen, and others. *Chan Comes West.* New York, Dharma Drum Publications, 2002.

Sheng-yen. *Hoofprints of the Ox.* Oxford, Oxford University Press, 2001.

Shibayama, Zenkei. *The Gateless Barrier: Zen Comments on the Mumonkan.* Boston, Shambhala Publications, 2000.

Shimano, Eido T. *Endless Vow: The Zen Path of Soen Nakagawa.* Boston, Shambhala Publications, 1996.

Soeng, Mu. *The Diamond Sutra: Transforming the Way We Perceive the World.* Boston, Wisdom Publications, 2000.

_____. *Trust in Mind: The Rebellion of Chinese Zen.* Boston, Wisdom Publications, 2004.

Steger, Manfred B., and Perle Besserman. *Grassroots Zen.* Boston, Tuttle Publishing, 2001.

Stevens, John. *Lust for Enlightenment: Buddhism and Sex.* Boston, Shambhala Publications, 1990.

Stone, Jacqueline I. *Original Enlightenment and the Transformation of Medieval Japanese Buddhism.* Honolulu, University of Hawai'i Press, 1999.

Storlie, Erik Fraser. *Nothing on My Mind: Berkeley, LSD, Two Zen Masters, and a Life on the Dharma Trail.* Boston, Shambhala Publications, 1996.

Streng, Frederick J. *Emptiness: A Study in Religious Meaning.* Nashville, Abingdon Press, 1967.

Suzuki, Daisetz Teitaro. *Essays in Zen Buddhism (First Series).* London, Rider & Company, 1926.

_____. *Essays in Zen Buddhism (Second Series).* London, Rider & Company, 1950.

_____. *Essays in Zen Buddhism (Third Series).* London, Rider & Company, 1953.

_____, Translator. *The Lankavatara Sutra: A Mahayana Text.* London, Routledge & Kegan Paul, 1932.

Suzuki, Shunryu. *Branching Streams Flow in the Darkness.* Berkeley, University of California Press, 1999.

_____. *Not Always So: Practicing the True Spirit of Zen.* New York, HarperCollins, 2002.

_____. *Zen Mind, Beginner's Mind: Informal Talks on Zen Meditation and Practice*. New York, Weatherhill, 1970.

T'aego. J. C. Cleary, Translator. *A Buddha from Korea: The Zen Teachings of T'aego*. Boston, Shambhala Publications, 1988.

Ta Hui. Christopher Cleary, Translator. *Swampland Flowers: The Letters and Lectures of Zen Master Ta Hui*. New York, Grove Press, 1977.

Tanahashi, Kazuaki. *Enlightenment Unfolds: The Essential Teachings of Zen Master Dogen*. Boston, Shambhala Publications, 1999.

_____, Editor. *Moon in a Dewdrop: Writings of Zen Master Dogen*. San Francisco, North Point Press, 1985.

Tanahashi, Kazuaki, and Peter Levitt, Translators. *A Flock of Fools: Ancient Buddhist Tales of Wisdom and Laughter from the One Hundred Parable Sutra*. New York, Grove Press, 2004.

Tarrant, John. *Bring Me the Rhinoceros: And Other Zen Koans to Bring You Joy*. New York, Harmony Books, 2004.

_____. *The Light inside the Dark: Zen, Soul, and the Spiritual Life*. New York, HarperCollins, 1998.

Thien-An, Thich. *Buddhism and Zen in Vietnam*. Rutland, Charles Tuttle, 1975.

_____. *Zen Philosophy, Zen Practice*. Emeryville, Dharma Publishing, 1975.

Tung-shan. William Powell, Translator. *The Record of Tung-shan*. Honolulu, University of Hawai'i Press, 1986.

Tweed, Thomas. *The American Encounter with Buddhism: 1844–1912: Victorian Culture and the Limits of Dissent*. Bloomington, Indiana University Press, 1992.

Tworkov, Helen. *Zen in America: Profiles of Five Teachers*. San Francisco, North Point Press, 1989.

van de Wetering, Janwillem. *Afterzen: Experiences of a Zen Student Out on His Ear*. New York, St. Martin's Press, 1999.

Victoria, Brian. *Zen at War*. New York, Weatherhill, 1997.

Warner, Brad. *Hardcore Zen: Punk Rock, Monster Movies and the Truth about Reality*. Boston, Wisdom Publications, 2003.

Watson, Burton, Translator. *The Vimalakirti Sutra*. New York, Columbia University Press, 1997.

Watts, Alan. *In My Own Way: An Autobiography*. New York, Pantheon Books, 1972.

_____. *The Way of Zen*. New York, Pantheon Books, 1957.

Welbon, Guy Richard. *The Buddhist Nirvana and Its Western Interpreters.* Chicago, The University of Chicago Press, 1968.

Welch, Holmes. *The Practice of Chinese Buddhism 1900–1950.* Cambridge, Harvard University Press, 1967.

Wenger, Michael, Editor. *Wind Bell: Teachings from the San Francisco Zen Center 1968–2001.* Berkeley, North Atlantic Books, 2002.

Wick, Gerry Shishin. *The Book of Equanimity: Illuminating Classic Zen Koans.* Boston, Wisdom Publications, 2005.

Williams, Angel Kyodo. *Being Black: Zen and the Art of Living with Fearlessness and Grace.* New York, Viking Compass, 2000.

Yamada, Koun. *The Gateless Gate: The Classic Book of Zen Koans.* Boston, Wisdom Publications, 2004.

Yampolsky, Philip B., Translator. *The Platform Sutra of the Sixth Patriarch: The Text of the Tun-Huang Manuscript.* New York, Columbia University Press, 1967.

Yasutani, Haku'un. *Flowers Fall: A Commentary on Zen Master Dogen's Genjokoan.* Boston, Shambhala Publications, 1996.

Yunmen. Urs App, Translator. *Master Yunmen: From the Record of the Chan Teacher "Gate of the Clouds."* New York, Kodansha International, 1994.

INDEX

ABOUT THE AUTHOR

*J*AMES ISHMAEL FORD is the founding teacher of Boundless Way Zen, a network of Zen centers currently based mostly in New England. James is also an adjunct teacher with the Pacific Zen Institute, and a member of the American Zen Teachers Association.

He has has been a student and teacher of Zen for nearly forty years. James was ordained an *unsui* and received Dharma transmission from the late Jiyu Kennett Roshi, and later completed koan study within the Harada/Yasutani tradition and received authorization to teach from John Tarrant Roshi. In 2004 he participated in the first Dharma Heritage ceremony of the nascent Soto Zen Buddhist Association of North America. This event was a public acknowledgment of James as well as other long-time Zen teachers as a senior member of the North American Zen community.

James is also a Unitarian Universalist minister, currently serving as senior minister of the First Unitarian Society in Newton, Massachusetts. He holds degrees in Psychology, Divinity, and the the Philosophy of Religion.

He lives with his family in Auburndale, Massachusetts.

ABOUT WISDOM PUBLICATIONS

Wisdom Publications, a nonprofit publisher, is dedicated to making available authentic works relating to Buddhism for the benefit of all. We publish books by ancient and modern masters in all traditions of Buddhism, translations of important texts, and original scholarship. Additionally, we offer books that explore East-West themes unfolding as traditional Buddhism encounters our modern culture in all its aspects. Our titles are published with the appreciation of Buddhism as a living philosophy, and with the special commitment to preserve and transmit important works from Buddhism's many traditions.

To learn more about Wisdom, or to browse books online, visit our website at www.wisdompubs.org.

You may request a copy of our catalog online or by writing to this address:

Wisdom Publications
199 Elm Street
Somerville, Massachusetts 02144 USA
Telephone: 617-776-7416
Fax: 617-776-7841
Email: info@wisdompubs.org
www.wisdompubs.org

The Wisdom Trust

As a nonprofit publisher, Wisdom is dedicated to the publication of Dharma books for the benefit of all sentient beings and dependent upon the kindness and generosity of sponsors in order to do so. If you would like to make a donation to Wisdom, you may do so through our website or our Somerville office. If you would like to help sponsor the publication of a book, please write or email us at the address above.
Thank you.

Wisdom is a nonprofit, charitable 501(c)(3) organization affiliated with the Foundation for the Preservation of the Mahayana Tradition (FPMT).

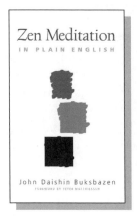

Zen Meditation in Plain English
John Daishin Buksbazen
Foreword by Peter Matthiessen
128 pp, ISBN 0-86171-316-8, $12.95

"Down-to-earth advice about the specifics of Zen meditation: how to position the body; how and when to breathe; what to think about. Includes helpful diagrams and even provides a checklist to help beginners remember all of the steps. A fine introduction, grounded in tradition yet adapted to contemporary life."—*Publishers Weekly*

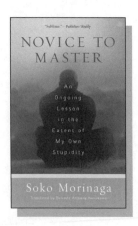

Novice to Master
An Ongoing Lesson in the Extent of My Own Stupidity
Soko Morinaga
Translated by Belenda Attaway Yamakawa
144 pp, ISBN 0-86171-393-1, $11.95

"I'm a real fan of *Novice to Master*. This wise and warm book should be read by all."
—Anthony Swofford, author of *Jarhead*

"Part memoir, part wisdom resource. A lively and enlightening overview of Zen."
—*Spirituality and Health*

Hardcore Zen
Punk Rock, Monster Movies, and the Truth
About Reality
Brad Warner
224 pp, ISBN 0-86171-380-X, $14.95

"Entertaining, bold and refreshingly direct; likely to change the way one experiences other books about Zen—and maybe even the way one experiences reality."—*Publishers Weekly* [starred review]

"Warner brings messages of substance on many introductory Buddhist topics: Zen retreat, meditation, the precepts, reincarnation etc. For my money, *Hardcore Zen* is worth two or three of those Buddhism-for-Young-People books."—*Shambhala Sun*

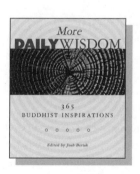

More Daily Wisdom
365 Daily Inspirations
Edited by Josh Bartok
384 pp, ISBN 0-86171-296-X, $16.95

Full of inspiration and surprises, *More Daily Wisdom* includes entries from the Dalai Lama, Eihei Dogen, Ezra Bayda, Sylvia Boorstein, Taizan Maezumi, Brad Warner, Kosho Uchiyama, Joan Halifax, and many more.

ALSO AVAILABLE:
Daily Wisdom: 365 Buddhist Inspirations
384 pp, ISBN 0-86171-300-1, $16.95

The Art of Just Sitting
Essential Writings on the Zen Practice of Shikantaz–Second Edition
Edited by John Daido Loori
Foreword by Taigen Dan Leighton
256 pp, ISBN 0-86171-394-X, $16.95

"The single most comprehensive treasury of writings on the subject in English."—John Daishin Buksbazen, author of *Zen Meditation in Plain English*

"A valuable collection from an authority on this subtle and profound form of Zen. We have needed a book like this for a long time."
—Professor Francis Dojun Cook, author of *How to Raise an Ox*

Sitting With Koans
Essential Writings on the Practice of Zen Koan Introspection
Edited by John Daido Loori
Introduction by Thomas Yuho Kirchner
352 pp, ISBN 0-86171-296-X, $16.95

"This collection of classic writings on koans will get you started and open up the treasure in your own heart."—John Tarrant, author of *Bring Me the Rhinoceros (And Other Zen Koans to Bring You Joy)*

"A remarkable collection brilliantly put together by a premier modern interpreter of koans."—Steven Heine, author of *The Zen Canon: Understanding Classic Texts*